AF605911

The Judiciary and American Democracy

SUNY series in American Constitutionalism

Robert J. Spitzer, Editor

The Judiciary and American Democracy

Alexander Bickel, the Countermajoritarian Difficulty, and Contemporary Constitutional Theory

Kenneth D. Ward and Cecilia R. Castillo, editors

State University of New York Press

Published by
State University of New York Press, Albany

Printed in the United States of America

For information, address State University of New York Press,
194 Washington Avenue, Suite 305, Albany, NY 12210–2384

Production by Kelli Williams
Marketing by Michael Campochiaro

Library of Congress Cataloging-in-Publication Data

The judiciary and American democracy: Alexander Bickel, the countermajoritarian difficulty, and contemporary constitutional theory / edited by Kenneth D. Ward and Cecilia R. Castillo.
p. cm. – (SUNY series in American constitutionalism)
Includes bibliographical references and index.
ISBN-13: 978-0-7914–6555–4 (hardcover : alk. paper)
ISBN 0-7914–6555–1 (hardcover : alk. paper)
1. Political questions and judicial power–United States. 2. Bickel, Alexander M. 3. Consititutional law–United States–Philosophy. I. Ward, Kenneth D. II. Castillo, Cecilia Rodriguez. III. Series.

KF8748.J83 2005
347.73'12–dc22 2004066245

10 9 8 7 6 5 4 3 2 1

Contents

Introduction

Alexander Bickel is perhaps the most influential constitutional theorist of the last half century. He sought to explain how judicial review, a nondemocratic institution, could be justified in a government that derives its legitimacy from majority rule. He describes the problem as the countermajoritarian difficulty, and with this memorable phrase he sets it at the center of constitutional theory's scholarly agenda. Moreover, *The Least Dangerous Branch,* his seminal work, became a model for approaching the problem. Bickel used recent U.S. Supreme Court decisions to illustrate how Justices can decide cases in a manner that contributes to a legitimate system of democratic government. Nonetheless, theorists have rejected Bickel's defense of judicial review. Indeed, for a considerable time Bickel became the symbol of past failures to solve the countermajoritarian difficulty. Theorists would criticize Bickel before venturing fresh solutions to the problem or putting forth claims about why such solutions would inevitably fail. Writing about ten years after Bickel's death, Anthony T. Kronman thought it curious that a scholar of Bickel's stature would have so little influence on the work of his successors.[1]

This book addresses the interesting question of Bickel's legacy. Does Bickel have any significance for contemporary debates forty years after the publication of *The Least Dangerous Branch*? Nine scholars address this question. They consider different aspects of Bickel's work and apply a variety of disciplinary perspectives. Although their contributions indicate that Bickel continues to capture the attention of theorists, an answer to our question remains elusive.

The contributions illustrate how the countermajoritarian difficulty and Bickel's response to it have animated and continue to animate prominent work in constitutional theory: the proceduralisms of John

Hart Ely and Jeremy Waldron; the republicanisms of Bruce Ackerman and Cass Sunstein; and the originalisms of Raoul Berger, Robert Bork, and Keith E. Whittington. Moreover, as in the broader literature in constitutional theory, the particular Bickel who emerges depends on the theorist who engages him. Some view his commitment to constitutional principle as licensing judicial activism; others see it as legitimating a contested status quo. Some join the quest to identify principles that judges can enforce in a government committed to majority rule; others emphasize the role the judiciary might play in a constitutional democracy. Lastly, the contributions reflect concern about whether Bickel addresses the right issue when he frames the question of judicial review, and whether the debate concerning this question has been detrimental to the broader constitutional culture.

Perhaps we should attribute Bickel's elusiveness to the breadth of his project. This breadth contributes to the difficulty of specifying exactly what it is that Bickel argued. His argument encompasses both abstract claims about how to conceptualize judicial authority and concrete strategies about how the Court should minimize conflicts with other institutions of government. He describes the Court not only as a dynamic force distilling society's principles and introducing them into the political process, but also as a conservative force embodying and sustaining society's traditions. Thus, we can see how Bickel became a target for both conservative and liberal theorists. Bork, for example, attacked Bickel for justifying the Court's lawmaking role, while Skelly Wright criticized Bickel for arguing that the Court should avoid most important policy questions. The tensions in Bickel's argument remain evident in the contributions to this book just as they have been present in the wider discussion of his place in constitutional theory.

The contributors emphasize three aspects of Bickel's work. First, he frames the problem of justifying judicial review from a perspective that focuses on constitutional adjudication. He asked why a nonelected judiciary should be able to substitute its judgment for that of elected institutions. In so doing, he puts the Court at the center of constitutional theory. This volume reflects the tension between theorists who define the Court's role in terms of the particular principles of constitutional law that it enforces and those who assess the Court as a single component in a broader system of constitutional government.

Bickel's focus on the Court explains the second aspect of his work. He believed that the judiciary contributes to a legitimate system of government by enforcing those constitutional principles that elected institutions tend to ignore. This claim leads scholars to assign great importance to questions of constitutional interpretation, and, consequently, the debate about the countermajoritarian difficulty has evolved into a quest to identify judicially enforceable principles. According to this view, the Court gains democratic legitimacy by enforcing principles that should supplant those advanced by elected institutions. Scholars looked to reason, nature, and tradition to defend potential principles. They also defended principles that they claimed were supported by popular consensus; they sought consensus in the political community's past, present, and even its future.

The third aspect of Bickel's argument follows from his recognition of limits on the Justices' authority to resolve disputes about the meaning of the Constitution. He asserted that the principles that judges enforce must be acceptable to a contemporary majority. He examined techniques the Court might use to delay the enforcement of an asserted principle, mainly jurisdictional devices that allow the Court to avoid issuing a decision. Such delay could advance a broader discussion among the Court, elected institutions, and the public and thereby help citizens to embrace the principle the Court seeks to enforce. Bickel described these techniques as "passive virtues," and the core of *The Least Dangerous Branch* illustrates their use.

Robert F. Nagel's contribution reflects the first aspect of Bickel's work. He addresses the question of how we should resolve disputes about the meaning of the Constitution, and describes *The Least the Dangerous Branch* as one of the intellectual fountainheads of the judicial activism that characterized the post-*Brown* Supreme Court. He rejects Bickel's defense of broad judicial authority to resolve such disputes; he contends that Bickel exaggerated the Court's willingness to subject itself to the discipline of the passive virtues. Nagel suggests that Bickel underestimated the attraction of the reformist principles that animated both the Warren Court and Bickel's defense of its jurisprudence. He believes that the nature of one's commitment to such principles would inevitably weaken the restraining force of the passive virtues. Therefore, in contrast to early critics who criticized Bickel's discussion of the passive virtues for sacrificing principle to prudence, Nagel contends that Bickel's concern for principle spawns unrestrained activism.

Mark Tushnet also considers Bickel's argument from a perspective that emphasizes the Court's role in resolving conflicts about the meaning of the Constitution. But rather than consider constitutional theory's influence on the broader political culture, he explores how such political forces influence constitutional theory. Tushnet agrees with Nagel that the passive virtues pose at best a limited restraint on judicial power. He contends that Bickel's defense of judicial review failed, because it assumed a societal consensus about constitutional principles. According to Tushnet, the weakness of Bickel's approach became evident as the emergence of a new regime exposed the dissensus underlying the old one. Similarly, he contends that the recent trend toward judicial minimalism, particularly the work of Sunstein, reflects a different epoch. Sunstein, he argues, transforms Bickel's conception of the passive virtues to suit the needs of the current regime, one in which there are manifest divisions concerning questions of constitutional principle. Although Tushnet believes that Sunstein fails to sustain his defense of minimalism as a theory of constitutional adjudication, he concludes that minimalism describes the diminished aspirations of this regime.

The contribution of Christopher Peters and Neal Devins focuses on the third aspect of Bickel's work. In contrast to Nagel and Tushnet, they suggest that his discussion of the passive virtues supports an attractive conception of judicial restraint. Peters and Devins distinguish Bickel's "procedural minimalism" from the substantive minimalism that characterized traditional constitutional theory and from the recent trend that Tushnet discusses. They endorse Bickel's attempt to define a role for the Court in which it plays an active though not dictatorial role in identifying constitutional values. While earlier proponents of restraint thought that the Court should defer to the substantive decisions of elected institutions, Bickel believed the Court should check the will of the majority when it is in conflict with constitutional principle. But the Justices also should use the passive virtues to mitigate the impact of such intervention. Peters and Devins criticize the "New Minimalists" to the extent that they return to the substantive minimalism of old, and conversely, because they are not adequately sensitive to the political antagonisms that arise when the Justices make decisions beyond their competence.

The contributions of David M. Golove and Stanley C. Brubaker address the second aspect of Bickel's argument: both seek to identify the types of principles that the Justices should enforce to sustain their authority in a democratic government. Golove explores the relationship between Bickel and Ackerman. He illustrates that their conceptions of democratic constitutionalism complement one another. Bickel, according to Golove, views constitutional change as a fluid process; he believes that the Court satisfies a test of democratic legitimacy when it enforces constitutional principles that reflect the evolution of our political tradition. Ackerman, on the other hand, emphasizes the importance of rare moments of heightened popular mobilization. He believes that the Court derives authority when it enforces principles that express a popular will, principles defined in periods in which citizens have engaged in intense deliberations about constitutional meaning. Golove claims that Bickel and Ackerman capture different dimensions of democratic constitutionalism and that a defensible conception should draw from both views.

Brubaker contrasts Bickel's traditionalist approach with originalist attempts to justify judicial authority. Brubaker considers two originalist critiques of Bickel: that his approach requires judges to play a nonjudicial—political—role, and that it fails to recognize the authority of the popular will expressed in enacting and amending the Constitution. Brubaker argues that neither Bickel nor the originalists provide an adequate solution to the countermajoritarian difficulty because they fail to provide an account of what the Constitution really means, an account that takes seriously the notion of a moral reality that is independent of our ideas about and descriptions of moral subjects. Brubaker, however, believes that their arguments point to the existence of such a reality and indicate the direction in which we must move to find a solution.

The remaining contributions consider how constitutional theory might move beyond Bickel and the countermajoritarian difficulty. Terri Peretti and Kenneth D. Ward retain the Court-centered focus that characterizes the first aspect of Bickel's work; they consider the countermajoritarian difficulty as a framework for assessing judicial authority. Keith E. Whittington directs constitutional theorists to a scholarly agenda that encompasses a richer idea of constitutionalism.

Peretti argues that Bickel's failure to reconcile judicial review and democratic values follows from empirical error. She identifies key assumptions that underlie Bickel's conception of the countermajoritarian difficulty: that (1) legislation reflects majority preferences; (2) Supreme Court decisions are inconsistent with majority preferences; (3) Supreme Court decisions are final; and (4) the Supreme Court, by virtue of its countermajoritarianism, is a deviant institution in American government. Peretti draws on recent work in political science to illustrate that these assumptions fail to reflect the reality of American constitutional politics. She concludes that this failure explains why the countermajoritarian difficulty has been a dead end for constitutional theory.

Ward picks up this theme, suggesting that the quest to solve the countermajoritarian difficulty leads right back to Bickel's starting point. Most commentators, he argues, assume that the countermajoritarian difficulty is resolved by identifying the substantive principles that judges should enforce. Bickel, by contrast, viewed the difficulty as the Court preempting political participation that strengthens citizens' commitment to the political community. The discussion of the passive virtues, according to this view, illustrates how the Court can complement elected institutions while maintaining sufficient opportunities for participation. Ward also notes a tendency among contemporary theorists to reject the conventional view of the countermajoritarian difficulty and to pursue Bickel's original path: they assess judicial authority based on its contribution to a system of legitimate government and not based on the particular principles that judges enforce. Nonetheless, many of these theorists retain the Court-centered perspective that characterizes Bickel's argument. Ward argues that it is Bickel's focus on the Court that leads theorists to misread his argument, and that this perspective continues to confuse contemporary debates. He examines the recent work of Ronald Dworkin and Jeremy Waldron to illustrate how a focus on the Court makes it difficult to grasp arguments that ground judicial authority in considerations that are independent of adjudication.

In the concluding contribution, Whittington introduces an agenda for constitutional theorists that moves beyond adjudication. He believes that constitutional theory has been decisively shaped by the image of conflict between the Court and the political branches during the New Deal. Scholars have concentrated on the ways the Constitution acts as a higher law constraining political actors and the benefits and problems associated with a countermajoritarian Court armed with a judicial veto. Whittington illustrates how constitutions also shape political outcomes by other means. Notably, constitutions help structure how political preferences are expressed and help constitute such preferences. Whittington contends that constitutional theorists need to examine these other faces of constitutionalism.

Taken together, the contributions provide a sense of where constitutional theory has been and some indication of where it might go. We see that Bickel has influenced various aspects of its development. He even anticipated its future evolution when he justified judicial authority based on its contribution to a legitimate system of government. We, alas, also see that he has shaped the perspective from which theorists view this development and that to progress, the discipline must transcend this perspective.

Notes

1. Anthony T. Kronman, "Alexander Bickel's Philosophy of Prudence," *Yale Law Journal* 94 (1985): 1567.

Chapter 1

PRINCIPLE, PRUDENCE, AND JUDICIAL POWER

Robert F. Nagel

I

The Least Dangerous Branch was published in the same year that the Supreme Court issued two stunningly audacious decisions, one holding that voluntary school prayers violate the Establishment Clause and the other that equal protection challenges to malapportioned state legislative districts are justiciable. Moreover, Bickel was writing the book during a period when the traditionalists among the constitutional law establishment were reeling from *Brown v. Board of Education*, a decision that profoundly challenged basic jurisprudential norms, as well as from *Cooper v. Aaron*, which made unprecedented claims for judicial supremacy. During this same period, there were also signs of increasing boldness in judicial efforts to protect freedom of speech and the rights of criminal defendants. Taken together, these extensions of judicial power might, to put it mildly, have made Bickel's title a bit puzzling. Indeed, for the benefit of those readers who might somehow have missed the ironic undertone to the proclamation on the cover, the book opens with this sentence: "The least dangerous branch of the American government is the most extraordinarily powerful court of law the world has ever known."

Nevertheless, if the measure is the scope of judicial power, in some respects 1962 was an innocent time. On issues like the extent of the national power over commerce and of the power of states to regulate businesses, the Supreme Court had decided to defer to the political process. More importantly, the aggressive use of judicial power, striking as it had been on occasion, was not yet routine. Consider the amazing record that still lay in the future: cases establishing the right to use contraceptives and to terminate pregnancies, decades of school busing, the crusade against sex discrimination, the extension of free speech protections to defamation and commercial speech and political contributions, the welfare reform movement, the campaign against aid to parochial schools, most of the criminal procedure revolution, energetic efforts to enforce separation of powers (including a momentous decision leading to a presidential resignation), an audacious revival of states' rights, and—as if to top off the century—a decision that effectively determined the outcome of a presidential election. In short, the forty years since Bickel's book first appeared have made its title sound downright strange.

Indeed, the initial reaction to *The Least Dangerous Branch* suggested in ominous terms that Bickel's ideas were themselves a potential cause of judicial adventurism. Herbert Wechsler argued that Bickel's positions would "divorce the Court entirely from the text that it interprets . . . and ultimately . . . equate completely what is constitutional and what is good."[1] Gerald Gunther charged that Bickel endorsed "conjecture about the complexities of political reactions as a primary ingredient of Court deliberations" and that "a virulent variety of free-wheeling interventionism lies at the core of his devices of restraint."[2] These early criticisms suggest the arresting possibility that the forty years of judicial ferment that followed the publication of *The Least Dangerous Branch* might be consistent with or even partially attributable to Bickel's ideas.

The excesses of modern judicial power, however, take a form that appears to be the opposite of what Bickel endorsed. That is, he thought that the Court should exercise political prudence when deciding *not* to intervene but that it should operate on the basis of principle on the rare occasions when it *did* intervene. The subsequent judicial record consists largely of imprudent and frequent decisions to intervene accompanied by constitutional judgments that are essentially pragmatic and devoid of principle. Moreover, Bickel emphasized that the Court's constitutional interpretations were only one part of an ongoing dialogue with other institutions of government, while a striking aspect of the subsequent record of the Supreme Court has been its recurrent and heartfelt claims to supreme interpretive authority.

Despite these departures from Bickel's positions, it remains possible that his book was—whether as a progenitor or as a legitimator—one of the intellectual fountainheads of four decades of interpretive daring. If this is true, there should be some aspect of Bickel's thinking that is inherently destructive of the limitations he recommended. For the most part, Wechsler and Gunther did not deal with this question, thinking it sufficient to demonstrate that the exercise of prudent judgment in deciding against intervention was itself lawless. Even assuming the truth of this important criticism, it would not necessarily follow that Bickel promoted the unmoored interventions that he specifically and emphatically disavowed—unless there is some reason to think that lawless judgment, once legitimated at the margin, cannot be cabined.

There is, I want to suggest, an element to Bickel's thinking that does undermine the qualifications and limitations that he proposes. Paradoxically, this element does not arise from his enthusiasm for political prudence; it arises from his commitment to principle. If Bickel's ideas have helped to promote forty years of constitutional adventurism, it has been because he believed too strongly in principle. But we should be clear as to what principle meant to Bickel. His view of principle was anchored in a commitment to reformist politics, and it was this commitment that, in turn, drove his conception of judicial authority.

II

It is a testament to the complexity and richness of Bickel's mind that by 1975, when the Court's wild constitutional ride was fully underway, he had located the problematic aspect in his own thinking.[3] He noted the tendency for a commitment to principle to breed arrogance. Writing in *The Morality of Consent* about the war in Vietnam, Bickel commented: "What propelled us into this war was a corruption of the . . . idealistic, liberal impulse. . . ."[4] He went on, ". . . [T]he altruistic impulse decayed into self-assurance and self-righteousness. . . ." Bickel rejected the notion that this decay was caused by individual excesses. He concluded:

> [T]he seeds of decay are within the ideologies themselves, in their pretensions to universality, in their over-confident assaults on the variety and unruliness of the human condition, in the intellectual and emotional imperialism of concepts like freedom, equality, even peace. (MC, 11)

Reacting not only to the cruelty of the military action in Vietnam, but also to the arrogance and lawlessness of Watergate, Bickel observed that the legal order "cannot sustain the continuous assault of moral imperatives. . . ." And he charged that this assault had been mounted not only from "the outside," but from "within," from "the Supreme Court headed for fifteen years by Earl Warren" (MC, 120).

The full force of Bickel's indictment can be appreciated by applying it to his earlier defense of the passive virtues, an argument that was grounded in a commitment to a progressive political ideology. After all, the purpose of judicial passivity was delay and the purpose of delay was to avoid legitimating (and thus entrenching) immoral political practices. The historical model was Lincoln's support for the Missouri Compromise. Bickel noted that because of prudential political considerations Lincoln could not support the immediate abolition of slavery; these considerations, however, did not induce Lincoln to abandon principle and concede the morality of the "evil institution." On the contrary, by opposing the spread of slavery into the territories, Lincoln could remain true to the principle that chattel slavery is incompatible with free government. The realization of the goal of abolition—which as a principle "made sense only as an absolute"—remained for the future, but the goal, the principle, could be asserted in the present (LDB, 68). What Bickel called the "educational" value of enunciated principle could influence political events and hasten the day of liberation.

Bickel's idea that imprudent haste can undermine the integrity of moral principle and thus obstruct political progress has as its central juridical model what he termed *Plessy v. Ferguson*'s Error (LDB, 197). Because the Court did not avoid the question of the constitutionality of segregation in 1896, it undermined the principle of equal protection and helped to entrench Jim Crow. In contrast, Bickel provided a veritable pantheon of progressive political goals that he claimed were or might have been advanced by avoidance and delay: the elimination of aid to parochial schools (LDB, 130), the desegregation of public schools (LDB, 132, 174), the reduction of censorship (LDB, 139), the right to use birth control devices (LDB, 155–56), the protection of membership in the Communist Party (LDB, 157), the right to equal voting representation (LDB, 195), and the elimination of the death penalty (LDB, 243).

In itemizing these political goals, I am certainly not suggesting that Bickel's objectives were merely ideological. He clearly thought that delay and avoidance served other important kinds of purposes, including responsible democratic decision making and full deliberation about the content of principles. But neither of these concerns about process nor Bickel's later explicit embrace of Burkean conservativism should obscure the fact that one of the fundamental impulses behind *The Least Dangerous Branch* was the urge to achieve liberal reform.

If Bickel was right in 1975 about the seeds of decay inherent in ideology itself, it would be peculiar if his earlier prescriptions for the Supreme Court's role—so clearly animated by his own reformist ideology—should show no evidence of authoritarian potential. This potential is manifest in the inflated significance that Bickel attributed to the concept of constitutional principle and to the Justices who enunciate them. Bickel claimed that by announcing a principle the Supreme Court supplements democracy by "inject[ing] into representative government something that is not already there . . ." (LDB, 58). Moreover, this supplementation is essential, for "[n]o good society can be unprincipled" (LDB, 64). While the Supreme Court should assert grand principles only sparingly, those principles that are finally announced must be enforced "without adjustment or concession and without let-up" (LDB, 59). And how do, in Bickel's evocative words, "nine lawyers . . . derive principles which they are prepared to impose without recourse upon . . . society" (LDB, 235)? Not merely by consulting conventional legal sources such as constitutional text or history or precedent. No, Justices must find "fundamental presuppositions rooted in history to which widespread acceptance may fairly be attributed." To achieve such insight, the nine lawyers must "immerse themselves in the tradition of our society and of kindred societies that have gone before, in history . . . and . . . in the thought and the vision of the philosophers and the poets." They will then be "fit to extract 'fundamental presuppositions' from their deepest selves . . ." (LDB, 236). The ambitiousness and seriousness of this process of derivation justify the dominion of the constitutional principles that emerge.

Just as Bickel conceived of the Court's principles as politically essential, deeply moral, and uncompromisingly authoritative, he depicted them as being in opposition not only to relatively unimportant considerations ("expediency") but also to weak, sometimes dangerous impulses. Thus, principles stand in the way of legislative irrationality, which ". . . only takes a legislature more than normally whipped up, . . . acting under severe pressure, rushed, tired, lazy, mistaken, or, forsooth, ignorant" (LDB, 39). The contrast is between "rationality and uncontrolled emotion . . ." (LDB, 41). The Court should impose a "test of a calm judgment resting on allowable inferences drawn from common human experience" (LDB, 41). How should a justice decide what inferences are "allowable"? What is constitutional, said Bickel, is what "rests on an unquestioned, shared choice of values . . ." (LDB, 43).

Contrast this exalted conception of constitutional principle with the more conventional and legalistic conception that it partly displaced. Consider, for example, Herbert Wechsler's view of principle, a view that Bickel discussed in *The Least Dangerous Branch.* Wechsler thought of principle as a minimal criterion, as a basic intellectual test meant to ensure the integrity of judicial reasoning, not as an expression of values that characterize a good society. Indeed, Wechsler's austere understanding of principle famously stood as a challenge to the moralism of the school desegregation decision, *Brown v. Board of Education* (LDB, 56). In contrast, Bickel extracted the moralism from his conventional reformist ideology and poured it into the idea of principle. For him, principles "derive their worth from a long view of society's spiritual as well as material needs . . ." (LDB, 58).

From this position, it was a short but necessary step to elevate the avatars of principle—those nine lawyers—to a superior moral status. This Bickel accomplished in part by idealizing the institutional context of adjudication. Cases, he said, present problems in a concrete setting far removed from the agitation surrounding the initial political decision. Thus, "insulation and the marvelous mystery of time give courts the capacity to appeal to men's better natures . . ." (LDB, 26). Bickel also relied on a skillful melding of assertion and prescription to make a rather surprising claim: "Judges have, or should have, the leisure, the training, and the insulation to follow the ways of the scholar in pursuing the ends of government" (LDB, 25–26). Presumably equipped with a "habit of mind" not unlike that which Bickel himself enjoyed, judges have the skills "crucial in sorting out the enduring values of a society . . ." (LDB, 25–26).

The Bickel of 1975 might well have asked the Bickel of 1962 how the Justices—assigned the task of identifying society's enduring and unquestioned values, and urged to believe they enjoyed an almost unique capacity to do so, and instructed to enforce these principles "without concession or let-up"—could avoid "intellectual and emotional imperialism" (MC, 11). Indeed, if Bickel had lived until 2002, he might well have wondered whether *The Least Dangerous Branch* had contributed to four decades of moral imperialism on the part of the federal judiciary.

To imagine this kind of self-criticism no doubt seems unfair, since it ignores the fact that Bickel's appreciation for the virtue of prudence was a central aspect of his thinking from the beginning.[5] The richly ambivalent, sometimes tortured intellectualizations about judicial review that make up *The Least Dangerous Branch* represent a protracted struggle between *two* impulses: on the one hand, the dangerous implications of Bickel's moral self-assurance but, on the other, his recognition of the need for prudence. The answer to the puzzle presented by the title of his book lay in his complicated and audacious argument that it is possible for a governmental institution to pursue high moral purposes safely, if it is hedged in by practices and understandings that assure prudence.

III

Bickel argued that the Supreme Court can safely be trusted with a role saturated by moralism because deep legalistic norms and practices assure humility, discretion, and restraint. The first of these was Thayer's "clear mistake" rule under which judges do not declare a statute unconstitutional unless the judgment of unconstitutionality is "not open to rational question" (LDB, 35). The second was Wechsler's requirement of neutrality, by which a court's determination must rest on a constitutional principle of general application (LDB, 50). And, of course, Bickel's own contribution was to describe at length how an array of devices, "passive virtues," allow judges to avoid decisions and thus delay the enforcement of principle until those rare moments when times are propitious.

Bickel argued that these norms and practices would restrain morally imperious judges. Indeed, he seemed to think they would cause judges to *be* prudent. Thayer's clear mistake rule, for example, dictates that judges defer to the reasonable judgments of other officials, and thus entails patience and caution and tolerance. Bickel contended that decisions must be made slowly and carefully (LDB, 41). The viewpoints of others must be considered imaginatively and respectfully. All this means that the judge will be inclined to appreciate the full complexity of public issues, to consult all of human experience, and to intervene only with reluctance (LDB, 41).

Similarly, Wechsler's requirement of neutrality forces a judge to render a decision that transcends interests of the moment, to be disinterested both politically and psychologically (LDB, 50). The testing of reasons and the striving for intellectual coherence that are inherently a part of neutrality necessitate rigor and self-discipline (LDB, 51). Because neutral principles must be enforced uniformly—without "adjustment or concession" (LDB, 59)—they are intrinsically sobering. Plainly, their announcement involves considerable risk and, so, it should be obvious that "there can be but very few such principles" (LDB, 59).

And lastly, Bickel's passive virtues entail judicial self-control in part because their very purpose is delay. The avoidance devices also require that judges attend to the widest array of social and cultural factors, including most especially attention to the opinions of others. One purpose of delay, after all, is to ensure that the judges impose principles at a time when society might be ready to accept them. Moreover, delay allows events and consequences to take form so that the content of principle can be shaped by experience (LDB, 116). Indeed, Bickel went so far as to argue that this experience includes the opinions and objections that develop in response to principles that the Court has already enunciated and imposed (LDB, 258–59). Humbled by all this unruly information, then, the Justices will not be authoritarian moralists; they will be teachers of society, learning as well as speaking, engaged in nothing more dangerous than a continuing "colloquy" (LDB, 68, 70).

In short, while Bickel freely blended description and prescription, his argument suggests that the practice of judging gradually instills capacities for caution, self-restraint, circumspection, and humility. His argument, then, is not merely an exhortation to the Justices that prudence is necessary in order to resist the dangers inherent in a profoundly moralistic role. It is a claim that, at least if institutional practices are understood and respected, the Court *can* be trusted with the "grand function" (LDB, 71) of protecting principle because its members will tend to develop an adequate capacity for prudence. The prudent character of the Justices will domesticate the moralistic nature of constitutional principle. That is why the most powerful court on earth is also the least dangerous branch.

The great difficulty with this subtle and powerful position is that prudent individuals would not want to exercise, indeed, would not be capable of exercising, the role that Bickel assigned to the Supreme Court. A judge who assigned principle the high meaning and purpose that Bickel urged would not be a prudent person. One imprudent enough to try to impose enduring, universal values would act imprudently even while utilizing the various devices intended to domesticate principle. This is to say that the principled reformer, rather than a capacious scholar who civilizes moralism through wide and respectful colloquy, is likely to be self-absorbed.

Consider Bickel's claim that in holding out and enforcing timeless principles, the Supreme Court is providing the democratic process something that it cannot provide for itself. This assertion is plainly untrue, as Bickel's own account of Abraham Lincoln's position on the Missouri Compromise demonstrates. Even without this striking instance, on what basis would anyone believe that politics is somehow incompatible with the articulation of enduring values? If such values are timeless, they must have long been recognized to be so—and not primarily by federal judges. Indeed, this is implicit in the judicial methodology that Bickel himself proposed, inasmuch as he claimed that the justices' task is to steep themselves in the work of the great thinkers and in society's shared, unquestioned choice of values. And since Bickel claimed that these values are truly fundamental to both national identity and political morality, their importance presumably could be apparent even to ordinary people and political arguments on their behalf at least sometimes widely persuasive.

It is difficult to account for Bickel's improbable insistence that only the Court can be depended upon to articulate and enforce enduring principles except as an instance of the authoritarian dynamic inherent in abstract idealism. If principles are primarily intellectualizations, it is natural to devalue or even shut out voices that speak concretely or experientially. And Bickel did write as if the common vocabulary of politics—the language of self-interest and emotion and pragmatism—were irrelevant to understanding or formulating the great goals of a polity.[6] What is clear about Bickel's sharp demarcation between principle and politics, then, is that it drastically restricts the kinds of colloquy thought to be appropriate.

In addition, judges who deign to participate in such colloquies are not likely to be responsive participants, given the nature of the principles that Bickel thinks should guide them. Principles define an ideal of a good life, one that judges seek to impose on those with competing views. Judges, thus, have reason to suspect such views as a step towards ignorance or evil. Moreover, because principles are universal, those who argue for exceptions and qualifications will be seen as compromisers and carpers. Because principles are conceptualizations, empirical information about practicalities and costs will be resisted. In fact, because principles are timeless, there will be a tendency to classify all competing information as temporary, short-run, or otherwise unimportant.

We have already seen that *The Least Dangerous Branch* contains copious signs that principled judges have the potential to become imperious guardians. Recall that judges immerse themselves in the political culture to ascertain "unquestioned" truths (LDB, 43). They stand as a bulwark against society's "uncontrolled emotions" (LDB, 41). True, these judicial moralists are to come to the point of action only slowly and then only in rare instances of indefensible irrationality and then only on the basis of considerations that transcend any immediate circumstance. But Bickel viewed the factors that require delay as generally regrettable, since the main purpose of delay is to allow conditions for reform to ripen. Certainly, Bickel wanted judges to assess social conditions and common understandings, but they are to do so mainly to determine whether these frustrating impediments have subsided to a manageable level. When that moment arrives, he insisted that there is no longer any reason not to impose principle, notwithstanding lingering objections in the political arena. It is true that the obligation of colloquy persists after the imposition of principle. But because such principles were arrived at through difficult reflection, are timeless and so clear as to be beyond rational dispute, even intellectualized objections raised after the Court's decrees necessarily carry a heavy presumption of illegitimacy. For Bickel, after all, the advantage of judicial review is that it gives consistent voice to enduring principles.

IV

Alexander Bickel helped to make respectable the idea that the function of the Supreme Court is to inject into our political life sufficient appreciation for enduring, essential, unquestionable moral principles. He proposed that this educational role could be fulfilled by imposing the principles without remorse or compromise. He made this imperious role seem safe by insisting that Justices imprudent enough to attempt it would nevertheless become prudent in exercising it. This transformation would be accomplished through the benignly cautionary influence of certain poorly understood but deeply rooted judicial practices. The difficulty is that these practices, in the hands of imprudent judges, only spur on the kind of moral imperialism that Bickel was seeking to avoid.

No one can say, of course, whether *The Least Dangerous Branch* is in any measure responsible for the four decades of judicial imperialism that followed its publication. It is entirely possible that Bickel and the Justices were independently moved by the same great institutional and jurisprudential currents. However, given Bickel's prominence and given how flatteringly seductive his depiction of the judicial role must have been, it is also possible that his book encouraged the Justices on their path. What can be said with assurance, I think, is that the general contours of the Court's record have a striking resemblance to what I have argued should be expected if restraining legal norms are consumed by the ideological fires of abstract moral principles.

Consider again one of the most striking aspects of constitutional law during the decades after 1962: its pervasiveness. Almost no aspect of modern life has been exempt from judicial oversight and intervention—not the decision making process used to expel public school students, not the methods by which police interrogate suspects, not a municipality's decisions on the appropriateness of signs and billboards, not the medical procedures by which abortions are performed, and not the standards by which votes are counted. The promiscuousness of constitutional interpretation is a natural outgrowth of the moral idealism that characterizes the modern Court. Because the Court's goals—equality, autonomy, liberation, and so on—are thought to represent profound and timeless moral principles, the need for their realization is felt urgently and the opportunity for their realization is perceived everywhere.

The Justices, of course, sometimes acknowledge the wisdom of selectivity and caution, and these considerations are occasionally decisive.[7] But this impulse is limited by the Justices' inability to see or respect disagreement. Since the seductive power of principle makes disagreement largely unthinkable, for the most part the Justices perceive the public as compliant. Even when the issue is undeniably controversial as a moral matter, like abortion or homosexuality, or when it is politically controversial, like presidential confidentiality or selection, they tend to believe their decisions will gain sufficient consent.[8] Given the scale of their mission, the Justices see objections that fall short of outright defiance as unimportant and, often, profoundly misguided or even improper.[9] The time for reform, consequently, usually seems propitious.

The second characteristic of the Court's modern record is that, despite the moral and institutional hubris that drives the Court's campaigns, the decisions themselves do not seem highly principled. Lofty goals are often stated but not consistently implemented. Instead, the articulation of goals is accompanied by pages devoted to pragmatic considerations, potential qualifications, and inconclusive doctrines.[10] To some extent, this hesitation and instrumentalism are also a consequence of the exalted educative role that the Court has assumed. Since it is thought to be crucial that society be made to understand, say, that women must be free to choose their own destinies or that people must be judged as individuals rather than as members of racial groups, the Court is naturally tempted to make such pronouncements before the time for consistent imposition has arrived.[11] After all, realization can be postponed, but—without immediate articulation of principle by the courts—society will lose sight of essential truths. Thus, when the fact of serious disagreement does register, the Justices are inclined to see it as reason to plunge ahead on articulation even while hedging on implementation.

Oddly, when the Court *is* ready to implement its lofty goals, its decisions are still often characterized by narrowness and by protracted utilitarian analysis.[12] This, too, is a consequence of the Court's exalted role. Its intellectual burden, after all, is to demonstrate that nothing justifies the law under review, that the law is unconstitutional beyond any rational dispute. The elaborate consideration of justifications, then, is not so much part of a colloquy as a sustained effort to disparage the political aspirations and judgments that stand in the way of principle.

Perhaps the most surprising aspect of constitutional jurisprudence at the turn of the century is that the Court has not retreated from enforcing principles, even those that subsequent experience makes clear society was not ready to affirm. Despite opposition strong enough to cause presidents and senators to call for judicial "restraint" and to install judicial "conservatives" and "moderates" on the Court, no landmark decision has been reversed and many have been validated and expanded. Far from being humbled or restrained by political controversy, the Justices have reacted to political agitation by asserting repeatedly that their constitutional interpretations are supreme and that disagreement is illegitimate.[13] Moreover, for substantial periods of time and on significant issues (ranging from school desegregation, to abortion, to school prayer) the Court's reaction to disagreement has been to widen, not constrict, its contested holdings.[14] Like the other prominent characteristics of the Supreme Court's record, this is not what Bickel recommended. But it, too, reflects the exalted sense of purpose that he did endorse.

The modern Court accepts the idea that its role is central to civilized government, and that it provides ideals which are both essential and otherwise unavailable. Maintaining the Court's authority, therefore, is thought to be more important than any justice's particular interpretive commitments.[15] And maintaining that authority is far more important than learning from clamoring political opposition; indeed, the Justices are less inclined to listen to or learn from this opposition to the extent that its criticisms are heartfelt and to the extent that the constitutional issue is fundamental. Fervent challenges on fundamentals might make for a good seminar, but they represent a strong threat to the Court's authority.[16]

Since the publication of *The Least Dangerous Branch*, the Supreme Court has been both powerful and dangerous. It has intervened often because pervasive oversight has seemed prudent. It has held out high principles while explaining itself pragmatically. It has taken on an exalted educative function without engaging in respectful colloquy. It has demonstrated that judicial norms and practices which might otherwise be expected to produce intellectual discipline and personal restraint become so much fuel when set afire by the idealism of principle.

Notes

1. Herbert Wechsler, "Reviews," *Yale Law Journal* 75 (1966): 672, 674.

2. Gerald Gunther, "The Subtle Vices of the 'Passive Virtues'—A Comment on Principle and Expediency in Judicial Review," *Columbia Law Review* 64 (1964): 1, 7, 25.

3. Needless to say, Bickel's thinking evolved gradually. Of particular relevance is *The Supreme Court and the Idea of Progress* (New Haven, CT: Yale University Press, 1970) where Bickel began to doubt the political practicability of high principle. He suggested that with respect to complex problems, perhaps "society is best allowed to develop its own strands out of its tradition; it moves forward most effectively, perhaps, in empirical fashion" (175).

4. Alexander Bickel, *The Morality of Consent* (New Haven, CT: Yale University Press, 1975), 11. Subsequent references to this work are cited in the text and notes with the following abbreviation: MC.

5. See generally Anthony T. Kronman, "Alexander Bickel's Philosophy of Prudence," *Yale Law Journal* 94 (1985): 1567.

6. In *The Least Dangerous Branch*, 2d ed. (New Haven, CT: Yale University Press, 1986), Bickel defends the intellectualized version of southern resistance to *Brown v. Board of Education* as represented by the Congressional Manifesto (256). Significantly, in *The Morality of Consent*, he widens his defense to include a sympathetic account of a private individual's concrete decisions about obtaining an adequate education for his children (MC, 104–05). Subsequent references to *The Least Dangerous Branch* are cited in the text and notes with the following abbreviation: LDB.

7. See, e.g., *Washington v. Glucksberg*, 521 U.S. 707 (1997). This is a decision turning aside, at least for the present, claims of a constitutional right to assisted suicide.

8. Especially striking in this regard was the Supreme Court's apparent assumption that a political resolution to the 2000 presidential election dispute would impart inadequate legitimacy while its own intervention would provide a satisfactory solution. *Bush v. Gore*, 121 S. Ct. 525, 532 (2000).

9. See, e.g., *City of Boerne v. P.F. Flores*, 521 U.S. 507 (1997). The fact that Congress had disagreed with the Court on the meaning of the Free Exercise Clause was a decisive factor in leading to invalidation of the Religious Freedom Restoration Act.

10. A detailed description can be found in Robert F. Nagel, *Constitutional Cultures: The Mentality and Consequences of Judicial Review* (Berkeley, CA: University of California Press, 1989), 121–55.

11. In *Planned Parenthood of Southeastern Pennsylvania v. Casey*, 505 U.S. 833 (1992), the Court went grandly on about the destiny of women but left many questions about the scope of the right to abortion unanswered. Similarly, its pronouncements on how the Equal Protection Clause protects individuals rather than groups have been lofty, but the actual consequences to affirmative action programs have been quite limited. See *Adarand Constructors, Inc. v. Pena*, 515 U.S. 200 (1995); *City of Richmond v. J.A. Croson Co.*, 488 U.S. 469 (1989).

12. A good example is *Romer v. Evans*, 517 U.S. 620 (1996). The Court protected the equal protection rights of homosexuals after engaging in a protracted analysis about whether any possible instrumental justification for the discrimination existed and emphasizing the sui generis nature of the case.

13. *City of Boerne v. P.F. Flores*, 494 U.S. 872 (1990*); Dickerson v. United States*, 120 S. Ct. 2326 (2000); *United States v. Morrison*, 529 U.S. 598 (2000); *Kimel v. Florida Bd. of Regents*, 528 U.S. 62 (2000); *College Savings Bank v. Florida Prepaid Postsecondary Education Expense Board*, 527 U.S. 666 (1999); *Planned Parenthood of Southeastern Pennsylvania v. Casey*, 505 U.S. 833 (1992).

14. This phenomenon is described in Robert F. Nagel, *Judicial Power and American Character: Censoring Ourselves in an Anxious Age* (New York: Oxford University Press, 1994), 71–80.

15. Justices who acknowledged serious reservations about both the right to abortion and the right to *Miranda* warnings voted to re-affirm each. *Planned Parenthood of Southeastern Pennsylvania v. Casey*, 505 U.S. 833, 853 (1992); *Dickerson v. U.S.*, 120 S. Ct. 2326 (2000).

16. For a discussion of the nature of the fears that drive the Court to suppress political disagreement about deep moral disputes, see Robert F. Nagel, *The Implosion of American Federalism* (Oxford: New York: Oxford Press, 2001), 106–07.

Chapter 2

The Jurisprudence of Constitutional Regimes

Alexander Bickel and Cass Sunstein

Mark Tushnet

Constitutional regimes elicit theories of adjudication that explain and justify the Supreme Court's role in each particular regime.[1] This essay examines Alexander Bickel's account of constitutional adjudication in *The Least Dangerous Branch,* and its relationship to the Warren Court and, more generally, to the New Deal-Great Society regime of which the Warren Court was a part. Bickel's theory of adjudication contributed to advancing that regime's substantive commitments to a liberalism of equality and political participation while attempting to validate the ordinary interest-group bargains struck in the political arena. With an interpretation of Bickel's jurisprudence in hand, I turn to the constitutional jurisprudence of the present regime,[2] as represented in Cass Sunstein's discussion of judicial minimalism. Sunstein's analysis descends from, but also transforms Bickel's, in ways that illuminate the new constitutional regime.

Bickel's theory of adjudication reflects his commitment to the New Deal-Great Society regime. This is so despite some obvious qualifications. Bickel was, in part, a critic of the Warren Court. Moreover, *The Least Dangerous Branch* was written well before the Warren Court came into its own after the retirements in 1962 of Felix Frankfurter, Bickel's mentor, and Charles Whittaker.[3] Further, the book was completed before Lyndon Johnson's Great Society programs confirmed that the New Deal-Great Society regime should be thought of as blending interest group pluralism with liberal commitments to equality and political participation. Despite these qualifications, the conceptual underpinnings of *The Least Dangerous Branch* could be taken to support the Warren Court's programmatic liberalism, though the book's ambivalences and internal tensions mean that the work could also be taken as a partial critique of that program.

Bickel's account of the proper occasions for, and the content and scope of, substantive judicial review emerged from his reflections on two dimensions of the Court's history and current performance. First, his jurisprudence had to account for how the New Deal Justices, particularly Felix Frankfurter, understood the lessons of the crisis that preceded the Court's transformation by President Franklin D. Roosevelt. Second, the jurisprudence also had to assimilate the Court's substantive commitments, and especially the Court's insistence on achieving what the Justices and their political culture understood to be equal protection in the aftermath of *Brown v. Board of Education*. These two dimensions reflected different aspects of the New Deal-Great Society regime—its commitment to interest group pluralism and its commitment to programmatic liberalism—and no jurisprudence that failed to take both into account could serve as the jurisprudence of that regime.

Frankfurter had responded to the New Deal crisis by articulating a general theory of judicial restraint. Such a theory responded directly to the events that provoked the crisis—the Court's refusal to treat legislation affecting the distribution of economic power as the product of ordinary interest group politics.[4] But it was less suitable for the liberal commitments of the nascent regime as was made clear by Frankfurter's discomfort with the Court's articulation of a theory under which some constitutional rights were said to have a preferred status.[5]

Frankfurter's difficulty, and derivatively Bickel's, lay in drawing the line between politics, the domain of interest group pluralism, and law potentially the source of liberal rights.[6] A generalized theory of judicial restraint failed to draw such a line, and even Frankfurter was wont to cross it to defend such rights. Frankfurter was a vigorous advocate of restrictions on police practices that he thought violated the Fourth Amendment, and endorsed the Warren Court's efforts to achieve racial justice.[7] More significantly to the extent that Frankfurter's jurisprudence incorporated a generalized stance of judicial restraint, that jurisprudence had been displaced by the time Bickel began to develop the argument that culminated in *The Least Dangerous Branch*.

An alternative approach, that of the Legal Process school, provided a better foundation for the New Deal-Great Society regime. Legal

Process theorists sought stability and social order.[8] Law, according to these theorists, could secure a stable social order by allocating different types of legal decisions to the institutions with the characteristics most suitable for developing results appropriate to the issues presented. Legislatures had the capacity to address novel problems based on some degree of factual investigation. More important, however, they could develop policy based on the preferences and values of their constituents. An elected legislature could promote stability by ensuring that those who were represented had a stake in the governing process: And people who were defeated on some particular issue still had a chance to raise it again, and in any event they could prevail on other issues of interest to them. Its conception of legislation, then, embraced and provided a jurisprudential rationale for the interest group pluralism that characterized the New Deal-Great Society regime.

The Legal Process school linked courts to the elaboration of constitutional principles, principles that could be used to justify the emerging commitment to substantive rights. For Legal Process theorists, courts were distinguished by their ability to articulate principled bases for the results they reached. By *principle* Legal Process theorists meant reasons that transcended the particular conflict before the courts, and that would also guide the resolution of other conflicts that implicated similar interests. In Legal Process terms, courts had a duty to consider the implications of their actions for future controversies in a way that legislatures did not. Otherwise the *distinctive* contribution of courts to lawmaking in a stable social order would disappear.[9] Legal Process theorists gave no particular substantive content to the principles that courts should articulate, but their notion of principle could be used to articulate the liberal commitments of the New Deal-Great Society regime.

Bickel attempted to meld a defense of the early Warren Court's commitment to liberal justice and the Legal Process school's conception of principled judging. His essay on the passive virtues, incorporated into *The Least Dangerous Branch*, pointed out that principles sometime undermine stability. A principled decision in a particular case might imply that some other controversy would have to be resolved in a way society was as yet unwilling to accept.[10] For Bickel, *Naim v. Naim* was a pivotal example of a principle undermining stability and the way courts could avoid excessive commitment to principle.[11] *Naim* was a challenge to Virginia's law prohibiting interracial marriage, which came to the Supreme Court in 1955, just after *Brown v. Board of Education.*[12] Whatever principle justified *Brown*, whether it be that statutory distinctions based upon race were almost necessarily invalid or that statutory classifications that perpetuated racial subordination were unconstitutional or any other, that same principle would certainly invalidate laws against racial intermarriage. Taking his cue from Frankfurter's arguments to his Supreme Court colleagues, Bickel argued that applying principle in *Naim*—that is, acting in the distinctive way courts act—would contribute to domestic instability. The Court therefore had to avoid deciding the case.

Bickel's overall argument gained much of its force by emphasizing the discretion the Court had to decide which cases to decide on the merits. His innovation was to point out that, precisely because grants of certiorari were discretionary, the Court would not violate principles of legality in taking political considerations into account in determining whether to grant or deny review in such cases. What made *Naim* so striking was that it came to the Supreme Court as an appeal from the Virginia Supreme Court. As a technical matter, the U.S. Supreme Court was required to decide all appeals on the merits. In contrast to the discretion the Court had in deciding whether to grant certiorari, it had no discretion to avoid deciding such appeals. The Court attempted to jawbone the Virginia Supreme Court into reconsidering its endorsement of the state's antimiscegenation law, but when that failed the Court dismissed the appeal for failing to present a federal question in the proper manner. As Herbert Wechsler put it, the Court's decision was "wholly without basis in the law."[13] It was an unprincipled decision in a context where Congress appeared to require principle.

As Bickel's endorsement of *Naim* showed, his argument operated mainly within Legal Process theory, but at points moved outside it. He directed attention to the various justiciability doctrines the Court had—mootness, the requirement that a federal question be properly presented, and others—that allowed the Court to avoid decisions when invoking principle would promote instability. The justiciability doctrines posed no conceptual problems within Legal Process theory, however. As doctrines, they could be applied in a principled way, thereby reducing the number of occasions on which principled substantive doctrines might produce instability.[14] But Bickel went further. As his position on *Naim* showed, he would allow the Court to be unprincipled in avoiding decisions in these troublesome areas.

In Gerald Gunther's words, Bickel insisted that the Court be 100 percent principled 20 percent of the time.[15] As Gunther's observation suggests, Bickel's approach was in deep tension with the Legal Process assumption that courts were different from legislatures in their commitment to principle alone.[16] As Bickel presented the Court's role, the Justices were to be politically sensitive in *selecting* the cases they chose to decide, and then were to abjure politics in *deciding* the cases they chose. How could the Court sustain that combination of approaches?

The first part of Bickel's analysis, in which political judgment played a large role, made sense for the Court as it was constituted during the New Deal-Great Society regime. The long Democratic Party dominance of the national policy-making process had two important implications for judicial selection. Presidents could nominate justices who were personally committed to programmatic liberalism, knowing that those commitments would not become controversial in the confirmation process. In addition, they could nominate justices who had substantial national political experience, in part because the New Deal crisis had taught the New Deal-Great Society Democratic Party that political judgment was essential to sound constitutional decision making and in part because judicial appointments were a form of patronage compatible with interest group bargaining. Together, these aspects of the nomination and confirmation process meant that the New Deal-Great Society Court would be staffed by people who could sustain the proper line between adjudication and legislation.

Consider President John F. Kennedy's Supreme Court appointments. Byron White had played a large role in Kennedy's campaign for the presidency and held a high policy and managerial position in the Department of Justice, and Arthur Goldberg was a labor lawyer, close to the leadership of organized labor, and his Secretary of Labor. These are appointments of the sort one would expect in the New Deal-Great Society regime. But, even President Dwight D. Eisenhower's appointments were largely compatible with the characteristics of the New Deal-Great Society regime. Earl Warren received the Chief Justiceship because Eisenhower had promised him a Supreme Court position as a reward for his support at the 1952 Republican convention.[17] Warren was a major national political figure, the Republican candidate for Vice President in 1948, Governor of California and a serious aspirant for the presidency himself. He was a leader of the progressive wing of the Republican Party, which accepted the New Deal's major programmatic elements. William J. Brennan was a state supreme court justice, who was nominated in 1956, an election year, because Eisenhower thought that nominating an urban Catholic with Democratic Party ties would strengthen his electoral prospects.[18] John Marshall Harlan was a leading New York corporate lawyer serving on the

Court of Appeals for the Second Circuit when he was nominated to the Supreme Court.[19] Harlan was close to Herbert Brownell and William Rogers, the leaders of the Department of Justice, and themselves at the heart of the northeastern liberal internationalist wing of the Republican Party. Potter Stewart was also associated with the "country club" wing of the Republican Party. Only the appointment of Charles Whittaker does not readily fit into an account that treats Supreme Court nominations as an aspect of the New Deal-Great Society regime.

In the end, however, Bickel could not adequately separate the political judgment judges were to exercise in choosing whether to decide cases, and the legal judgment they were to exercise that was to guide their actual decisions. His argument presupposes a conception of principle in which judges could follow the principles they articulated to their necessary conclusions. But the Legal Process school's conception of a principled decision failed to take adequate account of some insights of Legal Realism. For the Realists, conclusions did not flow from principles: In a mature legal system whose doctrinal space was thickly populated, a judge given a principle articulated in some prior case could faithfully deploy that principle along with others equally available in the doctrinal universe to reach whatever result the judge thought socially desirable. This doctrinal richness makes it possible for judges to deploy principle in ways that undermine the stability achieved in the legislative process: Where Legal Process thought that principles could transcend the conflicts of pluralist politics, Legal Realism recognized that these conflicts would only be transformed into a fight over the meaning of constitutional principle.

Although some Legal Process theorists criticized key Warren Court decisions as unprincipled, the Court's defenders responded that the critics had misunderstood the true set of principles the Warren Court was pursuing.[20] We can turn one of Bickel's phrases against the Warren Court critics and sometimes against Bickel himself, by the critics, under the guise of asserting that the Warren Court was unprincipled, were simply expressing moral disapproval of the lines.[21]

The Legal Realist conception of principle, then, undermines Bickel's argument. If judges could *always* satisfy the requirement that adjudication be principled in the Legal Process sense, there is no way to sustain the distinction between the political judgment exercised in deciding not to decide and the judgments of social value expressed in the fully principled decisions on the merits. And the vulnerability of the distinction seems to be confirmed by the background in politics of the

Warren Court's justices, and the Warren Court's behavior. With the Legal Realist understanding of principle in hand, we can invert Gunther's critique by saying that, in practice, the Warren Court was simultaneously 100 percent principled and 0 percent principled all of the time. It exercised political judgment both in deciding whether to decide and in deciding on the merits, and it was fully principled at both stages.

The limitations suggest why Legal Process theory proved inadequate as a constitutional jurisprudence for the New Deal-Great Society regime. In part its difficulties arose from the theory's foundational concern with social stability. The civil rights movement of the 1950s and 1960s pointedly raised the question: What is so desirable about stability when the social order rests on background conditions of injustice? John Hart Ely's elaboration of Legal Process theory went a long way toward addressing the particular concerns of the civil rights movement.[22] Legal Process theory accepted the civil rights critique insofar as it rested on the effective disfranchisement of African Americans in the 1950s and 1960s South. But the more general concern about stability against background injustice remained. As disagreement persisted over whether the background in the United States was one of justice with some exceptions, or was it rather one of pervasive injustice with occasional bright moments, the Legal Process assumption that stability in itself justified legal decisions came under pressure. As Jan Vetter observed, Bickel himself "had come to disbelieve in the possibility of resolving current constitutional controversies by rational argument.[23] This, according to Vetter, was a result of his reflection on the social disorder occasioned by the civil rights movement.

Moreover this disorder indicated that the liberal commitments of the New Deal-Great Society regime were not supported by the social consensus suggested by the Legal Process conception of principle. It is therefore not surprising that Legal Process approaches could not incorporate all of these commitments.[24] And, finally, when considered in light of Legal Realism's insights, dissensus over principle ensures that no decision could be applied in a principled manner and that Legal Process could not sustain its distinction between courts and legislatures.

The social and intellectual trends created two related problems within a generally Bickelian approach to constitutional adjudication. Retaining the insistence on principled adjudication, courts sensitive to political concerns could develop large-scale principles sweeping across a wide range of policy areas. As Robert Burt put it, the Warren Court articulated an "ambiti[ous]" program that accepted the proposition that "the judiciary acts properly when, and only when, it can invoke abstract principles of sufficient generality and logical force to impose definitive resolution on social disputes."[25] Having been taught that adjudication must be principled, the Warren Court adopted programmatic liberalism as its guiding principle. But this led people to view the Court as a participant in pluralist politics rather than a protector of values that transcend partisanship. Second, Bickel's approach required that judges have the capacity to make sound political judgments, whether in connection with decisions to avoid the merits, or in connection with decisions on the merits. This might be true once a constitutional regime is in place, for judges might be chosen whose principled ambitions comport with those of the rest of that regime's institutions.[26] Times of regime transition, however, place the Court's principles under stress. What was sound political judgment under the old regime can become political folly under the new one, as holdover judges insist on implementing political principles no longer in harmony with the principles of the new regime.

We appear to be in such a time of regime transition, and a new jurisprudence might be appropriate. The New Deal-Great Society regime has disappeared, replaced by a system in which government appears to be permanently divided, with different political parties often controlling Congress and the presidency. Further, the political parties seem to have become more coherent ideologically, with people who formerly might have been conservative Democrats becoming Republicans and people who might have been liberal Republicans becoming Democrats. With this sort of divided government, public policy is unlikely to embody any particularly distinctive substantive values, for the only legislation that can be enacted will reflect values shared across the ideological spectrum. Cass Sunstein's arguments for judicial minimalism fit well into the new regime, capturing the lowered expectations we should have for policy in the new regime. We can expect the processes of judicial selection and appointment to reflect the stresses of divided government. But the breakdown of consensus makes the Legal Process concern for stability relevant to the emerging regime. We can expect the processes of judicial selection and appointment to reflect this stress. As Mark Silverstein and David Yalof have argued, these processes have indeed changed since the decay of the New Deal-Great Society constitutional regime.[27] The constraints on judicial selection are complex, but one can summarize them in this way. Some participants in the selection process, usually located in the Department of Justice, will press for the choice of a nominee who will be programmatically committed to the principles of the present constitutional regime. Other participants, usually in the White House, will be more sensitive to the reception the nominee will receive in the Senate. In light of what appears to be a near-permanent close division in the Senate, mobilized interest groups today are in a position to inflict substantial political cost on a president who puts forward a nominee with obvious programmatic commitments, and a smaller cost if the nominee lacks such commitments. The most likely nominees, then, are those with short paper trails, and preferably records that can be explained as resulting from their adherence to directives from higher courts. But such nominees are unlikely to be politically astute.

Yet, they may be astute *enough* to serve in the present constitutional regime. The reason is that the regime's programmatic commitments are substantively modest.[28] This is not to say that particular political factions lack ambitious agendas, and indeed all factions might have such agendas. Nonetheless, the persistence of effectively divided government means that the principles advanced by the regime, taken as a whole, will be modest. With programmatic liberalism in retreat, the Legal Process concern for stability regains its importance. The judgment needed by a judge in the present constitutional regime need only be a cautious reluctance to take bold steps.

Cass Sunstein offers a constitutional jurisprudence well-suited to the current constitutional order. If Bickel's jurisprudence was appropriate for the New Deal-Great Society regime, Sunstein's is equally appropriate for the present one. As one reviewer put it: "It is rare that a work of constitutional theory so precisely expresses . . . the mood of a particular Supreme Court."[29] Sunstein describes a style of opinion writing that he calls "minimalism," and defends that style as appropriate in those many situations in modern society where people disagree about fundamental propositions regarding the proper role of government but may agree about particular results. Sunstein's analysis derives from Bickel's, as he acknowledges, but transforms it as well: Where Bickel urged the Court to exercise political judgment in deciding which cases to decide and then to make fully principled decisions on the merits, Sunstein asks the Court to exercise political judgment at both stages.[30]

What is the relation between minimalism and the new constitutional regime? First, minimalism is not a different term for Bickel's passive virtues, for it is a technique courts can use in deciding the merits, and it therefore is responsive to the need (after the Legal Realist challenge to Legal Process) for an account of adjudication that allows courts to make substantive decisions. Second, Sunstein does not defend minimalism as a method fit for all occasions. Rather, minimalism is appropriate, he argues, when judges accurately assess political circumstances and discover a degree of social dissensus, and yet believe that some normative claims being urged on them should not be disregarded. In other circumstances, maximalist decisions are appropriate. Political judgment, then, pervades Sunstein's prescription for the courts: The justices are to consider the degree of social consensus on the issue before them, the degree to which there is an on going democratic debate about it, and the like. Questions then arise that parallel those that arose in connection with Bickel's analysis seen in the light cast by Legal Realism. Can minimalist and maximalist opinions have the beneficial effects Sunstein says they can? Do the justices in the new constitutional regime have the background and political astuteness to engage in the political calculations Sunstein says they should?

Consider first how minimalist decision making is said to promote democratic deliberation. Shallow opinions drawing on a variety of principles for support resemble the compromises legislators make in working out the details of a statute. To that extent, Sunstein's analysis weakens the distinction between courts and legislatures, as, of course, does his insistence that courts engage in political analysis to determine whether their opinions should be shallow or deep, narrow or broad. Indeed, Sunstein reduces that distinctiveness even more by insisting that *legislatures* are forums of principle as well.[31] This immediately raises the question: Why should the courts ever invalidate legislation, even in minimalist opinions?[32]

Sunstein's answer is that such invalidations can be democracy-promoting by forcing legislatures to consider problems they have been ignoring.[33] The difficulty here is that democracy-promoting is unrelated to whether an opinion is minimalist or maximalist, because minimalism and maximalism are not intrinsic characteristics of opinions themselves.[34] Rather, they are characterizations the opinions receive in retrospect.[35] As Sunstein puts it: "Courts deciding particular cases have only limited authority over the subsequent reach of their opinions. . . . A court that is determined to be maximalist may fill its opinion with broad pronouncements, but those pronouncements may subsequently appear as 'dicta' and be disregarded by future courts. . . . A court may write a self-consciously minimalist opinion, but subsequent courts may take the case to stand for a broad principle that covers many other cases as well."[36]

Sunstein concludes that "[t]he public reception of a judicial opinion may matter as much as the applicable theory of stare decisis."[37] Or, I would add, as much as the opinion's minimalism or maximalism: "Public officials may take an opinion as settling a range of issues . . . despite the Court's determined effort to proceed narrowly. . . . Alternatively, public officials may take an opinion to be narrow, or distinguishable, despite the Court's effort at breadth."[38] But if this is so, it is hard to see how an opinion's minimalism can be democracy-promoting rather than democracy-obstructing, or how its maximalism can be democracy-obstructing rather than democracy-promoting. Everything depends on the opinion's reception, over which the Justices have little control, not its intrinsic character, which they might control.

Sunstein for example, treats *Romer v. Evans*[39] as a minimalist opinion invalidating legislation. But the decision might obstruct democratic dialogue because it rhetorically associated proponents of anti-gay legislation with advocates of racial segregation,[40] and attributed the particular anti-gay initiative involved in the case, and perhaps by extension all anti-gay proposals, to "animosity toward the class of persons affected,"[41] He also treats the assisted suicide decisions as minimalist opinions upholding legislation, but they could be seen as a broad assertion of the absence of federal constitutional controls over state legislation, or as indicating that a majority of the justices believe there to be some circumstances in which a state *would* violate the Constitution by denying assistance to a person seeking to commit suicide.

In addition, it is possible that maximalist invalidations too can be democracy-promoting in one important sense. They can foster discussion among the public broadly both about the particular issue the Court purported to foreclose, and about the deep theory on which the Court rested its judgment. *Dred Scott* might have contributed to the outbreak of the Civil War, but it did so by providing an impetus to the growth of the Republican Party and its campaign for the limitation of slavery's spread. *Roe* may have made it impossible to *enact* a range of restrictions on the availability of abortion, but I confess that it is not clear to me that the quality of public debate over abortion and privacy was better before *Roe*.[42]

Further, minimalist opinions purport to leave much open for resolution in the democratic process, but they may be inserted into a political environment where they have precisely the same effect as a maximal one. The Canadian experience with the law of abortion is suggestive. The Canadian Supreme Court overturned a conviction for violating the nation's ban on performing abortions because the ban was accompanied by exceptions that were in fact unavailable in the real world.[43] Criminal laws could not be enforced if they offered such illusory defenses, according to the Court. This appeared to leave open the way for a substantial reenactment of the general ban on abortion. But the political terrain was such that *no* legislation could be enacted after *Morgentaler*, leaving Canada without any criminal laws dealing specifically with abortion.[44] As Sunstein points out, "[t]he choice between minimalism and the alternatives depends partly on pragmatic considerations and partly on *judgments about the capacities of various institutional actors*."[45] Positive political theory suggests that, particularly in circumstances of divided government, a minimalist invalidation may well have maximalist effects: The legislature will be unable to come to agreement on *anything* to replace the invalidated statute, leaving the subject of the Court's action completely unregulated, just as would occur had the Court adopted a maximalist position.

Minimalism, then, may not be democracy-promoting or even minimal in its effects. There may also be more fundamental Legal Process questions about stability in the face of disagreement. Robert Burt suggested that Bickel's interest in principled adjudication drew upon a vision of social order in which "violent conflict seemed the only plausible outcome unless some authoritative body, somewhere, somehow, would impose a conclusive end to the dispute."[46] Minimalism leaves things undecided while allowing for accommodations among contesting parties, thereby achieving a temporary solution to a permanent problem. But, according to Sunstein, courts must make political judgments in deciding when minimalism is appropriate and when it is not. Those judgments reflect the courts' assessment of the degree and depth of social division.

Those assessments, in turn, will sometimes themselves be controversial, particularly because one issue may be the level of abstraction on which to describe social practices. The abortion controversy provides one example: There may be little division over the abstract principle of personal privacy invoked by pro-choice advocates, but there obviously is great division over the appropriate characterization of that principle in the abortion setting. Sunstein's analysis asks the courts to interpret social practices with respect to disagreement on the level at which substantive disagreements are presented. But to do so they must take some position on the controversial question of characterization. If they can do that, perhaps they can resolve the underlying substantive issues on the merits, which is what Professor Sunstein's minimalism seeks to avoid. Or, perhaps the courts are not able to make the needed political determinations with much accuracy.

The Supreme Court's actions in the presidential election cases of 2000 provide a helpful example of many of the problems associated with minimalism. In *Bush v. Palm Beach County Canvassing Bd.*, the Court asked the Florida Supreme Court to reconsider its interpretation of the state's statutes dealing with election certification deadlines, indicating that the U.S. Supreme Court was unsure of the extent to which the state supreme court had considered the relevance of a federal statute and constitutional provision in construing the state statutes.[47] Sunstein praised the unanimous decision as appropriately minimalist, "a triumph for good sense and even for the rule of law" because "unanimity can go a long way toward deflecting political passions."[48] In the context of the rapidly developing election litigation, however, the Court's intervention, nominally neutral between the parties, actually reinforced the claims of then-Governor Bush. As one critic of Sunstein's column observed, Republicans took the Court's action as a criticism of the Florida Supreme Court, so that the Court's decision "unintentionally help[ed] confirm the intemperate attacks made on the state court and on judicial independence generally."[49] More generally, the political effects of minimalist decisions depend on their context. *Bush I* suggests that minimalist decisions can have larger political consequences than Sunstein's general characterization suggests.

Bush v. Gore, the decision in which the Supreme Court determined who the president would be, purported to be minimalist too, with the Court referring to the "special instance of a statewide recount under the authority of a single state judicial authority" and expressly asserting, "Our consideration is limited to the present circumstances, for the problem of equal protection in election processes generally presents many complexities."[50] Sunstein calls the decision "subminimalist" because of its narrowness and the lack of substantial precedent supporting the Court's holding.[51] Subminimalist holdings are, for Sunstein, improper because they are inconsistent with the most modest demands of a rule of law regime. It bears noting, however, that the relation between acceptable minimalism and unacceptable subminimalism resembles the relation between the two stages of decision Bickel wrote about. Having authorized judges to think politically at stage one, Bickel had little ground to stand on when judges thought politically at stage two. Similarly, judges may find it easy to deploy the reasons Sunstein gives them for making a minimalist decision when they wish to make a subminimalist one.

In addition, *Bush v. Gore*, minimalist though it purported to be, did impose a conclusive end to the only real dispute that generated it: The equal protection issue remained open, but not the office of the presidency. The consensus among legal commentators appears to be that the Court acted to avoid the continuation of what it believed to be a chaotic and perhaps lawless state of affairs in Florida. Its judgment about that state of affairs remains controversial, and the accuracy of its overall political judgment will be determined not by anything intrinsic to *Bush v. Gore* but by the success or failure of the Bush administration: A successful presidency will vindicate the Court's judgment, and an unsuccessful one will show that the Court was wrong. Again, minimalism's merits are closely tied to questions of political judgment.

Minimalism may not, therefore, have the characteristics Sunstein attributes to it.[52] But, as the term suggests, minimalism can be described as the form that doctrinal downsizing takes. Big courts issue big—maximalist—opinions, but a Court that is part of a smaller government should issue smaller—minimalist—ones. At the same time, however, minimalism enhances judicial power, as debates over the proper form of constitutional adjudication in the 1950s and 1960s showed. One side of the argument was taken by proponents of ad hoc balancing, who believed that the courts were to take every relevant detail of a case into account, carefully identify the precise interests that competed for vindication, and finally balance those interests.[53] Their critics, led by Justices Black and Douglas, argued that ad hoc balancing gave judges too much power, in part because the metaphor of balancing concealed the necessary elements of judgment that went into constitutional adjudication but in part because opinions justifying outcomes as the result of ad hoc balancing gave too little guidance to other lawmakers.[54]

As Sunstein suggests,[55] minimalism is subject to the same criticism. Perhaps the most pithy critique was offered by one of Justice Thurgood Marshall's law clerks in a memorandum explaining why it was hard to tell whether a lower court had followed the Court's affirmative action holding in *Wygant v. Jackson Board of Education*:[56] "[N]obody knows what that opinion stands for now that Justice Powell has retired."[57] That is, to know what a minimalist opinion means one must go to the source. In a world where minimalist opinions are the general rule, no one can be confident that a statute is constitutional until we ask the Supreme Court. Minimalist opinions thus make the Court the focal point with respect to *every* statute, hardly the position that a Court that aimed at reducing its role in public life would seek.[58]

Nor is this accidental. It is only a slight overstatement to say that if Bickel asked the Court to be 100 percent principled 20 percent of the time, Sunstein hopes that the Court will be 5 percent principled 75 percent of the time, with the degree of and occasions for the use of principle determined by the judges' prudential assessment of political circumstances. For Legal Process adherents, *principle* meant some verbal formulation used to justify a result in the case at hand that implied how other reasonably imaginable cases should be resolved. Minimalist opinions are not principled in that sense, in part because they are self-consciously narrow and in part because they may draw eclectically on a variety of deeper theories to demonstrate that people of diverse views may converge on a result in the case at hand. Minimalist opinions maximize judicial power because they have few discernable implications for other cases.

Perhaps, then, we should consider whether the reduced scope of recent opinions can be traced to a shift in regimes. Substantively the Court's minimalist invalidations enforce a reduction in the scope of national power. A Court firmly embedded in what I have been describing as the new constitutional regime might confidently develop doctrines, not necessarily minimalist, that would define the new contours of national power.[59] That, however, is not what the present Court has done as yet.[60] Instead, the Court, like the other institutions of the new constitutional regime, takes small steps. The most important thing about minimalism may be the word itself. It is precisely the word one would choose to describe the practices of courts in a constitutional regime whose aspirations have diminished.

Notes

1. I use the term "constitutional regime" to refer to a reasonably stable set of institutional practices engaged in by political actors in political parties, legislatures, the executive branch, the courts, and elsewhere.

2. I defend the proposition that we are in a new constitutional regime, and my account of its institutional characteristics, in Mark Tushnet, "The Supreme Court 1998 Term—Foreword: The New Constitutional Order and the Chastening of Constitutional Aspirations," *Harvard Law Review* 113 (1999): 29, which is a preview of a longer work, *The New Constitutional Order* (Princeton, NJ: Princeton University Press, 2003).

3. For a discussion of the three eras of the Warren Court, only the last of which is the programmatic liberal Warren Court, see Lucas A. Powe, *The Warren Court and American Politics* (Cambridge, MA: Belknap Press, 2000).

4. See Robert A. Burt, "Alex Bickel's Law School and Ours," *Yale Law Journal* 104 (1995): 1853, 1860. Noting that by the 1950s the "proper goal . . . for governance institutions [was] to foster mutual accommodations among conflicting parties" in the arena of labor-capital struggle.

5. See *Kovacs v. Cooper*, 336 U.S. 77, 90–95 (1949) [J. Frankfurter, concurring]. The case criticizes the argument that the First Amendment has a preferred position in constitutional adjudication.

6. For a discussion of the way in which the Court-packing struggle during the New Deal shaped understanding of the law-politics distinction, see Barry Friedman, "The History of the Countermajoritarian Difficulty, Part Four: Law's Politics," *University of Pennsylvania Law Review* 148 (2000): 971. The next installment of Friedman's work addresses the dilemma, explored in this essay as well, faced by liberals in the 1950s. Barry Friedman, "The Birth of an Academic Obsession: The History of The Countermajoritarian Difficulty, Part Five," *Yale Law Journal* 112 (2002).

7. For a discussion of the tortuous path by which Frankfurter reached the result of endorsing *Brown*, a journey on which Bickel accompanied him, see Mark Tushnet, *Making Civil Rights Law: Thurgood Marshall and the Supreme Court, 1935–1961* (New York: Oxford University Press, 1994), 203–04.

8. What follows is a thumbnail sketch of Legal Process theory and its conceptual structure. I ignore many details and, in particular, ignore the sequence in which the elements of Legal Process theory's analysis of constitutional adjudication actually developed.

9. To say that courts contribute to lawmaking in this way does not imply, however, that legislatures may not develop policy based on principle in the Legal Process sense. The point is that legislatures may do so, but they need not, whereas courts must.

10. The Legal Process approach came to be understood as specifying institutional arrangements that would support stability in *any* society. In invoking the actual conditions of American society, Bickel may have modified the approach in an important way. But cf. Henry M. Hart, Jr. and Albert M. Sacks, *The Legal Process, Basic Problems in the Making And Application of Law*, eds. William N. Eskridge, Jr., and Philip P. Frickey (Westbury, New York: Foundation Press, 1994), 113.

11. 350 U.S. 891 (1955), after remand, 350 U.S. 985 (1956), discussed in Alexander Bickel, *The Least Dangerous Branch*, 2d ed. (New Haven, CT: Yale University Press, 1986), 174.

12. Richard H. Fallon, Henry Melvin Hart, Herbert Wechsler, Daniel J. Meltzer, and David L. Shapiro, *The Federal Courts and the Federal System*, 4th ed. (Westbury, New York: Foundation Press, 1996), 653–55, provides a convenient summary of the *Naim* litigation and its jurisprudential context.

13. Herbert Wechsler, *Principle, Politics and Fundamental Law* (Cambridge, MA: Harvard University Press, 1961), 47, originally published as "Toward Neutral Principles of Constitutional Law," *Harvard Law Review* 73 (1959): 1.

14. Of course, principled application of justiciability doctrines might require that the Court decline to decide some cases where invoking principle would not produce instability.

15. Gerald Gunther, "The Subtle Vices of the "Passive Virtues": A Comment on Principle and Expediency in Judicial Review," *Columbia Law Review* 64 (1964): 1, 3.

16. In addition, Bickel's analysis was in tension with the Legal Process idea that courts lacked the capacity to do a good job in making political judgments.

17. On Warren's appointment, see Powe, *The Warren Court*, 24.

18. On Brennan's appointment, ibid., 89–90.

19. On Harlan's appointment, ibid., 48–49.

20. A representative response is J. Skelly Wright, "Professor Bickel, The Scholarly Tradition, and the Supreme Court," *Harvard Law Review* 84 (1971): 769.

21. Bickel, *The Least Dangerous Branch*, 23. Bickel drew the phrase from James Bradley Thayer, who took it from William Wordsworth. The best example of this phenomenon is probably Philip B. Kurland, "Foreword: "Equal in Origin and Equal in Title to the Legislative and Executive Branches of the Government," *Harvard Law Review* 78 (1964): 143.

22. Ely pointed out that Legal Process theory imputed characteristics to legislatures that need not always be satisfied. Legislatures, for example, would not respond to the interests, preferences, or values of those who were not represented. An incomplete or partial democracy was unlikely to be stable, and therefore could not satisfy Legal Process theory's foundational requirement. Ely argued that courts could promote stability by invoking the Constitution to guarantee that legislatures fairly represented all in the society. John Hart Ely, *Democracy and Distrust* (Cambridge, MA: Harvard University Press, 1980).

23. Jan Vetter, "Postwar Legal Scholarship on Judicial Decision Making," *Journal of Legal Education* 33 (1983): 412, 420.

24. Ely's critique of *Roe v. Wade* exemplifies the difficulty. John Hart Ely, "The Wages of Crying Wolf: A Comment on *Roe v. Wade*," *Yale Law Journal* 82 (1973): 920. For Ely, *Roe* was simply not constitutional law as he understood it, for two related reasons: It was unprincipled in the Legal Process sense, and it identified no problem of democratic representation that justified judicial intervention.

25. Burt, "Alex Bickel's Law School and Ours," 1864, 1859.

26. At least if, as was true during the New Deal-Great Society regime, the regime principles point to choosing judges who combine political judgment with a committment to principle.

27. Mark Silverstein, *Judicious Choices: The New Politics of the Supreme Court Confirmations* (New York: W. W. Norton, 1994); David Alistair Yalof, *Pursuit of Justice: Presidential Politics and The Selection of Supreme Court Nominees* (Chicago: University of Chicago Press, 1999).

28. For a more extended discussion of this point, see Tushnet, "The Supreme Court 1998 Term."

29. Jeffrey Rosen, "The Age of Mixed Results," review of *One Case at a Time: Judicial Minimalism on the Supreme Court*, by Cass Sunstein, *The New Republic*, June 28, 1999, 43.

30. See Cass Sunstein, *One Case at a Time: Judicial Minimalism on the Supreme Court* (Cambridge, MA: Harvard University Press, 1999), 267–68 n.5. Whereas Bickel believed that "once assumed, jurisdiction should result in the most principled and full of opinions," Sunstein's view is that "opinions should be self-consciously narrow and shallow, at least some of the time."

31. See, e.g., Sunstein, *One Case at a Time*, 267 n. 5. "My argument . . . finds its foundations in the aspiration to deliberative democracy, with an insistence that the principal vehicle is the legislature, not the judiciary; the judiciary is to play a catalytic and supplementary role" (162). "The original understanding was that deliberation about the Constitution's meaning would be part of the function of the President and legislators as well." Christopher J. Peters, "Assessing the New Judicial Minimalism," *Columbia Law Review* 100 (2000): 1400, argues, with the aim of undermining any claimed democratic superiority of legislatures to courts, that courts are at least as representative as legislatures. If Sunstein's arguments raise questions about the justifications for judicial review, Peters's arguments raise questions, oddly enough, about the justifications for legislative decision making.

32. For example, Sunstein urges minimalism when "things will be quite different in the near future," *One Case at a Time*, 48. When one of the things that might change is "relevant . . . values," ibid., it is unclear what is gained by invalidating a statute in such a situation; the invalidated statute would become a derelict anyway.

33. Sunstein, *One Case at a Time*, 5. "Certain forms of minimalism can be democracy-promoting, not only in the sense that they leave issues open for democratic deliberation, but also and more fundamentally in the sense that they promote reason-giving and ensure that certain important decisions are made by democratically accountable actors." Minimalist decisions *upholding* statutes, that is, finding that they do not violate the Constitution, may have a similar effect if legislatures understand the courts to be saying that they *might* invalidate the statute if it is unchanged when a slightly different case is presented to them.

34. A slightly more detailed version of the argument that follows can be found in Mark Tushnet, "How to Deny a Constitutional Right: Reflections on the Assisted-Suicide Cases," *Green Bag* 2d 1 (1997): 55. See also Rosen, "The Age of Mixed Results," 44. "Whether a decision is characterized as narrow or shallow, or deep or broad, seems entirely in the eye of the beholder."

35. Sunstein addresses this problem under the heading of stare decisis. Sunstein, *One Case at a Time*, 19–23. I believe the better label would be *ratio decidendi*. The most acute analysis of the problem is Jan G. Deutsch, "Precedent and Adjudication," *Yale Law Journal* 83 (1974): 1553. See also Richard Primus,

"Canon, Anti-Canon, and Judicial Dissent," *Duke Law Journal* 48 (1998): 243, 263. ("Holdings . . . are retrospectively constructed) [283], (noting "the degree to which the meaning of a judicial opinion is determined by its later construction.")

36. Sunstein, *One Case at a Time*, 21.

37. Ibid., 22.

38. Ibid., 22.

39. *Romer v. Evans* 517 U.S. 620 (1996).

40. Sunstein, *One Case at a Time*, 623.

41. Ibid., 634.

42. Of course, the public's democratic deliberations cannot be immediately effective if they reach a different conclusion from the Court's maximalist one. See Sunstein, *One Case at a Time*, 30 (makes this point in connection with *Dred Scott* and *Roe*). But obstacles to legislative action mean that such deliberations are rarely immediately effective anyway. The real question is how large is the difference between the time it takes to secure legislation after a minimalist decision and the time it takes to do so after a maximalist one. Here all I can report is my sense that the difference is not as large as the terms *minimal* and *maximal* suggest.

43. *Morgentaler v. The Queen*, [1988] S.C.R. 30.

44. For a brief discussion of the legislative aftermath, see F. L. Morton, *Pro-Choice Vs. Pro-Life: Abortion and The Courts in Canada* (Norman, OK: University of Oklahoma, 1992): 290–93.

45. Sunstein, *One Case at a Time*, 56 (emphasis added). See generally Neil K. Komesar, *Imperfect Alternatives: Choosing Institutions in Law, Economics, and Public Policy* (Chicago: University of Chicago Press, 1994).

46. Burt, "Alex Bickel's Law School and Ours, " 1869.

47. *Bush v. Palm Beach County Canvassing Bd.* 121 S. Ct. 471 (2000).

48. Cass Sunstein, "The Broad Virtue in a Modest Ruling," *New York Times*, December 5, 2000, p. A29. Sunstein reiterated his praise for the decision in "Order Without Law," in *The Vote: Bush, Gore, and the Supreme Court*, ed. Cass R. Sunstein and Richard A. Epstein (Chicago: University of Chicago Press, 2001).

49. Martin Flaherty, letter to the editor, *New York Times*, December 7, 2000, p. A38.

50. *Bush v. Gore*, 121 S. Ct. 525, 532 (2000). The decision illustrates as well the fact that minimalism is not an intrinsic characteristic of decisions, as Sunstein recognizes. See "Order Without Law." The Court articulated an equal protection *doctrine*, which remains available for later courts to use more expansively if they choose. The decision's apparent minimalism, that is, is hostage to what courts do with it in the future.

51. Sunstein, "Order Without Law."

52. For this reason, I find unconvincing Sunstein's specification of the circumstances under which courts should prefer minimalism or maximalism.

Because they are not intrinsic characteristics of an opinion, the analysis must focus not on judicial capacity or the nature of the problem posed to the courts, but on the reaction of public officials to the courts' decision. Sunstein provides little account of the variables affecting these reactions.

53. See, e.g., Wallace Mendelson, "On the Meaning of the First Amendment: Absolutes in the Balance," *Southern California Law Review* 50 (1962): 821. Sunstein, *One Case at a Time*, 53.

54. See, e.g., Laurent B. Frantz, The First Amendment in the Balance, *Yale Law Journal* 71 (1962): 1424.

55. Sunstein, *One Case at a Time*, 48. "A court that economizes on decision costs for itself may in the process 'export' decision costs to other people, including litigants and judges in subsequent cases who must give content to the law."

56. *Wygant v. Jackson Board of Education* 476 U.S. 267 (1986).

57. Carol Steiker, bench memorandum for Thurgood Marshall, no. 87–998, Thurgood Marshall Papers, Library of Congress, box 429, file 4, cited in Mark V. Tushnet, *Making Constitutional Law: Thurgood Marshall and the Supreme Court, 1961–1991* (New York: Oxford University Press, 1997), 137. Sunstein commends the narrowness of Justice Powell's affirmative action opinion in *Regents of the University of California v. Bakke*, 438 U.S. 165 (1978). See Sunstein, *One Case at a Time*, 131.

58. Cf. Sunstein, *One Case at a Time*, 22. Describes "width as a judicial virtue" because "it creates a reliable backdrop for use by citizens and legislators."); Rosen, "The Age of Mixed Results," 46. Notes the power-enhancing aspects of Justice O'Connor's minimalism in cases involving challenges to districting as impermissibly based on race.

59. We might impute a more strategic view to the Court. I have argued that there are reasons to believe that a new constitutional order has emerged, but those reasons are certainly not conclusive. One might think that the new order is struggling to be born, and may not ever fully emerge. In such circumstances, it would be imprudent to project today a rule that is to guide the national government in the new constitutional order, because that rule might turn out to be incompatible with what in fact takes place. This is one way of understanding Sunstein's arguments for minimalism: When political society is sharply divided over some issue, minimalist positions are strategically desirable for the Court. Resolving the issue definitively would generate severe criticism of the Court by the (large) losing side, and the Court might resolve the issue in a way inconsistent with the way society ends up resolving it. Minimalist decisions allow the Court to endorse a vision of a more limited national government without, however, committing the Court to enforcing strict rules in the event that the new order never consolidates and the old one continues.

Some have suggested that Sunstein's analysis should be understood as strategic in another sense. See, e.g., D. W. Miller, "Book Says Bolder Isn't Better in Rulings by the Supreme Court," *Chronicle of Higher Education*, March 5, 1999,

p. A19. Miller quotes Professor Michael Klarman: "To a neutral observer, it is suspicious that all of us liberals are making these claims about limited judicial power at a time when we don't control the power." According to this view, Sunstein is taken to be a political liberal facing a relatively conservative Supreme Court. The best he can hope for in a liberal direction are minimalist decisions like *Romer*. The worst, from his imputed political position, would be maximalist conservative decisions. The presumption in favor of minimalist decisions takes nothing away from what he and his allies can get from the Court anyway, and might deprive his opponents of some decisions they might get. This interpretation unattractively attributes disingenuousness to Sunstein, and implausibly attributes an inability on the part of conservative justices to see through the purported Machiavellian strategy.

60. See Mark Tushnet, "Symposium: Federalism and the Supreme Court: The 1999 Term: What Is the Supreme Court's New Federalism?", *Oklahoma City University Law Review* 25 (2001): 927. I argue that the present Court is neither revolutionary nor restorationist.

Chapter 3

Alexander Bickel and the New Judicial Minimalism

Christopher J. Peters and Neal Devins

I. Introduction

Starting with *Marbury v. Madison*, the Supreme Court frequently has been attacked for addressing issues not before it. No doubt, when the Court "seek[s] to decide cases in a way that sets broad rules for the future and that also gives ambitious theoretical justifications for outcomes,"[1] the Court risks making costly mistakes. For this reason, the Court long has been encouraged by some to steer clear of political fights by issuing minimalist decisions upholding elected government decision making. Others, of course, have been more sanguine about aggressive judicial intervention.

In *The Least Dangerous Branch*,[2] Alexander Bickel transformed this debate over judicial minimalism. Seeking to defend *Brown v. Board of Education*,[3] Bickel needed to justify the existence, within a supposed representative democracy, of a nonelected, life-tenured Supreme Court—a Court with the power to override local, state, and perhaps even national majorities on issues about which people felt passionately enough to require, on occasion, the mobilization of the National Guard. Bickel believed that this "countermajoritarian difficulty" ought not to prevent the Court from deciding constitutional questions. And in deciding them, Bickel thought, the Court should pay no deference whatsoever to the political branches, for the Court's special role was precisely to enforce the demands of principle where necessary, even against the current will of the majority. But Bickel also argued that the Court should not always *decide* constitutional questions when given the opportunity to do so. Instead, the Court should make frequent and strategic use of what he called the "passive virtues"—techniques of avoiding decision of substantive constitutional issues—and should wait until the appropriate principle has suitably "ripened" before finally applying it to the issue in question. Thus, Bickel, in a chiding phrase of Gerald Gunther's, advocated for the Court something like "100 percent insistence on principle, 20 percent of the time."[4]

The revolutionary part of Bickel's prescription was not his counsel of judicial restraint, but the nature of the restraint he counseled. Previous advocates of judicial minimalism had argued, in various ways, that the Court should *substantively* defer to decisions made by the political branches—by, for instance, indulging a strong presumption of constitutional validity or deferring entirely to political decisions in certain subject areas. In contrast, Bickel argued for *procedural* deference: the use of process-based judicial techniques to avoid ruling on the constitutionality of a political decision unless, and until, the constitutional principle in question became relatively clear. Bickel's brand of judicial minimalism had to do with the timing and scope of judicial review, while previous forms had dealt primarily with its content.

Turn-of-the-millenium constitutional theory in America has rediscovered Bickel's procedural minimalism, and a small but influential school, which we refer to here as "the New Judicial Minimalism," has taken up Bickel's central themes: that the Court can and should choose the occasions and mitigate the impact of its constitutional decision making, and that its proper role is that of a participant in an ongoing conversation with the political branches, not that of a dictatorial proclaimer of values. At the same time, the New Judicial Minimalism has wandered from Bickel's message in at least two important respects. First of all, the New Minimalism in some ways revisits the substantive minimalism that Bickel rejected. Second and perhaps more significantly, the New Minimalism is animated by a different spirit than was Bickel's. Bickel's minimalist project was *juricentric*: It rested on a theory of the judiciary's independent, coequal institutional role in the American constitutional democracy. Much of the New Minimalism, however, is primarily *policentric*, grounded in a belief that the Court has value only as a secondary or supplemental institution vis-à-vis the political branches of government.

In part II of this chapter, we begin by situating Bickel's *The Least Dangerous Branch* against some of its minimalist precursors and then explain how Bickel added the concept of procedural minimalism to the debate about judicial review. In part III, we turn our focus to the New Judicial Minimalism, tracing some of its central themes back to Bickel and noting some important points of divergence from Bickel's work. In part IV, we critique the New Minimalism for being too policentric. In particular, we think that the Court ought not to be shy about speaking to basic questions of values on matters that divide the nation. Whether the issue is abortion, affirmative action, or the death penalty, the Court's unique voice ought not to be muted simply because its members are appointed, not elected. At the same time, adjudication as a process of social decision has limits, and these limits support the use of certiorari denials and other "passive virtues" that delay Supreme Court review. To the extent that the New Minimalism eschews these delaying strategies, we think that the New Minimalism does not go far enough.

II. Bickel's Judicial Minimalism

Judicial minimalism is the most recent label for an idea that has been around in some form for a long time: that the judiciary—at least the nonelected, life-tenured federal judiciary, and most particularly the Supreme Court—should interfere as little as possible with decisions made by the political branches of government. At the turn of the twentieth century, James Bradley Thayer noted the danger of legislative atrophy created by aggressive judicial review[5] and proposed what Bickel would later call "the rule of the clear mistake": a strong presumption that a court uphold a political decision against constitutional challenge unless the legislature (or other responsible political branch) clearly has crossed the bounds of rationality.[6] In the middle of the twentieth century, Judge Learned Hand, who had been Thayer's student at Harvard,[7] suggested that courts should enforce only structural limitations on political power—the boundaries between the branches of the federal government, and between the federal government and those of the states—but should never override a political decision on the ground that it interferes with one of the Constitution's enumerated rights.[8] Clashes between exercises of political power and individual rights, Hand contended, always involve the balancing of competing values, and courts are no better equipped to perform that balancing than are the political branches; besides, "a society so driven that the spirit of moderation is gone, no court *can* save."[9]

These and similar early expressions of judicial minimalism, however, were *substantive* in nature; they demanded some form of judicial deference to politics in deciding constitutional issues on their merits. Both Thayer and Hand thought the Court should affirmatively validate most political decisions, save those that were patently irrational (Thayer) or self-aggrandizing with respect to competing political institutions (Hand). On this view, where the Court was not absolutely certain that a political decision was unconstitutional, the Court was required to defer to politics and enter a substantive ruling upholding that decision. Of course, in following this approach, the Court necessarily would foreclose, or at least erect significant obstacles to, any later reconsideration of the constitutionality of a political decision it had deferentially approved.

Bickel's revolutionary move was to justify a limited role for the judiciary, while at the same time rejecting the notion that courts should presumptively defer to the political branches in deciding substantive constitutional issues. He criticized Thayer and Hand for failing to recognize the deep legitimating impact that the Court's *validation* of a constitutionally questionable political decision might have: Rather than "removing the Court from the political arena," substantive minimalism simply "works an uncertain and uncontrolled change in the degree of the Court's intervention, and it shifts the direction" of that intervention (LDB, 131). Bickel, that is, understood that presumptively upholding political decisions on their constitutional merits was in fact a type of judicial maximalism, because it inoculated such decisions from later constitutional attack should principled opposition to them develop.

But Bickel noticed that constitutional validation or invalidation of a political action rarely are the only options available to the Court. Often the Court can avoid altogether the decision of constitutional issues:

> The essentially important fact, so often missed, is that the Court wields a threefold power. It may strike down legislation as inconsistent with principle. It may validate, or, in Charles L. Black's better word, "legitimate" legislation as consistent with principle. *Or it may do neither.* [Bickel's emphasis] It may do neither, and therein lies the secret of its ability to maintain itself in the tension between principle and expediency. (LDB, 69)

The Court can "do neither"—avoiding a decision on the constitutional merits—through the use of a wide range of procedural techniques that

Bickel famously referred to as "the passive virtues" (LDB, 111–98). The Court can decline to hear a case altogether, through denial of certiorari, through strict invocation of the "case or controversy" requirements of standing and ripeness, or through the political question doctrine. It can decide a case without getting to the constitutional issues by narrowly construing applicable statutes to avoid constitutional jeopardy. Or it can avoid conclusive pronouncements on core constitutional questions by invalidating political decisions for remediable procedural defects—on grounds of desuetude, improper delegation, statutory vagueness, or abuse of administrative discretion.

In *The Least Dangerous Branch*, Bickel argued that the Court should make frequent strategic use of these "passive virtues" to avoid premature head-on decisions of important constitutional questions. As Bickel saw it, the decision of substantive constitutional issues often puts the Court in a difficult bind. On the one hand, Bickel argued that decisions of principle are "peculiarly suited to the capabilities of the courts."[10] In contrast, to legislators, who are likely to be influenced by considerations of expediency, judges are well situated to inject considerations of principle into decision making. If so, then the substantive minimalism of Thayer and Hand had to be rejected as not giving the Court its due: Thayer's "clear mistake" rule was simply too permissive, substituting questions of rationality for questions of principle (LDB, 35–46); Hand's "therapy of nearly total abstinence" ignored the Court's special capacity as an interpreter of principle (LDB, 48). Moreover, substantive minimalism required affirmative validation of constitutionally questionable political decisions, validation that might be difficult to reverse in future cases (LDB, 131).

On the other hand, Bickel's conception of principled decision making creates difficulty for judges. Bickel believed that the Court, when it squarely decides a constitutional issue, is required to do so in a rigorously principled way. Consequently, he believed that the unflagging application of principle by the Court is unworkable in the actual conditions of political society, with its shifting alliances and its requirement of frequent compromise. Just as "no good society can be unprincipled . . . no viable society can be principle-ridden" (LDB, 64). It followed that an attempt by the Court always to enforce the strict dictates of principle would undercut the Court's ability to act in a political world. Bickel recognized that the Court's authority over the public will is limited: The Court "is a court of last resort presumptively only" (LDB, 258); the ultimate arbiter of principle is the "consistent and determined majority"

(LDB, 28) that is capable of nullifying an ill-considered Court decision by simply ignoring it. To ensure its own political viability, then, the Court has to temper principle with an expedient understanding of what the public is willing to accept from it. Thus, Bickel rejected as unrealistic Herbert Wechsler's insistence on complete application of "neutral" principles in every constitutional case—a form of judicial *maximalism* (although it might counsel against "unprincipled" judicial interventions in particular cases).[11]

Bickel therefore laid out a troublesome dilemma for the Court: It must somehow exercise "principle and expediency at once" (LDB, 69). But Bickel found a solution in a brand of minimalism that was procedural rather than substantive. The Court, Bickel held, must act scrupulously on principle in actually deciding constitutional issues, but also must choose carefully—taking full advantage of the passive virtues—the occasions upon which it will decide those issues, doing so only when expediency permits. This solution was procedural rather than substantive because it counseled choosing whether and when to decide rather than how to decide; it prescribed the avoidance or delay of constitutional decisions rather than the presumptive validation of political actions.

It is important to emphasize that Bickel's procedural minimalism was motivated by concerns entirely different from those felt by substantive minimalists like Thayer and Hand. The substantive minimalists had worried primarily about the Court's questionable democratic pedigree in comparison to the political branches. In their view, the role of judicial review should be limited to safeguarding the political process against irrationality (Thayer) or against power-grabbing by one political institution at the expense of others (Hand). The animating spirit behind substantive minimalism thus was policentric, focused on the Court's function as a safeguard against perceived defects in political decision making.

In contrast, Bickel's procedural minimalism was juricentric, grounded in a desire to preserve the quality and efficacy of the Court's own decision making. One prong of Bickel's juricentrism was his belief that the Court's constitutional decisions in fact would *better* reflect principle if they came only after the issues involved had percolated for a while in the political sphere and perhaps in the lower courts, "remain[ing] in abeyance and ripen[ing]" (LDB, 71). For Bickel, constitutional principle was something that was "evolved conversationally[,] not perfected unilaterally" (LDB, 244); it formed through the gradual coalescence of public opinion about an issue. Thus, the Court's duty, on those occasions when it articulated and applied constitutional principle, was to "declare as law only such principles as will—in time, but in a rather immediate foreseeable future—gain general assent" (LDB, 239). The Court was "a leader of opinion, not a mere register of it, but it must *lead* opinion, not merely impose its own" (LDB, 239; emphasis added).

The other, closely related prong of Bickel's juricentrism, already mentioned, was his particular understanding of the practical relationship between the Court and the political branches. The legislature had the power of the purse, the executive had the police and the army, but the judiciary had, in Alexander Hamilton's phrase, "neither force nor will."[12] The Court could not then simply impose its judgments upon an unwilling populace; those judgments had instead to earn acceptance, if not immediately then over time. This recognition, by Bickel, of the necessity that the Court's rulings ultimately be *acceptable* followed (as Bickel recognized) Andrew Jackson, Abraham Lincoln, and Franklin Roosevelt, each of whom (Lincoln most famously, with respect to *Dred Scott*) had taken the position that a Supreme Court decision is binding in the decided case only, not "as a political rule" forever determinative of the underlying issue.[13]

The recognition of the condition of ultimate acceptability implied also the practical impossibility of what might be called "judicial supremacy"—of the idea that the Court really is or can be the *final* arbiter on questions of constitutional principle. The Court, using the passive virtues, "shape[s] and reduce[s]" a question of principle rather than answering it bluntly and instantaneously, so that eventually the answer "has [been] rendered . . . familiar if not obvious" (LDB, 240). And the passive virtues allow the majority, through the political branches, the opportunity to participate actively (if sometimes antagonistically) in the shaping of the answer, rendering it not only "familiar," but also ultimately acceptable and satisfying.[14]

For Bickel, then, strategic use by the Court of the passive virtues was both a constitutive element of its decision-making process and a necessary survival technique. Deferring conclusive resolution of a constitutional issue until the problem had been "lived with"[15] a while allowed the contours of a principled solution to take shape, giving the Court the raw material it needed for its ultimate decision of that issue. The process of deferral also protected the Court by reducing the likelihood that its ultimate decision would trigger severe and widespread public antagonism, which might harm the Court's standing and impair its subsequent ability to render authoritative constitutional decisions.

III. Bickel and the New Minimalists

Although Bickel's thinking in *The Least Dangerous Branch* seems to have been driven, or at least spurred, largely by the author's desire to justify the result in *Brown v. Board of Education*—hardly a conservative motivation at the time—the torch of judicial minimalism for thirty years after the book's publication was carried mostly by political conservatives.[16] On the one hand, the major constitutional decisions of the Warren and Burger Courts tended to sit well with the left-leaning mass of the legal academy, making calls for judicial restraint seem self-defeating. On the other hand, the Court's most controversial ruling since the *Brown* case, *Roe v. Wade*, the 1973 decision recognizing a constitutional right to abortion,[17] along with some of the Warren Court's more aggressive criminal procedure decisions,[18] mobilized conservatives against what was popularly derided as "judicial activism."[19] Thus, Robert Bork, arguably the most prominent critic of judicial review during those years, advocated a brand of judicial minimalism that combined Thayer's rule of the clear mistake with Wechsler's insistence on the application of neutral principles.[20] Bork, however, expressly rejected two central components of Bickel's minimalism: Bickel's premise of special judicial competence to make decisions of principle, and his prescription for strategic use of the passive virtues. Unlike Bickel's minimalism, Bork's variety was substantive rather than procedural, advocating considerable deference to the political process through affirmative constitutional validation of political decisions.[21] Bork's minimalism also was policentric rather than juricentric, emphasizing the Court's (limited) role as rectifier of the occasional legislative excess rather than its capacity as a coequal participant in the constitutional democratic enterprise.[22]

The advent in the 1980s and early 1990s of the Rehnquist Court, with its majority of Republican appointees, shook the Left's complacency about judicial review and reignited among American constitutional theorists a general interest in the idea of judicial minimalism. One product of this renaissance has been the emergence of the New Judicial Minimalism, a loosely allied school of theorists interested in reviving many of Bickel's central minimalist ideas. As we explain here, the New Minimalism owes much to Bickel's core themes of procedural restraint and interbranch colloquy, although its animus turns out to be considerably less juricentric than Bickel's.

Connections to Bickel

The New Judicial Minimalists have varied agendas, but they share Bickel's two main themes. First is an interest in techniques of procedural minimalism—methods, like Bickel's passive virtues, by which the Court can avoid or defer the decision of constitutional issues. Second is an emphasis on the idea of colloquy between the Court and the political branches of government, with a corresponding rejection of the notion of absolute judicial supremacy in constitutional decision making.

1. Procedural Minimalism. While contemporary conservative critics of judicial review like Robert Bork typically have advocated substantive minimalism in the tradition of Thayer and Hand, the New Judicial Minimalists follow Bickel in promoting the use of procedural minimalist techniques. For example, Cass Sunstein, probably the most influential New Minimalist, advocates what he calls "narrow" and "shallow" constitutional decision making by the Court: Narrow court decisions "try to decide cases rather than set down broad rules," while shallow court decisions form "concrete judgments on particular cases, unaccompanied by abstract accounts about what accounts for those judgments."[23] Put another way, narrow and shallow decisions limit their binding impact as closely as possible to the facts of the cases being decided.

The point of narrow and shallow decision making for Sunstein is twofold. First, narrow and shallow decisions leave many issues undecided, giving the political branches first crack at those issues and thus "allow[ing] democratic processes room to maneuver."[24] Such decisions reduce the costs of Court decision making, by allowing the Court to converge on a particular result without necessarily agreeing on the rationale or implications of that result. They also reduce both the costs and the risks of Court error, by leaving the Court free to reach different results in future cases involving similar issues. Faced with a narrow and shallow decision as a precedent, the Court can, in future cases, reason analogically from the result of the prior case without being strictly bound by the prior case's broad holding or deep reasoning.[25] Narrowness and shallowness thus allow flexibility and adaptability in both the judiciary and the political branches.

Second—and perhaps more important to Sunstein—narrow and shallow decisions often can be tailored to promote deliberation and accountability in political decision making. Rather than face a controversial constitutional question head-on, the Court can interpret or invalidate political decisions in ways that encourage the political branches to rethink them: striking down excessively vague provisions, invalidating insufficiently cabined delegations of legislative power, demanding a clear legislative statement before interpreting a statute in a particularly onerous way, declining to enforce statutes that have fallen victim to desuetude, or requiring evidence of "public-regarding justifications" for legislation.[26] (Sunstein's debt to Bickel here is obvious, both in the particular techniques Sunstein proposes for promoting democratic deliberation—Bickel had listed the doctrines of vagueness, improper delegation, clear statements, and desuetude among his passive virtues[27]—and in the very idea that the Court might use procedural-seeming techniques to encourage greater deliberation in the political branches, a notion at which Bickel strongly hinted.)[28]

The two primary goals Sunstein sets for procedural minimalism—limiting the impact of the Court's decision making vis-à-vis the political process and providing the impetus for that political process to more legitimately make its own decisions—are shared by other New Minimalists in various ways. Some, like Richard Fallon and Robert Burt, point to the utility of doctrinal "balancing tests" as ways to avoid permanent foreclosure of constitutional questions and to reinforce democratic values. Fallon, for example, articulates two minimalist justifications for doctrinal tests: They allow the Court to avoid deeply theorized grounds for its judgments, making agreement more attainable and allowing future decisions to be based upon different grounds;[29] they encourage deliberation in the political branches by requiring legitimate reasons for burdensome decisions.[30] For this latter reason, Burt similarly favors the use of so-called middle-tier or intermediate scrutiny under the Equal Protection Clause, which invalidates a discriminatory political decision where the government has not articulated an important state interest to justify it.[31] Burt also advocates the use of "void for vagueness" and ripeness doctrines and "clear statement" principles as means of avoiding a head-on decision of constitutional issues and of spurring democratic deliberation.[32]

Other New Minimalists pick up on Sunstein's devotion to narrow analogical reasoning as a way to avoid unnecessary foreclosure of constitutional issues. Michael Dorf goes even farther than Sunstein by proposing a form of "provisional adjudication" that involves a looser version of the common law method, in which the Court would "treat more of its precedents as provisional than is formally permitted under the doctrine of stare decisis,"[33] perhaps even "expressly designat[ing] some of its decisions . . . as subject to experiment . . . [or] as provisional, promising to revisit these matters at some future date."[34] Dorf's proposal implies, in effect, that some of the Court's decisions should be infinitely narrow, allowing not only for different resolutions of slightly different future cases (à la Sunstein), but even for different resolutions of virtually *identical* future cases. Neal Kumar Katyal takes a related approach, favoring a broader role for dicta in the decision of cases—a role that Katyal calls "advicegiving." For Katyal, "[a]dvicegiving occurs when judges recommend, but do not mandate, a particular course of action based on a rule or principle in a judicial case or controversy."[35] Katyal believes that judicial advicegiving combines the impact-limiting and democracy-promoting functions of procedural minimalism that Sunstein identifies, by allowing courts to avoid broad binding impacts of their decisions while at the same time signaling to the political branches the existence of potential constitutional problems.

A common theme of these New Minimalist efforts is their devotion to techniques of procedural minimalism, a devotion handed down by Bickel. Sunstein's narrow and shallow decision making, Dorf's "provisional adjudication," and Katyal's "judicial advicegiving" are, like the passive virtues, methods of avoiding unnecessary decision of constitutional issues; they speak to the timing and the scope of the Court's decision making, not to its substance. These techniques differ from the passive virtues only in their scope: Whereas Bickel advocated judicial avoidance of substantive constitutional issues altogether, the New Minimalists allow for the decision of such issues in the case at hand but warn against the unnecessary predecision of future cases that can arise from broad rules.

Other New Minimalist techniques—desuetude, clear statement principles, void-for-vagueness, and similar methodologies—derive directly from Bickel. Such doctrines seem on the surface to be more substantive than procedural; they dictate how actual constitutional cases should be decided. But in fact these devices are primarily procedural, as Bickel recognized, because they are ways of deciding *cases* while avoiding or deferring decisions of the central constitutional *issues* those cases seem to implicate. So, for example, both Sunstein and Bickel approve of the decision in *Kent v. Dulles*,[36] in which the Supreme Court forbade the secretary of state to deny passports to citizens found to be communists, not on the controversial ground, asserted by the plaintiff, that such denial violated the "right to travel" implicit in the Due Process Clause of the

Fifth Amendment, but for the more mundane reason that the secretary did not have clear statutory authorization to deny passports on the basis of communist affiliation.[37]

An important aspect of the New Minimalism, then, is a Bickelian shift in emphasis away from substantive deference to political decision making and toward procedural ways of skirting core constitutional issues. At the same time, as we explain in more detail in part IV, the New Minimalists generally ignore some of the more passive of Bickel's passive virtues: those methods of avoiding adjudication altogether, like strict enforcement of standing requirements, use of the political question doctrine, and parsimonious exercise of the Supreme Court's certiorari power. Most of the New Minimalists' procedural techniques are ways of deciding constitutional cases without deciding difficult constitutional issues, rather than ways of avoiding the decision of constitutional cases in the first place. Thus, in critical respects, the New Minimalists do not take procedural minimalism as far as Bickel was willing to take it.

2. Colloquy vs. Judicial Supremacy. Bickel saw judicial supremacy—the idea that the Supreme Court's constitutional decisions would be finally and conclusively binding on the other branches—as both undesirable and impracticable. He recognized that the authority of the Court's constitutional decisions relies ultimately on the general political acceptability of those decisions, and he believed that the constitutional principle the Court applies derives in part from political practice—from the public realization, after opportunity for discussion and experimentation, that a particular principle must apply to a particular circumstance in a particular way. These themes are what Bickel meant to invoke by his dictum that "principle is evolved conversationally[,] not perfected unilaterally" (LDB, 244).

Many of the New Judicial Minimalists have taken up this theme of inter-branch colloquy (some more than others). Robert Burt in particular has advanced "an egalitarian conception of authority among the branches" in constitutional interpretation,[38] one in which the Court uses procedural minimalism as a way to avoid finally trumping the political process. For Burt, the Court's primary mission should be to encourage unanimity among the three branches on issues of constitutional principle rather than to impose, dictatorially, its own vision of principle on the other branches.[39]

Other New Minimalists advocate similar conversational approaches. The point of Katyal's "advice giving" is precisely to stimulate colloquy between the Court and the political branches about constitutional issues, by calling upon the Court to make clear (if nonbinding) pronouncements of constitutional values. Michael Dorf's "provisional adjudication" is likewise intended to allow for experimentation and deliberation in the political branches before constitutional issues are "finally" decided. And Sunstein's emphasis on "democracy-promoting" minimalism assumes a conversational political culture, one in which the political branches pay attention and respond to both the results and the rationales of Court decisions.

Thus, the New Minimalists have learned from Bickel the desirability of inter-branch colloquy rather than naked judicial supremacy—although, as we contend below, their motives for rejecting judicial supremacy tend ultimately to differ in an important way from Bickel's.

Departures from Bickel

Bickel's procedural minimalism was juricentric—grounded in a vision of the judiciary as an independent and coequal component, with the political branches, in a holistic scheme of constitutional decision making. The New Minimalism, in contrast, is primarily policentric—based on a conception of the judiciary as a threat to the supposedly more legitimate decision-making authority of the political branches. We explain this philosophical contrast in this section, and then connect it to a more practical divergence between Bickel's procedural minimalism and the New Minimalists' occasional forays into substantive minimalism.

1. Policentrism. Bickel combined an appreciation of the Court's dependence on the political branches with an understanding that the Court is uniquely capable of interpreting constitutional principle. For Bickel, again, the Court was dependent upon the political branches in two interrelated ways. As a practical matter, Bickel recognized that the Court's authority ultimately extends only so far as the political process chooses to recognize it. More philosophically, Bickel believed that the principles from which good constitutional decisions are wrought come ultimately from colloquy among the three branches of government. Thus, Bickel advocated procedural minimalism as a means of allowing constitutional principle to develop, to ripen, thereby becoming more politically palatable when finally articulated by the Court.

But Bickel also believed that, once principle has suitably ripened, the Court should not shy away from implementing it out of deference to the political branches. Courts, after all, "have certain capacities for dealing with matters of principle that legislatures and executives do not possess" (LDB, 25). Of the three branches, Bickel believed, the judiciary, as the most deliberative and the most politically insulated, was best equipped to synthesize constitutional principle from diverse political and judicial experience and to apply it in particular cases. At bottom, then, Bickel championed judicial deference to politics in constitutional decision making, but deference of a particular, holistic kind—deference to the political system as a whole, of which the Court was a vital and coequal part, rather than deference to particular decisions made by particular political institutions.

The result was a view that the Court is neither superior in practice nor subservient in political pedigree to the elected branches of government. Procedural minimalism was, for Bickel, both a necessary implication of the Court's practical lack of supremacy and a strategic device for maintaining its decision making legitimacy within the political system. It was, in other words, an approach motivated by juricentrism—by a desire to preserve the Court's position as a coequal institution with inherent importance in the constitutional scheme.

In sharp contrast, the New Minimalism is motivated primarily by policentrism—by a desire to preserve the supposed prerogative of the political branches to make most constitutional decisions, unimpeded by interference from the judiciary. The New Minimalist policentrism arises from the adoption of a central premise that Bickel rejected: the belief that political decision making is generally preferable to judicial decision making on constitutional issues, including issues involving rights. Consider Sunstein's statement of the difference between his approach and that of Bickel:

> My argument here [Sunstein writes] finds its foundations in the aspiration to deliberative democracy, with an insistence that the principal vehicle is the legislature, not the judiciary. . . . For Bickel, the Court was the basic repository of principle in American government; because of its insulation, it was the central deliberative institution. By contrast, a central point here is that the Court's understanding of the (constitutionally relevant) principle may well be wrong; I think Bickel erred in seeing the Court as having a systematically better understanding of "principle" than other branches.[40]

Sunstein, it should be noted, elides here a crucial component of Bickel's theory. Although Bickel held that the Court should apply constitutional principles even in the face of contemporaneous political disagreement, he believed that those principles themselves were best developed not unilaterally but holistically, through trial and error and discourse among the three governmental branches (and often the states). Thus, it is somewhat inaccurate to ascribe to Bickel a view that the Court "understands" principle better than the political branches. Bickel rather believed that the Court, as a deliberative institution, could *interpret* principle better than the political branches (principle that, nonetheless, arose through colloquy *with* the political branches) and then, as a politically insulated institution, could *apply* principle better on the facts of particular cases.

Nonetheless, Sunstein is correct to identify an elemental distinction between Bickel's juricentric faith in the competency and, thus the legitimacy, of judicial decision making and his own policentric preference for decision making by the political branches. This latter preference is shared by other New Minimalists. Fallon in particular asserts that where "reasonable disagreement" exists on constitutional issues, "the basic commitment of the Constitution is to permit decision by democratic majorities and their elected representatives."[41] Dorf criticizes adjudication partly because he believes it is slower than the political process in responding to changing social conditions.[42] Katyal counsels judicial advicegiving as a way to "avoid interference with legislative power."[43] Each of these expressions of the New Minimalism is underwritten by a distrust of judicial decision making vis-à-vis decision making by political institutions.

Animated by their policentric preference for political branch decision making, the New Minimalists have sought ways to limit the occasions on which the Court interferes with the political process. Bickel's brand of minimalism, in contrast, was motivated by a juricentric desire to maintain the Court's ability to *participate* in what he saw as a larger political process, one that produces constitutional principles through colloquy and experimentalism rather than unilateral decree.

2. SUBSTANTIVE MINIMALISM. One consequence of the New Minimalism's policentric focus is an amenability to substantive minimalism that Bickel, the juricentrist, did not share. If one believes that political decision making is preferable, all else being equal, to judicial decision making, then one is inclined to promote substantive (and not

just procedural) minimalism on occasion, as most of the New Minimalists in fact do. One is inclined to believe that there are at least some issues of constitutional principle with respect to which the Court will never be a superior decision maker to the political branches, and, if so, then in cases involving those issues the Court should simply defer to the result reached by the political process.

Sunstein again serves as a prime exemplar of this tendency. While Sunstein's theoretical defense of miminalism is mostly procedural—focusing on techniques of avoiding unnecessary constitutional decisions and encouraging deliberative and accountable political decision making—his applications of minimalism in particular cases often reveal a substantive aspect. For example, Sunstein defends the Supreme Court's decisions in *Washington v. Glucksberg*[44] and *Vacco v. Quill*,[45] which upheld state laws forbidding physician-assisted suicide, partly on the ground that the Court should be "wary of recognizing rights of this kind amid complex issues of fact and value."[46] Similarly, Sunstein suggests that the constitutional permissibility of affirmative action ultimately "should be settled democratically, not judicially,"[47] and he defends recent First Amendment decisions involving new communications technologies partly on the grounds that factual and moral "flux" in this area "argues in favor of judicial caution in invalidating regulatory controls."[48] In each of these contexts, Sunstein advocates not judicial avoidance or deferral of constitutional decision making in particular areas—procedural minimalist techniques—but rather substantive deference to "reasonable" political judgments in those areas.[49]

Fallon and Dorf similarly favor limited use of substantive minimalism. Fallon is enthusiastic about what he calls "nonsuspect-content" tests in constitutional adjudication, including rational basis review of legislation under the Due Process and Equal Protection Clauses; he believes that such tests appropriately defer to political decision making in areas of "reasonable disagreement" about constitutional norms.[50] This approach is reminiscent both of Thayer's dictate that the Court overrule political decisions only in cases of "clear mistake," and of Hand's insistence that the Court is no better able to make difficult value judgments than is the political process.

For his part, Dorf thinks the Court should "give greater deference to state policies that arguably infringe constitutional rights than to equivalent uniform national policies" and should generally limit itself to "the articulation of fundamental . . . values," leaving the implementation of those values mostly to the political process.[51] These recommendations too are substantively minimalist, in that they counsel not judicial avoidance of constitutional issues but presumptive judicial validation of certain political decisions on their merits.

In sum, then, Bickel's underlying juricentrism animated his choice of procedural over substantive minimalism; Bickel believed the Court should preserve its authority by choosing carefully whether and when to decide a constitutional issue, but then should decide it unabashedly, with reference but not deference to politics. In contrast, the New Minimalists' underlying policentrism animates their willingness to indulge substantive minimalism; they believe there are some (perhaps many) constitutional issues with respect to which the Court simply should not override political decisions.

IV. Assessing the New Judicial Minimalism

The New Judicial Minimalism goes both too far and not far enough. On the one hand, substantive minimalism, with its policentric emphasis, does not recognize how it is that courts participate in constitutional dialogues with the political branches and the people—dialogues which make the Constitution more relevant and stable. For these dialogues to occur, the Court must play a part in shaping political and popular discourse. On the other hand, by deemphasizing certiorari denials and other delaying strategies, the New Minimalists do not recognize how inherent limits in judicial capacity sometimes stand in the way of judicial review of governmental decision making.

The Costs of Substantive Minimalism

Courts often play a profound and beneficial role in the shaping of constitutional values. Judges, thanks principally to life tenure, are less likely to be driven by political expediency than elected officials. Moreover, because courts must offer reasons for their decisions, judges are apt to take seriously their responsibility to advance logical coherent arguments. In other words, courts are more likely than other parts of government "to appeal to men's better natures, to call forth aspirations" (LDB, 26), and "to be a voice of reason . . . articulating and developing impersonal and durable principles."[52]

Judges, of course, are not philosopher kings. But their willingness to speak about principle can be salutary, even if the principles they identify are wrongheaded. And, by sometimes invoking high-sounding principles when striking down elected government action, court decisions upholding governmental decision making have greater force.[53]

Beyond these institutional advantages, there can be severe costs when judges fail to enforce constitutional principle, or when they deferentially legitimatize an erroneous principle defined by the political branches. Consider, for example, *Plessy v. Ferguson*.[54] By leaving the issue of racial segregation to the political process (a substantively minimalist outcome), the Court did little more than "inflict unnecessary pain" for over half a century.[55] In sharp contrast, *Brown v. Board* (a decision which recognized that courts must participate in the shaping of constitutional values) was a first step in ending state-sponsored segregation. And while the New Minimalists do not dispute—how could they?—that the Court must sometimes stand against the majority to articulate rights, their policentric approach discounts the ways that courts sometimes prod elected government into action.

The saga of abortion rights likewise underscores how constitutional decision making is improved by Court-elected government dialogues. *Roe v. Wade* served as a critical trigger to abortion rights, overcoming politically potent pro-life interests that have always stood in the way of populist abortion reform.[56] *Roe* also prompted elected government into action. From 1973 to 1989, 306 abortion-restricting measures were passed by forty-eight states.[57] During that same period, the Court responded to these pressures in piecemeal fashion and cut back on *Roe*'s broad holding, returning some of the decision-making power relating to this divisive issue back to the states.[58] This gradual judicial adjustment of *Roe* culminated in the Court's 1992 decision in *Planned Parenthood v. Casey*, which, while reaffirming "the central holding of *Roe*," repudiated *Roe*'s stringent trimester test in favor of a more deferential "undue burden" standard which thus signaled the Court's increasing willingness to uphold much (if not all) state regulation of abortion.[59]

Without question, to a pro-choice advocate, *Casey*'s balance sells out important interests of women, and, to a pro-lifer, it permits moral outrages to continue. But there is no realistic alternative to *Casey's* balancing act. The political upheaval that followed *Roe* reveals the unworkability of a strident, substantively maximalist pro-choice jurisprudence. Conversely, a substantively minimalist jurisprudence, allowing the outright prohibition of abortions, is equally unworkable; in the years before *Roe*, when nontherapeutic abortions were prohibited in nearly every state, abortions were almost as common as they are in the post-*Roe* period (albeit less safe).[60] Ultimately, abortion is too divisive for either pro-choice or pro-life absolutism to rule the day. *Roe* may have gone too far, but through narrow construction of *Roe*'s precedential impact, the Court eventually succeeded in mitigating the harsh absolutism of that decision. And the history of the abortion debate demonstrates that the judiciary needs to play a leadership role, if a flexible one, in recognizing constitutional rights. To be sure, a workable approach towards abortion rights also has required elected government participation; but the Court has provided the leading voice in the shaping of constitutional values—a role that substantive minimalism unduly discounts.

Reinvigorating "The Passive Virtues"

In arguing that courts should be active, forceful interpreters of the Constitution, we do not mean to suggest that courts should not look before they leap. Inherent limits in judicial fact-finding and the need for Court decision making to take social and political forces into account both suggest that—at least sometimes—the Court would be well advised to employ procedurally minimalist delaying strategies, including certiorari denials and the strict enforcement of standing requirements.

Courts, notwithstanding their institutional strengths, cannot escape "the unfortunate consequences of judicial ignorance of the social realities behind the issues with which they grapple."[61] Specifically, with judges and advocates relying on precedent-based legal arguments, courts rarely can engage in thorough cost-benefit analysis. Courts may also be hamstrung in that they decide cases at a single moment in time, so that a changed understanding of the underlying facts sometimes can only be corrected through a reversal. Moreover, notwithstanding *amicus curiae* filings, the Court often relies on the arguments made by the parties before it, and the parties before it frequently frame the issues that the Court will consider. Correspondingly, the Court may "anchor" its decision making in its perceptions of whether the parties before it are sympathetic or not. Problems may arise, however, when different parties, raising identical legal issues, appear more or less sympathetic and, as such, the Court's decision may well be tied to the accident of which plaintiff presents its case to the Court.[62]

It is true that these shortcomings often can be mitigated by the kind of procedural minimalism advocated by the New Minimalists, particularly Sunstein. A narrow and shallow decision, limited as closely as possible to the facts of the case, can allow the Court room to maneuver in future cases if changed understandings and more or less sympathetic litigants present themselves. Sometimes, however, the Court will not be able to prevent its decision from having a broad impact. For example, the decisions in *Brown v. Board of Education*—despite the Court's caution to avoid prescribing an immediate, one size fits all remedy for school segregation—necessarily controlled the policies of hundreds of school districts across the country that enforced racial segregation, and in so doing profoundly affected the lives of millions of interested citizens well into the future. Where this kind of impact cannot be avoided (as in many constitutional contexts), narrowness and shallowness in decision-making will not be enough to escape the potentially severe costs of a Supreme Court's misjudgment.

Beyond the prospect of getting the facts wrong, the risks of elected government reprisal also suggest that courts should sometimes delay a definitive ruling (or, for that matter, any ruling—however narrow or shallow it may be). Following its decisions in *Brown*, for example, the Court steered clear of the school desegregation issue for more than a decade. Indeed, well aware of the "momentum of history" and the "deep feeling" people had about school segregation, the Court refused to hear a 1955 challenge to Virginia's antimiscegenation law rather than risk "thwarting or seriously handicapping" its decision in *Brown* and, with it, its institutional prestige.[63] By 1964, however, Congress and the White House—through the monumental 1964 Civil Rights Act—had made it clear that they were prepared to lend their institutional support to the dismantling of single-race schools. It was against this backdrop that the Warren Court finally returned to school desegregation. In 1964, it finally recognized that "the time for mere deliberate speed has run out"[64] and, in 1968, it returned to school desegregation in earnest, demanding that school boards "come forward with a plan that promises realistically to work, and promises realistically to work now."[65] And in 1967, with the principle of desegregation safely established, the Justices revisited the miscegenation question, unanimously striking down the Virginia statute.[66]

The Court's ability to navigate desegregation (at least before forced busing) is truly remarkable. It reveals that the Court can pursue radical social change while taking into account inherent limits in its authority. In particular, by seeing each decision (including a decision not to decide) as part of a broader mosaic, the Court can allow time for cultural norms to change and settle so that its decision can win wider acceptability.

Delay, as Alexander Bickel put it, has the advantage of allowing the "full political and historical context, the relationship between the Court and the representative institutions of government" to be made clearer (LDB, 124). To their credit, the New Judicial Minimalists embrace certain strategies for delaying decision of issues and—no less important—for avoiding foreclosure of further discussion and reevaluation of those issues. Nevertheless, by failing to take into account the appropriate uses of certiorari denials and findings of no standing, the New Minimalists commit error. The Court sometimes is best off avoiding an issue altogether, to revisit it only when sufficient factual data and moral consensus have emerged. (This, after all, is what the political branches often do in the face of conflict or uncertainty.) More to the point, if the Court is to play an active role in shaping constitutional values (by issuing nonminimalist substantive decisions), the Court must be especially careful to take into account both limitations in its own fact-finding and a case's sociopolitical setting. By utilizing *all* of the passive virtues, the Court can combat its inherent institutional disabilities and take the long view on the issues before it.

V. Conclusion

Constitutional decision making is a never ending process involving all parts of the government and the people, too. For this reason, as Ruth Bader Ginsburg observed, "[J]udges play an interdependent part in our democracy. They do not alone shape legal doctrine but . . . they participate in a dialogue with other organs of government, and with the people as well."[67] In participating in constitutional dialogues, judges cannot simply sit on the sidelines rubber-stamping government. Rather, they must be full-throttled participants, sometimes upholding and other times rejecting elected government decision making.

By giving short shrift to the critical role that courts can and should play in constitutional dialogues, the New Judicial Minimalism is too policentric. In particular, today's minimalists are wrong in assuming that the judiciary should play a role subordinate to the political branches, and then defending or attacking judicial review on the basis of its success or failure in preserving that subordination. Unlike the work of Alexander Bickel that they invoke, the New Minimalists demand judicial restraint solely as a means of permitting as many decisions as possible to be made politically and of increasing the extent to which those political decisions are deliberative and accountable. This is an unnecessarily crabbed vision of the judicial role.

On the other hand, the New Minimalism commits a different type of error by emphasizing ways in which the Supreme Court can decide cases without issuing far-ranging opinions on the Constitution's meaning. Sometimes the Court should simply steer clear of an issue. In this way, as Alexander Bickel well understood, the Court can take both politics and its institutional weaknesses into account while trying to preserve its role as the oracle of principle in the American constitutional system.

Notes

1. Cass R. Sunstein, *One Case at a Time: Judicial Minimalism on the Supreme Court* (Cambridge, MA: Harvard University Press, 1999), 9.

2. Alexander M. Bickel, *The Least Dangerous Branch*, 2d ed. (Princeton, NJ: Princeton University Press, 1986). Subsequent references to this work are cited in the text and notes with the following abbreviation: LDB.

3. *Brown v. Board of Education*, 347 U.S. 483 (1954).

4. Gerald Gunther, "The Subtle Vices of the "Passive Virtues"—A Comment on Principle and Expediency in Judicial Review," *Columbia Law Review* 64 (1964): 1, 3.

5. See James Bradley Thayer, *John Marshall* (Boston, MA: Houghton Mifflin, 1901), 103–07.

6. See James Bradley Thayer, "The Origin and Scope of the American Doctrine of Constitutional Law," *Harvard Law Review* 7 (1893): 129. Bickel discusses and critiques Thayer's "rule" in Bickel, LDB, 35–46.

7. See Gerald Gunther, *Learned Hand: The Man and the Judge* (New York: Knopf, 1994), xvi, 50–52.

8. See Learned Hand, *The Bill of Rights* (Cambridge, MA: Harvard University Press, 1958).

9. Learned Hand, "The Contribution of an Independent Judiciary to Civilization," in *The Spirit of Liberty*, ed. I. Dilliard (New York: Knopf, 1952), 155–65.

10. Bickel, LDB, 24; see also ibid., 69. "When it strikes down legislative policy, the Court must act rigorously on principle, else it undermines the justification for its power"; ibid., 188. "The role of the Court and its raison d'être are to evolve 'to preserve, protect and defend' principle."

11. Indeed, Wechsler himself famously applied his theory of neutral principles to question the decision in *Brown v. Board of Education*. See Herbert "Wechsler, Toward Neutral Principles of Constitutional Law," *Harvard Law Review* 73 (1959): 1, 31–34.

12. *The Federalist* No. 78 (Alexander Hamilton), ed. Isaac Kramnick (New York: Viking Penguin, 1987), 437.

13. The particular phrase "as a political rule" was used several times by Lincoln in his debates with Stephen Douglas. See, e.g., Abraham Lincoln, Speech at Chicago, Illinois (July 10, 1858), in *Abraham Lincoln: His Speeches and Writings*, ed. Roy P. Basler (Cleveland, NY: World Publishing Co., 1946), 385, 396. See also Bickel, LDB, 260 (quoting Lincoln).

14. For Bickel, the paradigmatic example of this back and forth process is *Brown v. Board of Education*. See LDB, 244–72.

15. This phrase is Bickel's. See LDB, 240.

16. One arguable exception to this generalization was John Hart Ely's germinal 1980 book *Democracy and Distrust* (Cambridge, MA: Harvard University Press, 1980), a work that, like Bickel's *The Least Dangerous Branch*, sought both to justify judicial review and to imply from that justification certain limits upon its legitimate exercise.

17. *Roe v. Wade*, 410 U.S. 113 (1973).

18. *See, e.g.*, *Mapp v. Ohio*, 367 U.S. 643 (1961) (excluding evidence obtained by unconstitutional search); *Miranda v. Arizona*, 384 U.S. 436 (1966) (excluding defendant statements obtained without appropriate safeguards of rights to counsel and against self-incrimination).

19. For some diverse discussions from this period of the imprecise concept of "judicial activism," see the essays collected in *Supreme Court Activism and Restraint*, eds. Stephen C. Halpern and Charles M. Lamb (Lexington, MA: Lexington Books, 1982). See also, e.g., Archibald Cox, "The Role of the Supreme Court: Judicial Activism or Self-Restraint?", *Maryland Law Review* 47 (1987): 118; Mark V. Tushnet, "Comment on Cox," *Maryland Law Review* 47 (1987): 147; William Wayne Justice, "The Two Faces of Judicial Activism," 61 (1992): 1.

20. See Robert H. Bork, *The Tempting of America* (New York: Free Press, 1990); Robert H. Bork, "Neutral Principles and Some First Amendment Problems," *Indiana Law Journal* 47 (1971): 1.

21. The version of originalism that Bork advocates as the only legitimate approach to constitutional interpretation has a sort of "clear mistake" rule built in: A potential interpretation that cannot be "shown to be a constitutional principle" because "the historical evidence" that the principle was within the original understanding "is unclear" cannot, for that reason, be enforced by judges "against a current legislative majority's decision" Bork, *The Tempting of America*, 149–50. "Democratic choice must be accepted by the judge where the Constitution is silent," ibid., 150—which, for Bork, means in cases where a potentially

applicable constitutional principle is not "clearly" supported by "the historical evidence." Thus, a court must uphold—validate—a political decision (a "[d]emocratic choice") unless the historical evidence clearly demonstrates an original understanding that such a decision was not to be permitted. This is a standard potentially as deferential to political decision making as Thayer's clear mistake rule.

22. See, e.g., Bork, *The Tempting of America*, 4–5.

23. Sunstein, *One Case at a Time*, 10, 13, 25.

24. Ibid., 54.

25. See ibid., 42–45. Sunstein develops these ideas more extensively in Cass R. Sunstein, *Legal Reasoning and Political Conflict* (New York: Oxford University Press, 1996).

26. See Sunstein, *One Case At A Time*, 27.

27. On desuetude and vagueness, see Bickel, at LDB, 147–56; on delegation and clear statements, see ibid., 156–69. Bickel, however, did not approve of the kind of search for legislative "motive" that Sunstein's proposed requirement of "public-regarding justifications" might be thought to suggest. See ibid., 208–21.

28. See ibid., 155–56, in which Bickel approves of the Court's deferral of the Connecticut birth control prohibition case on the ground that "it is quite wrong for the Court to relieve [Connecticut citizens and officials] of th[e] burden of self-government."

29. See Richard H. Fallon, Jr., "The Supreme Court, 1996 Term—Foreword: Implementing the Constitution," *Harvard Law Review* 111 (1997): 54, 116. This argument echoes one made by Sunstein. See, e.g., Sunstein, *One Case at a Time*, 11–14; Sunstein, *Legal Reasoning*, 35–61.

30. See Fallon, "The Supreme Court, 1996 Term," 76.

31. See Robert A. Burt, *The Constitution in Conflict* (Cambridge, MA: Belknap Press, 1992), 362–67.

32. Ibid., 359–62.

33. Michael C. Dorf, "The Supreme Court, 1997 Term—Foreword: The Limits of Socratic Deliberation," *Harvard Law Review* 112 (1998): 11.

34. Ibid., 73.

35. Neal Kumar Katyal, "Judges as Advicegivers," *Stanford Law Review* 50 (1998): 1709, 1710.

36. *Kent v. Dulles*, 357 U.S. 116 (1958).

37. See Bickel, LDB, 164–67; Sunstein, *One Case at a Time*, 27.

38. Burt, *The Constitution in Conflict*, 5.

39. Unlike most of the New Minimalists, however, Burt is decidedly distrustful of the political process. His version of judicial minimalism is inspired not by a preference for political over judicial decision making, but by a conception of democracy as the absence of coercion. See Christopher J. Peters, "Assessing the New Judicial Minimalism," *Columbia Law Review* 100 (2000): 1454, 1470.

40. Sunstein, *One Case at a Time*, 6, n.5.
41. Fallon, "The Supreme Court 1996 Term," 89.
42. See Dorf, "The Supreme Court 1997 Term," 43–45, 53.
43. Katyal, "Judges as Advicegivers," 1711.
44. *Washington v. Glucksberg*, 521 U.S. 702 (1997).
45. *Vacco v. Quill*, 521 U.S. 793 (1997).
46. Sunstein, *One Case at a Time*, 76.
47. Ibid., 117.
48. Ibid., 174. The decisions Sunstein defends are *Denver Area Educational Telecommunications Consortium, Inc. v. FCC*, 518 U.S. 727 (1996); *Reno v. ACLU*, 521 U.S. 844 (1997); *Turner Broadcasting System, Inc. v. FCC*, 512 U.S. 622 (1994), reh'g denied 52 U.S. 1278 (1994); and *Turner Broadcasting System, Inc. v. FCC*, 520 U.S. 180 (1997).
49. Sunstein, *One Case at a Time*, 103.
50. See Fallon, "The Supreme Court 1996 Term," 88.
51. Dorf, "The Supreme Court 1997 Term," 10, 79; see also ibid., 62–65. The details of Dorf's proposal that the Court should mostly confine itself to the articulation of rather abstract values, leaving questions of implementation to political decision makers, are spelled out in Michael C. Dorf and Charles F. Sabel, "A Constitution of Democratic Experimentalism," *Columbia Law Review* 98 (1998): 267, 388–404, 444–69.
52. Henry M. Hart, Jr., "Foreword: The Time Chart of the Justices," *Harvard Law Review* 73 (1959): 84, 99.
53. In this way, the Court "through its history, has acted as a legitimator of government." Charles L. Black, Jr., *The People and the Courts* (Englewood Cliffs, NJ: Prentice-Hall, 1960), 52.
54. *Plessy v. Ferguson*, 163 U.S. 537 (1896).
55. Mark Tushnet, "How to Deny a Constitutional Right: Reflections on the Assisted-Suicide Cases," *Green Bag* 2d 1 (1997): 55, 60.
56. See David J. Garrow, *Liberty and Sexuality* (New York: Macmillan Publishing Co., 1993), 359, 374 (explaining that when Roe was decided, pro-choice activists had abandoned efforts to seek legislative repeal of criminal abortion statutes).
57. See Glen Halva-Neubauer, "Abortion Policy in the Post-Webster Age," *Publius* 20 (1990): 27, 43.
58. See, e.g., *Planned Parenthood of Central Missouri v. Danforth*, 428 U.S. 52, 63 (1976; *Maher v. Roe*, 432 U.S. 464 (1977; *Harris v. McRae*, 448 U.S. 297 (1980; *H.L. v. Matheson*, 450 U.S. 398 (1981); *Planned Parenthood Association of Kansas City v. Ashcroft*, 462 U.S. 476 (1983); *Webster v. Reproductive Health Services.*, 492 U.S. 490, 507–11 (1989); *Hodgson v. Minnesota*, 457 U.S. 417 (1990); *Ohio v. Akron Center for Reproductive Health*, 457 U.S. 502 (1990; *Rust v. Sullivan*, 500 U.S. 173 (1991.
59. See 505 U.S. 833, 878 (1992).

60. Gerald N. Rosenberg, *The Hollow Hope* (Chicago: University of Chicago Press, 1991), 353–55.

61. Richard A. Posner, "Against Constitutional Theory," 73 *New York University Law Review* 73 (1998): 1–12.

62. For extensive discussions of the representative aspects of adjudication, see Christopher J. Peters, "Adjudication as Representation," *Columbia Law Review* 97 (1997): 312; Peters, "Assessing The New Judicial Minimalism," 1477–92.

63. Del Dickson, "State Court Defiance and the Limits of Supreme Court Authority: *Williams v. Georgia* Revisited," *Yale Law Journal* 103 (1994): 1423, 1476, and n.317 (quoting a Nov. 4, 1955 memorandum from Justice Felix N. Frankfurter to the Conference).

64. *Griffin v. County School Bd.*, 377 U.S. 218, 234 (1964).

65. *Green v. County School Board*, 391 U.S. 430 (1968).

66. *Loving v. Virginia*, 388 U.S. 1 (1967).

67. Ruth Bader Ginsburg, "Speaking in a Judicial Voice," *New York University Law Review* 67 (1992): 1185, 1198.

Chapter 4

Democratic Constitutionalism
The Bickel-Ackerman Dialectic

David M. Golove

Any theory of constitutional law for a *constitutional democracy* must perforce offer an explanation of the relationship between basic democratic norms and constitutionalism and, at least in the American case, for the practice of judicial review. The enduring challenges are familiar: Why should we be ruled by the dead hand of the past, allowing judgments made by our forebears, even if by a majority or supermajority of them, to override democratic decisions we make today? And, why should a court have final say over the interpretation and application of the Constitution and hence the way we govern ourselves on fundamental issues? These questions collectively express the tension that Alexander Bickel famously captured in his phrase, "The Counter-Majoritarian Difficulty,"[1] and they have provoked a generation of theorists to offer a bewildering array of answers.

Yet, few of Bickel's successors have actually managed to meet the formidable goal which he set for himself—to articulate a theory that both sustains a robust role for constitutionalism and judicial review but still roots the ultimate justification for constitutional principles in the actual ongoing consent of (a majority of) the people. Without meaning to prejudge any larger issues in democratic theory, I will call a constitutional theory meeting the latter requirements *democratic* and the family of such theories *democratic constitutionalism*. Most constitutional theories are democratic in the minimal sense that they consider the approval of the people ab initio a necessary condition to the validity of a constitution. Far more controversial, however, is the proposition that consent must be ongoing. Under a constitutional system that permits ready amendment by a majority, ongoing consent does not present a special problem. In such a system, the absence of amendment gives rise to a presumption of ongoing consent. Because of the peculiar difficulty of amendment in the case of the American Constitution, however, no such presumption is available. Thus, for any theory which is democratic in the sense I have specified, the need to ensure ongoing consent will necessarily influence one or more of the theory's critical components: the choice of interpretive methodologies, the assignment of institutional responsibilities for constitutional interpretation, and the attitude towards constitutional change outside the formal amendment process.[2]

There are, of course, many familiar theories that are not democratic in my sense. They seek various other means to mitigate or resolve the tension between democracy and constitutionalism, including by advocating a broad construction of governmental powers, defending an aggressive judicial role when it comes to perfecting the democratic system itself, or insisting that the Constitution is, or should be, justice-seeking first and democratic second. Whatever the version, however, none are democratic because they do not insist that the principles of constitutional law must themselves ultimately be rooted in the ongoing consent of the people.

In this essay, I examine two competing efforts to meet this Bickelian ideal—Bickel's own theory and that of perhaps his most prominent student, Bruce Ackerman. Although both theories aspire to be democratic, they offer diverging accounts on many fundamental issues, most strikingly in their approaches to judicial review and constitutional interpretation. These differences, I will claim, are themselves rooted in contrasting accounts of democracy and popular sovereignty: Ackerman's republican dualism, with its emphasis on reasoned deliberation, leads him to endorse a strictly backwards looking, preservationist theory of interpretation and judicial review; Bickel's Burkean consensualism yields a more fluid interpretive methodology and room for a larger more creative role for the elite judiciary. Nevertheless, reconciliation of their accounts is both possible and desirable. I will argue that Ackerman is right in emphasizing the importance of rare moments of heightened popular mobilization in inaugurating new constitutional regimes, but wrong in thinking that the character of such new regimes can be fixed in single moments of enactment. Constitutionalism is an always ongoing project. Bickel, in turn, is right in viewing constitutional change as a fluid process, but wrong in insisting on gradualism and incremental change and in dismissing the possibility of self-conscious popular revision of fundamental law.

In the first section, I demonstrate how both Bickel and Ackerman are exemplars of democratic constitutionalism. In the next section, I show how their contrasting approaches to judicial review and constitutional interpretation are rooted in their differing accounts of democracy. In the final section, I offer some critical reflections and propose a tentative synthesis that combines the stronger aspects of both of their approaches.[3]

I. The Democratic Constitutionalism of Bickel and Ackerman

It may seem peculiar to lump Bickel and Ackerman into the same camp for any purpose. Notwithstanding their radically different temperaments and philosophical commitments, however, Ackerman in an especially fundamental way has taken to heart Bickel's core theoretical insight that constitutionalism and judicial review can only be justified if they can be made consistent with the fundamental democratic premises of the American political system.

Ackerman

Ackerman is explicit throughout about "the Constitution's foundational commitment to popular sovereignty."[4] He believes that the principles of American constitutional law obtain their validity in only one way—from their self-conscious affirmation by a clear majority of the citizenry in moments of mobilized deliberation.[5]

Ackerman's focus is on the moment of lawmaking—the moment when the Constitution is adopted or an amendment ratified. For Ackerman, the crucial point is that this moment of enactment represents, or should represent when working properly, the culminating achievement of a special kind of political process: The people as a whole (or at least a large portion of them) have engaged in serious deliberation about one or more aspects of their political values and have coalesced (or at least a clear majority of them have coalesced) around novel principles to express a new political identity. The moment of enactment (or, in Ackerman's terms, "codification" (WPF, 288)) is the moment when these novel principles become constitutional law, the successful conclusion of a period of "constitutional politics" (WPF, 7) or "higher lawmaking" (WPF, 6).[6]

But Ackerman is also an antiformalist. He insists that enactments of new constitutional law need not take the form of formal amendments. The political process leading to "amendment" of the Constitution need not, and historically has not, Ackerman claims, invariably followed the forms specified in Article V of the Constitution. To "amend" the Constitution, what is crucial is that there are sufficiently reliable indicia that a political movement has in fact provoked the sustained deliberation of the citizenry over a question of fundamental principle and has successfully mobilized a clear majority in favor of a new constitutional solution (WPF, 44–56, 266–94; WPT, 10–31, 69–88). Applying this model, Ackerman famously argues that the procedural illegalities attending the Founding and the adoption of the Fourteenth Amendment can appropriately be disregarded and, most strikingly, that the struggles between Franklin D. Roosevelt and the Old Court during the New Deal resulted in a transformative set of informal constitutional "amendments" in 1937.[7]

At the same time, Ackerman's theory retains a powerful strand of formalist thinking. Indeed, he has sought to define a rigorous set of formal criteria, derived in common law fashion from historical precedents, by which to test the claim that a political movement has successfully achieved an informal amendment.[8] These criteria act as an alternative to the "classical" set specified in Article V (WPF, 267) and seek to ensure that when a genuine act of popular sovereignty has occurred, its animating principles are incorporated into constitutional law, and, conversely, that when a movement fails to achieve the necessary deliberative support, its proposed principles are not (WPF, 266–90; WPT, 85–88, 403–06).

As a descriptive matter, Ackerman argues that there have been a number of (formal and informal) constitutional moments in American history. Only three—the Founding, Reconstruction, and the New Deal—have enacted far-reaching principles that have transformed the fundamental character of the constitutional system. These transformative moments, he argues, have inaugurated new "constitutional regimes" (WPF, 59, 58–130). The balance have only tinkered with more or less important, though ultimately relatively discrete, aspects of constitutional design.[9] In contrast, however, there have been countless failed constitutional moments (WPF, 50–55, 70–86, 101–13; WPT, 389–403, 471–74).

This pattern is not surprising because the criteria for informal amendment are strict, and in a society, as Ackerman says, devoted to "private citizenship," they are extraordinarily difficult to satisfy (WPF, 234, 6–7).

Finally, for Ackerman, constitutionalism need not pose a countermajoritarian difficulty. Striking down an act of Congress, for example, is not necessarily the overturning of the democratic choice of a majority of the people. Rather, if exercised properly, it is enforcing the will of the citizens expressed during a moment of mobilized deliberation against an ultra vires act of their temporary (and often fallible) agents (or "stand-ins") in Washington, D.C. (WPF, 236, 260, 9–10, 60, 139–40). As long as those charged with implementing the Constitution stick by the expressed will of the people, there is no countermajoritarian difficulty, only a problem of interpretation (WPF, 60–61, 131–62, 262–63). Which is not to underestimate the magnitude of the problem—especially because it requires the interpreter to synthesize the sometimes conflicting, and always complexly interrelated, judgments of the American people during three great transformative moments in our history as well as during a number of other more modest moments of successful constitutional politics (WPF, 86–104, 113–29, 142–62).

Bickel

For Bickel, self-government is a first principle of political morality.[10] Yet, he also believed that self-rule, although necessary, is not alone sufficient to constitute a good society. A good society must have self-rule, but, at the same time, it must also be principled.

> It is a premise we deduce not merely from the fact of a written constitution but from the history of the race, and ultimately as a moral judgment of the good society, that government should serve not only what we conceive from time to time to be our immediate material needs but also certain enduring values.[11]

Unless it rests on a foundation of moral values, democratic government degenerates into "a mindless, shameless thing, freely oppressing various minorities and ruining itself" (MC, 23).

The rule of principle, moreover, is not ultimately inconsistent with rule by the people. Indeed, they are mutually supporting, for unless it is principled, a democratic regime will ultimately prove incapable of maintaining itself. "A valueless politics and valueless institutions are shameful and shameless and, what is more, man's nature is such that he finds them, and life with and under them, insupportable" (MC, 24). A good regime, then, must be "principled as well as responsible; but it must be felt to be the one without having ceased to be the other," for unless it is also responsible, it "is not . . . morally supportable" (LDB, 29).

This dual regime of principle and responsibility thus defines, for Bickel, the core problem of constitutionalism, and it is precisely in this duality that judicial review finds its justification. Although far from cynical about the capacity of the political branches to uphold moral principle, Bickel nevertheless believed that our tradition offered up an alternative approach that was at least in some contexts more effective than relying solely on Congress, the presidency, and other electorally responsible institutions.[12] These institutions are ultimately limited in their capacity to safeguard principle, most especially because the task involves ensuring not only the observance of established principles, but also "the evolution of principle in novel circumstances . . . and the creative establishment and renewal of a coherent body of principled rules."[13] Hence, another sort of institution is needed to assume a central role. At the same time, because the enunciation and application of principled rules is necessarily and irreducibly political—"a high policy-making function"—it was also essential to show specifically why nonelected judges, exercising judicial review, are in fact better suited for the task than electorally responsible legislators and executives.[14]

Bickel's answer was multifaceted and drew heavily on ideas developed by Legal Process scholars. Judges, he noted, have "the leisure, the training, and the insulation to follow the ways of the scholar" in pursuing the development of principle, critical characteristics for sorting out "the enduring values of society" (LDB, 25–26). Moreover, because they enunciate and apply principle only in the concrete factual setting of an actual case, they are well positioned to take the longer view, in contrast to the legislature which considers legislation, *ex ante*, in the abstract (LDB, 26). Furthermore, their insulation, and the timing of the judicial process allows the judges to appeal to our better natures, to call forth a "sober second thought," and to act as teachers in "a vital national seminar."[15] Indeed, it is this conception of the Supreme Court as educator that is the crux of Bickel's vision. Judicial review is justified because a democracy—our democracy at any rate—needs an institution, suitably insulated from the political process and staffed by those most able to undertake the task, which by explaining and rigorously justifying the principles it pronounces, can offer the necessary guidance to make possible "a society dedicated both to the morality of government by consent and to moral self-government."[16]

But identifying the aim of judicial review did not yet explain how it could be made consistent with "the morality of government by consent." In order to find a "tolerable accommodation" between judicial review and democracy, Bickel needed to say much more about how judicial review was actually supposed to work (LDB, 28). Judicial review was not, and could not justifiably be, an exercise in purely abstract moral theorizing. Rather, he insisted that the moral theorizing of judges be rooted in tradition, not of a stale ossified sort, but in the evolving moral traditions of our society. The Court could pronounce only those principles which "rest on fundamental presuppositions rooted in history to which widespread acceptance may fairly be attributed."[17] Only then, he said, could "the conscientious judge . . . hope for the ultimate assent of those whom otherwise he governs irresponsibly" (LDB, 237). Indeed, in the final analysis, judicial review is possible only because of the "moral unity" which characterizes our society and which provides the materials from which a consensually based rule of principle can be derived. The function of judicial review is to make this purported "moral unity" manifest, to renew, sharpen, and bring it to bear.[18]

In carrying out its duties, moreover, the Court is also subject to important structural limits. It does not act wholly in isolation from the political branches. By exploiting the "passive virtues," the Court both reduces the number of occasions when it is called upon to adopt binding constitutional decisions and, even more important for present purposes, continually engages the political branches, and the people, in colloquies over questions of principle.[19] Important Supreme Court decisions are thus only the "beginnings of a conversation between the Court and the people and their representatives" (SCIP, 91). These conversations reshape the Court's doctrines in directions that can ultimately garner widespread consent.[20]

These conceptual and structural limits on the scope of judicial review go some distance in relieving the tension between judicial review and self-government. Nevertheless, Bickel did not contend that they were sufficient to provide a full reconciliation (LDB, 27). The defining feature of democratic rule is revisability by the people, and the conventional wisdom holds that the Court's constitutional decisions are revisable only through the Article V amendment process with its extreme minority veto (LDB, 17–21, 27). Justifying judicial review thus required rejecting this conventional view, and it was in doing so, both normatively and descriptively, that Bickel made his most original contribution. On the normative level, the conventional view would render us "a Platonic kingdom contrary to the morality of self-government" (LDB, 200).

> Having been checked, should the people persist; having been educated, should the people insist, must they not win over every fundamental principle save one—which is the principle that they must win? . . . Who will think it moral ultimately to direct the lives of men against the will of the greater number of them? (LDB, 28)

Indeed, throughout his career, Bickel was tenacious in his insistence on this point. In the absence of an opportunity through the democratic process to overrule the Court, he later said: "I for one would find it extremely difficult to defend the Supreme Court's function as ultimately consistent with democratic self-rule."[21] By the end of his career, as he became increasingly skeptical of the practical ability of the Court even tentatively to define moral progress for the nation, he asserted that "judicial supremacy would be intolerable if, in pursuance of their constitutional oath . . . , legislators and executives did not sometimes challenge the constitutional determinations of the Court—bending, supplementing, and finally displacing them."[22]

Nor did Bickel hesitate to recognize the far-reaching implications of this normative claim. In his view, opposition and resistance to the Court's doctrines—even, sometimes, civil disobedience—were perfectly appropriate.[23] White southern political leaders were thus fully within their rights in organizing political opposition to *Brown* and urging delay, relitigation, and refusal to comply in the absence of a court order (LDB, 263–64). Indeed, though many had, it was wrong to characterize (most of) their resistence as violating the rule of law. They were only following the great precedent that Lincoln himself had established (though not originated) during the Lincoln-Douglas debates: Although willing to respect the Court's specific judgment, Lincoln steadfastly refused to recognize *Dred Scott* as a political rule of decision for Congress or for the country at large and pledged to work assiduously for its demise.[24] What was wrong, then, with the conduct of the white southern leaders was not that in challenging the legitimacy of the Court's rulings they violated the rule of law, but that the political position they pursued was morally wrong where Lincoln's had been morally right—or, at least, that society widely came so to believe.[25]

Political revisability, moreover, was not only a normative ideal. Bickel argued vigorously that it was also an accurate description of the way judicial review actually works. Constitutional decisions, he claimed, open a colloquy with the public. But the Court only "proposes . . . [;] the nation disposes" (PWC, 147). "The Supreme Court's judgments may be put forth as universally prescriptive; but they actually become so only when they gain widespread consent" (SCIP, 90). Without the support of the political branches, whose resources and energies are needed to implement a judgment of any complexity, and without widespread acceptance by the public, the Court's decisions have not, and cannot, survive for long, lapsing either from desuetude or reversal. "This is why," he argued, "the Supreme Court is a court of last resort presumptively only."[26] Thus, a decision will be effectively overturned if it provokes the sustained opposition of far less than the supermajority needed to approve a formal amendment. Where there is such a majority, or sometimes even a committed minority, "the decision is doomed—wholly and totally doomed—without the need to amend the Constitution."[27]

II. Judicial Review, Constitutional Interpretation, and the Bickel-Ackerman Dialectic

Despite their common commitment to democratic constitutionalism, it is evident that Bickel and Ackerman offer widely differing accounts on many points. I turn now to a key dimension of their differences—their contrasting theories of judicial review and constitutional interpretation. These differences, I claim, arise out of their distinctive theories of popular sovereignty and democracy.

Ackerman

For Ackerman, constitutional interpretation, whether carried out by the courts or the political branches, must always be guided by the same goal: to preserve intact the constitutional judgments that the people endorsed in their last pertinent moment of mobilized deliberation. Preservation is thus key, and constitutional interpretation, correspondingly, is properly a backward-looking enterprise. Nevertheless, although all interpreters share the same duty, Ackerman recognizes the Supreme Court's special role in upholding constitutional values. In his view, the Court is today the most important "preservationist" institution.[28] To use Ackerman's metaphor, judges sit in the caboose of the train called the American Republic as it moves forward in time. When called upon to give constitutional judgment, they must resolutely focus their gaze backwards at a landscape formed by past successful efforts of the people to make constitutional law through self-conscious acts of popular sovereignty.[29]

But, why does Ackerman believe that judges must only gaze backwards and never succumb to the temptation to peek sideways from a passenger car or even, occasionally, to join the engineer in the locomotive?[30] Perhaps, they could learn something about how the present generation thinks about some fundamental question or even anticipate, or influence, future sensibilities.

The answer, for Ackerman, lies in his "dualist" theory of democracy (WPF, 6). According to Ackerman, American style politics comes in two modes—normal and constitutional.[31] This dichotomy is a pervasive feature of a political system in which most citizens place a relatively low value on political participation and a high value on their private pursuits. Such citizens ("private citizens," in Ackerman's terminology) are not to be condemned; indeed, Ackerman makes accommodating their needs the foundation of his theory.[32] Still, they simply cannot be expected to give their engaged attention to questions of fundamental principle except on rare occasions when some looming crisis, or perhaps a moment of idealistic insight, inspires them to forego their normal routines. At those moments, after a period of sustained public-regarding deliberation, they may sometimes come to widespread agreement (incorporated or not into a formal text) on a program for fundamental change—a program usually conceived initially, in Ackerman's model, by a group of public-spirited citizens; promoted by them through decades of organizing and struggle; and then finally appropriated, modified, and propelled forward to the attention of the national private citizenry by the president or a presidential aspirant.[33] In contrast, most of the time, private citizens give politics little of their time and attention. To be sure, they—or at least enough of them—vote, but they do so only halfheartedly, self-conscious that they have not done enough to educate themselves about the issues to have anything more than an untutored intuition about what really should be done.[34] Their elected representatives, moreover, though sorely tempted to do so, have no legitimate claim to a popular mandate on the basis of such "soft" votes (WPF, 240–43), and the laws they pass are not acts of popular sovereignty but only the best that can be expected given the realities of normal politics (WPF, 265, 234–65).

Thus, according to Ackerman, from a democratic point of view, normal politics are, albeit for good reasons, a shabby affair,[35] and true republican self-government, if it exists anywhere, can be found only during periods of constitutional politics when engaged citizens, through reasoned deliberation, collectively decide upon principles to guide their common political life.[36] Constitutional law, in turn, is the medium through which the democratic character of those heightened republican moments is transferred to normal political life.[37] Given this dualist conception, to uphold republican self-government, a theory of constitutional law will have no choice but to seek its principles in the judgments the citizenry make in those rare moments of constitutional politics. During periods of normal politics, the sad fact of the matter, according to Ackerman, is that the people are simply absent, doing other more interesting things, and their agents in Washington have only a most limited charge.[38] Their absence explains not only why there is nothing undemocratic in judges striking down statutes that violate the principles the people have affirmed in their moments of mobilized deliberation, but also why constitutional interpretation must be backward looking. It is delusory, Ackerman argues, to imagine judges "communing with a 'contemporary community consensus'" (WPF, 264). During periods of normal politics, there is no such consensus, at least no such consensus formed on the basis of considered judgments hammered out during a period of sustained deliberation. Without such deliberation, however, a judgment, if it exists at all, is simply not democratic, at least not sufficiently so to qualify, in Ackerman's republican vision, as an act of popular sovereignty.[39] Thus, judges who would indulge the temptation to glance sideways or forwards will find nothing of relevance to their task but only materials to confuse and confound—or worse, to undermine the democratic achievements of the American people.

Bickel

For Bickel, like Ackerman, judicial review is backward-looking, but, in contrast, it is neither simply nor exclusively so. As we have already seen, according to Bickel, the sources of constitutional meaning are found first of all in tradition and history—indeed, "the Court is typically the institution of government in which tradition should and does have the greatest weight."[40] The relevant history, however, is not limited, as for Ackerman, to a few extraordinary periods of mobilized popular deliberation. Rather, judges must consult all of our experience, pondering as many different sources, perspectives, and disciplines as possible. Only then will they discover "fundamental presuppositions rooted in history . . . to which widespread acceptance may be fairly attributed" (LDB, 236). Judges, he maintained,

> must immerse themselves in the tradition of our society . . . , in history and in the sediment of history which is law, and, as Judge Hand once suggested, in the thought and the vision of the philosophers and the poets. The Justices will then be fit to extract "fundamental presuppositions" from their deepest selves, but in fact from the evolving morality of our tradition. (LDB, 236)

For Bickel, history and tradition, though crucial, are not straitjackets, nor can they ultimately "displace judgment" (LDB, 108). The enduring scheme of values reflected in our constitutional law has "evolved, and should continue to evolve in the light of history and changing circumstance" (MC, 25). Moreover, although the courts are to look for principle "in the experience of the past, in our traditions, in the secular religion of the American republic" (MC, 25), these sources will not ultimately yield definite answers that can be mechanically or uncontroversially derived, but only conflicting strands of thought (LDB, 109–10). Just as Lincoln reasoned "not from the Framers' resignation to the fact of slavery, but from the abolition of the slave trade," so too, in choosing among the strands, we are necessarily guided by "our own aspirations and evolving principles," and we search for "principles that we can adopt or adapt, or ideals and aspirations that speak with contemporary relevance" (LDB, 109–10).

It should be evident, then, that while judicial review, for Bickel, is backward-looking, it is not so in Ackerman's more straightforward sense, for the experience of the past which judges consult must be filtered through a contemporary lens. Even this conception, moreover, is ultimately too confining. Although the Court should only pronounce principles to which "widespread acceptance may fairly be attributed," that does not mean, for Bickel, that the Court is limited to those principles supported by an existing consensus. Rather, on rare occasion, the Court might endorse a principle, sometimes of momentous significance, which, though still controversial, will ultimately "gain general assent" (LDB, 239). In doing so, it fulfills a crucial function as leader and shaper as well as "prophet of the opinion that will prevail and endure" (LDB, 239, SCIP, 94–95). At the same time, however, it is held to a strict standard. When it acts in this prophetic mode, it "labors under the obligation to succeed" and to succeed "in a rather immediate foreseeable future" (LDB, 239). In contrast to Ackerman's account, then, Bickel's conception of judicial review is not exclusively backward-looking but, sometimes, on critical occasions, is forward-looking as well. (MC, 26). When the Court takes "upon itself to strike a balance of values, it does so with an ear to the promptings of the past and an eye strained to a vision of the future much more than with close regard to the present" (MC, 26).

It remains to be explained, however, what motivates this complex conception of judicial review. In the same way that Ackerman's preservationist account of judicial review arises out of his republican dualism, so, too, Bickel's conception of judicial review arises out of his ideal of stable, principled, and benevolent government enjoying widespread societal consent. For present purposes, I focus on two critical elements of his account—his idea of consent and his conception of the role of deliberation—and attempt to bring out their relationship to his theory of judicial review. I also contrast them with Ackerman's account.

If the core of popular sovereignty for Ackerman is the considered judgment of the majority rendered during a period of mobilized deliberation, for Bickel it is the idea of actual, ongoing consent—consent of "as unified a population as possible" to "specific actions or to the authority to act."[41] "[C]oherent, stable—and *morally supportable*—government," he observed, "is possible only on the basis of consent, and . . . the secret of consent is the sense of common venture fostered by institutions that reflect and represent us and that we can call to account" (LDB, 20).[42] Representative institutions thus serve to make consent possible.[43] Although recognizing that it may perforce be necessary at times to settle for mere majority consent, Bickel nevertheless insisted that only "preponderant, not merely majority consent," was ultimately sufficient (MC, 18). This insistence was reflected in his oft-stated reluctance to sanction coercion against intense dissenting minorities who were to be persuaded instead by appeals to reason and interest.[44]

It should now be evident that this consensus-based conception of popular sovereignty underlies Bickel's emphasis on the role of tradition and history in constitutional interpretation. Long-standing practices and institutions, with their animating ideals, provide a rich source of interpretive materials for judges charged with discovering principles that have, or can achieve, "widespread acceptance." In contrast, a judge who undertakes to derive principles in isolation from tradition and history runs a far greater risk of failure. This same conception, moreover, also underlies Bickel's claim that judges should view tradition and history dynamically through the filter of contemporary values. The aim of judicial review is not to reproduce a static tradition but to uncover a consensual basis for moral self-government. That cannot be achieved by holding rigidly to the intentions of long dead framers. To provide a basis for widespread consent, constitutional principles must be permitted to evolve along with changing beliefs and circumstances. For similar reasons, Bickel would no doubt have rejected a fundamental premise of Ackerman's dualism. To uncover the values of the people of today, one cannot look only to extraordinary moments of political engagement. Rather, "the people," he observed, manifested "its temper in many ways and over a span of time . . . not speaking merely on occasion in momentary numerical majorities."[45]

Furthermore, though not normatively linked to the very idea of consent as for Ackerman, deliberation, for Bickel, nevertheless played a critical role in making widespread consent a viable possibility. For Bickel, deliberation was a necessary part of any process of debate that can uncover an existing consensus or forge a new one, and it was here that the Court had a crucial role to play. The first requirement imposed on judges, Bickel insisted unyieldingly, was that they conform to the strictest "standards of analytical candor, rigor, and clarity."[46] By rendering a reasoned decision, the Court was initiating a wider dialogue with the public at large and offering, as guidance, a rigorously justified position. The aim was both to persuade and to raise the standards of debate.

In contrast, for Ackerman, mobilized deliberation is as an essential feature of the idea of consent itself. His commitment to this republican ideal leads him to endorse a populist style of constitutional politics and a corresponding use of referenda to resolve questions of fundamental principle.[47] It also leads him to define a distinctive role for the Supreme Court in fostering democratic deliberation during such moments. According to Ackerman, in the modern Republic, movements for constitutional reform initiate their higher lawmaking proposals by securing passage of transformative statutes which are inconsistent with principles endorsed by the people in earlier moments of constitutional politics.[48]

What the Court can and should do to further citizen deliberation during the next round of constitutional politics is to stand firm against such would be constitutional reformers until they have earned the right to speak for the citizens at large. By striking down the first wave of transformative statutes, as the Court did in 1934–36, the Court performs an essential function, clarifying the questions of fundamental principle at stake as citizens deliberate upon the constitutional proposals placed before them for decision.[49]

In contrast, Bickel was deeply skeptical about the capacity of the people to engage in the mass-based deliberation Ackerman prizes.

> Masses of people do not make clear-cut, long-range decisions. They do not know enough about the issues, about themselves, their needs and wishes, or about what those needs and wishes will appear to them to be two months hence. (MC, 16)

Indeed, the idea of submitting questions of principle directly to the people by referendum was "the fallacy of the misplaced mystics, or the way of those who would use the forms of democracy to undemocratic ends" (LDB, 27). Hence arises the need for a specially situated institution, insulated from the political process, which can guide the people in the formulation and application of fundamental principle. Indeed, it is considerations like these that led Bickel, notwithstanding his democratic first premises, to endorse not only the practice of judicial review, but also specifically a prophetic role for the Supreme Court. In that mode, the Court was to serve an essential function—to grasp the tensions and conflicts within our existing scheme of values and to persuade the people to endorse new principles more suited to their evolving political morality. Although from Ackerman's perspective this elitist account of judicial review underestimates the deliberative capacities of the people at least within a well functioning higher lawmaking system (WPF, 139; RC, 525), for Bickel, it was essential to achieving a society that was at once both democratic and principled.

Nor is this to suggest that Bickel believed that the people were incapable of deliberation. That is why the Justices were teachers not Platonic Guardians. When the Court exercises the power of judicial review—as when it applies the passive virtues and avoids exercising its ultimate power—it initiates a dialogue with the people and their representatives. This deliberative dialogue, too, is an essential part of Bickel's conception of democracy, and it makes possible, though by no means inevitable, the forging and maintenance of the kind of consensus upon which moral self-government must be premised (PWC, 147). In a rare moment of abstract theorizing, Bickel provided a model:

> The Court proposes major ideas—they are relatively few in number—and a period of vigorous debate follows, during which the Court's proposed principles are far from stable. Eventually, and for a time, consensus is arrived at, which may or may not coincide in this or that degree with the principles initially broached by the Court. There follows a period during which the Court consolidates the position on the basis of the consensus, and this is normally a period of relatively placid acceptance of the Court's work. Then, before long, the Court tackles some other subject, or an old one once more, and the cycle begins again. (PWC, 147)

III. The Bickel-Ackerman Dialectic: Towards a Synthesis

Thus far my approach has been strictly interpretive. Now, however, I assume a more critical posture. After identifying weaknesses in the accounts of both Bickel and Ackerman, I conclude by offering a tentative synthesis of their views, which draws on the best aspects of each.

Ackerman

One central aim of Ackerman's theory is to demonstrate the possibility of genuine democratic self-rule despite the fact that citizens normally choose to pursue their private affairs, paying scant attention to politics. As we have seen, he solves this apparent dilemma by positing dualism. Democratic self-rule is possible because during periods of normal politics politicians are not free (or, at least, not completely free) to exploit the defects of normal politics but are instead constrained (via the Supreme Court) by the considered judgments of the people rendered during rare moments of constitutional politics.

This solution, of course, raises many important questions, but, for present purposes, I wish to focus on two related points. First, I question Ackerman's implicit assumption, which I take to be fundamental, that the judgments of the people rendered during moments of constitutional politics are the only available reflection of the considered views of the citizenry during later periods of normal politics and that consequently enforcing strict adherence to those judgments affords the most effective means for realizing self-rule by current majorities, which is the central aim of democratic constitutionalism. Second, I question whether the sense in which the Supreme Court acts as a preservationist institution in Ackerman's account is strong enough to do the democratic work his dualist theory requires.

1. THE INTERTEMPORAL DIFFICULTY. By insisting that the sole sources of legitimate constitutional meaning are the considered judgments the citizens make during periods of constitutional politics, Ackerman introduces a significant "intertemporal" (RC, 527) difficulty into his account: Citizens today, rather than living in accordance with their own considered judgments, are instead ruled by the considered judgments of generations past. Since the Founding, there have been only two moments, Reconstruction and the New Deal, in which the American people have undertaken large-scale, though still partial, reconsideration of their inherited political arrangements. From the perspective of a theory that aims to ensure that the people govern themselves in accordance with principles that reflect their considered judgments, this state of affairs should give pause. "The bad news," Ackerman concedes, "is that the Americans who made these considered constitutional judgments are dead."[50] Yet, he fails to acknowledge the depth of the problem. On many important questions, the likelihood that the judgments made by past generations will correspond with the considered judgments of today's generation—or whatever considered judgments would be reached after sustained deliberation—becomes ever more doubtful.

Of course, the people may simply be satisfied with the constitutional status quo. Perhaps they have undertaken large-scale reconsideration only twice, and altered more or less important but discrete matters on several other occasions, because the existing principles still conform to their considered judgments. Or, to put the point somewhat differently, so long as the people have the power to revise their existing constitutional arrangements, is it not fair to presume that their failure to act represents their affirmation of the status quo?

Were the only method for revising the Constitution the procedures specified in Article V, this rejoinder would be exceedingly weak. Article V's extreme minority veto over amendments makes it implausible to say that the failure to amend the Constitution reflects widespread satisfaction with existing doctrine, and Ackerman certainly does not claim otherwise. Indeed, as we have seen, he argues that there is in fact an alternative nontextual amendment procedure that mitigates this feature of the "classical" procedure. The problem, however, is that this alternative, as Ackerman describes it, poses obstacles that are only slightly less arduous for constitutional reformers successfully to navigate. In order to ensure the kind of sustained deliberation that he believes popular sovereignty demands, Ackerman sets the bar very high, and by his own account, it will consequently only be on rare occasions that a reform movement will ultimately succeed in earning the right to make new constitutional law (RC, 529). Whether it be the nature of normal politics, the nonideological character of the party structure, or the immense difficulty of obtaining a considered collective judgment "from a quarter of a billion people living a bewildering diversity of lives," the status quo will be extraordinarily difficult to change (RC, 529).

In any case, Ackerman does not claim that the absence of any successful large-scale constitutional moments since the New Deal reflects the people's considered judgment in favor of the status quo. On the contrary, in his view, what it reflects is that citizens today, and for the past sixty-plus years (with important, but still relatively discrete exceptions)[51] have not formed considered judgments on most important questions (WPF, 263). "[I]t is simply impossible to say how the people of today would decide an issue if they mobilized their political energies and successfully hammered out a new constitutional solution."[52] It is not, then, that Ackerman believes that the constitutional solutions of 1789, 1868, and 1937 reflect current considered judgments, but, rather, that there are no such judgments and that we simply have no access to what they might turn out to be were the people to engage in a process of serious deliberation. Thus, the reason the Supreme Court should preserve the prior considered judgments of the people is rather deflating: it is the best we can do under the circumstances. Even if those judgments may have become increasingly stale over time, it is preferable for the Court to enforce them rather than to attempt to divine the considered judgments of the citizenry today.[53]

It is this second best claim, then, that justifies Ackerman's refusal to allow the Court any room to update constitutional doctrine in accordance with evolving moral beliefs and changing circumstances. But the claim is, I believe, subject to serious objection. Even accepting a republican deliberative ideal, as I do, Ackerman simply places too much weight on an overly formalistic distinction between ordinary and constitutional politics.

During the extended periods of ordinary politics, the people are not entirely quiescent, incapable of reaching considered judgments. Although the kind of mobilized deliberation that Ackerman prizes may be less in evidence, the people can reveal their shifting moral judgments in myriad ways—in persistent courses of legislation sustained over time, for example, or in discernable long-term shifts in public attitudes arising from better education, actual experience, scientific and philosophical advances, or increased exposure to different kinds of people and conceptions of the good. These more evolutionary changes are also legitimate sources of constitutional meaning for a democratic constitutionalist and help those charged with interpreting the Constitution to ensure that doctrine keeps pace with changing values and circumstances. On rare occasions, they may even justify interpreters in superseding earlier Ackermanian judgments altogether. Ackerman seems to believe that mobilized deliberation will always yield judgments that are more thoroughly considered than those which result from other forms of deliberation. Even were this correct, however, it would not mean that the former must always prevail over the latter. Rather, it would only mean that we will sometimes face a difficult choice of whether to respect old but more fully considered judgments or, alternatively, more contemporary but less thoroughly considered judgments. Ackerman has not explained why the better choice from the perspective of securing genuine self-government will always be the former. Temporal proximity will at least sometimes be a powerful counterbalancing consideration.[54]

To be sure, despite his emphasis on the Founding, Reconstruction, and the New Deal, Ackerman has also identified other times in which the American people have engaged in constitutional politics and successfully altered existing constitutional arrangements in significant, if less global, respects. He has variously pointed to the Jeffersonian Revolution of 1800, the Jacksonian period, the internationalist movement of World War II, and the Civil Rights Movement as cases in point.[55] How far incorporating these and perhaps other moments may ameliorate the intertemporal objection remains to be seen. To be successful, however, Ackerman will, I suspect, have to soften his strict distinction between normal and constitutional politics, and this move, in turn, will further strengthen the argument for recognizing the kind of evolutionary developments that I have identified.

It should be noted, moreover, that there is a considerable gap between Ackerman's official theory, with its exclusive focus on successful constitutional moments, and the more flexible way in which he applies it in practice. At times, in fact, he seems open to finding support for court decisions in contemporaneous popular opinion rather than in the strict application of his synthetic interpretive method. His discussion of the Court's decision in *Lochner*[56] is particularly instructive. In the official account, *Lochner* is justified as a synthetic interpretation of Reconstruction and Founding principles (WPF, 63, 66, 94–104, 118). There is, however, an alternative version of the story, which is quite different. In this version, *Lochner* does not so much, or only, result from a synthetic reading of Reconstruction and the Founding, but from the political forces at play beginning in 1896, the year of Republican William McKinley's landslide victory over the Populist Williams Jennings Bryan.

> It is a large mistake to look upon 1905—the year that *Lochner* was decided—as if it were 1937. In 1905, the Justices were not confronting a New Deal Congress and a President who had just won decisive popular majorities in support of a decisive break with constitutional laissez-faire. To the contrary: the Justices had just lived through the failed Populist effort to mobilize the American people against the evils of laissez-faire capitalism—a movement that climaxed with the nomination of William Jennings Bryan as the Democratic candidate for the Presidency in 1896. Rather than leading to a Rooseveltian transformation, Bryan's nomination served only to catalyze a decisive popular counterreaction on behalf of William McKinley and the Republican Party.[57]

Indeed, Ackerman notes that both the formal incorporation of the Takings Clause into the Fourteenth Amendment and the beginning of more aggressive protection for freedom of contract occurred in 1897. "The inauguration of this more aggressive property-contract interpretation of constitutional liberty in 1897 was by no means accidental. It came immediately after the Populists tried to redefine the constitutional agenda in the election of 1896" (WPF, 118). Ackerman does not contend that 1896 represented a successful constitutional moment—indeed, it was a failed moment—and, thus, in the official account, it should have no bearing on the correctness of *Lochner*. Notwithstanding his official account, however, he also offers here a more plausible basis for the decision—that it was not only consistent with the Reconstruction Amendments, but that it also was accorded with widely held contemporaneous judgments as reflected in McKinley's decisive 1896 defeat of Bryan and the Populist program.

2. PRESERVATIONISM. A second difficulty with Ackerman's theory is his preservationist account of judicial review. It is not that preservationism is itself an incoherent ideal. Rather, even if we put aside the diminishing capacity of past constitutional moments to reflect current beliefs, the problem is that the sense in which Ackerman's interpretive approach is preservationist is too weak to ensure that constitutional doctrine remains faithful even to the past judgments he privileges.

Given his apparent commitment to a populist conception of popular sovereignty, it seems somewhat surprising that Ackerman endorses an expansive approach to interpreting the judgments made by the people during the three great transformative constitutional moments. He provides a three-step model, which, in his view, is both descriptively accurate and normatively appropriate: In the early period after a transformative moment, the Court takes a relatively particularistic approach, sticking close to the concrete judgments that animated the constitutional debate. With time, however, it begins to abstract from those concrete judgments until, ultimately, it comes to identify a small number of abstract principles as expressing the core meaning of a new constitutional regime.[58] In resolving concrete controversies thereafter, the Court synthesizes the abstract principles of the new regime with the abstract principles the Court previously assigned to earlier transformative regimes.[59]

This account would certainly be less vulnerable from a democratic point of view were it to limit interpreters to the first step—to identifying the concrete problems that motivated a movement for constitutional reform and interpreting the principles endorsed to accomplish results that were widely appreciated during the debate and that received widespread assent. The difficulties begin with the second step, with the interpretive move from the particular to the abstract. The danger is that in this process the voice of the people will quickly be lost. I share Ackerman's optimistic belief that the people can engage in meaningful deliberation over important political principles and that they can self-consciously choose to reshape their social practices, sometimes in momentous ways, as by banning slavery, or by empowering the national government to regulate the economy and redistribute wealth. But it is unrealistic to think that when the people deliberate, even when they express their judgments in abstract texts like the Fourteenth Amendment, that they do so without particular, concrete contexts in mind, which explain and qualify the principles that they endorse. When courts move beyond the concrete contexts that animated the people's deliberations and interpret their judgments at higher and higher levels of abstraction, the connection between the judgments of the people and the resulting constitutional law is likely to become increasingly attenuated. Indeed, by following such an interpretive practice, courts may well in the end enunciate principles that the people would, after serious deliberation, have flatly rejected.

This result is all the more probable, moreover, in light of the third step in Ackerman's methodology, the complex synthetic interpretive process in which the judges are to engage. Indeed, as best as I can understand it, this process is not designed to yield only those principles that can claim the deliberative endorsement of the most recent transformative generation or even of any of the previous transformative generations. Rather, in some cases, it will produce principles which were never contemplated by any generation but which are a synthesis of principles endorsed at different times by two or more of these generations. It is perfectly plausible, therefore, and Ackerman must assume, that the synthetic process will sometimes yield principles that all three transformative generations would, on reflection, separately have rejected. Consider in this regard Ackerman's reading of *Brown*,[60] which he claims is best understood as a synthesis of Reconstruction and New Deal principles. According to Ackerman, Reconstruction, understood at an abstract level, affirmed both the principle of political equality and the doctrine of laissez-faire, the latter of which denied in principle the responsibility of the state for unequal relationships resulting from private ordering. Hence, the Fourteenth Amendment led, albeit in a convoluted way, to *Plessy*.[61] The New Deal, in turn, did not reconsider the principle of political equality but did reject laissez-faire in favor of the activist state.[62] Thus, synthesizing these judgments, political equality still stands—only now shorn of the Reconstruction commitment to laissez-faire. Irrespective of whether both the Reconstruction and New Deal generations would, on reflection, have rejected the principle of equality affirmed in *Brown*, therefore, the decision was correct, "obviously so," as a synthesis of the commitments of both.[63]

Whatever else one might say about this claim, it underscores the gap that Ackerman's interpretive method opens up between the actual concrete judgments that the people make and the constitutional law that the Supreme Court ultimately frames in their name. Thus, for example, Ackerman construes the New Deal generation as having made a considered judgment to reject the abstract principle of laissez-faire, but it seems far closer to the facts to say that the New Dealers rejected the constitutional doctrine of laissez-faire in the marketplace and simply did not consider, let alone render, a considered judgment that laissez-faire was not still appropriate in other domains of social life—in race relations, for example.[64] Likewise, Ackerman interprets Reconstruction as having affirmed the abstract principle of political equality, but his own story more strongly suggests the impossibility of separating out Reconstruction's commitment to political equality from its commitment to laissez-faire.[65] The Reconstruction generation did not give its considered affirmation to political equality simpliciter, but to political equality in certain spheres, those consistent with laissez-faire. Thus, even if the New Deal rejected laissez-faire *tout court*, the process of synthetic judgment would not produce a more extended commitment to political equality, a commitment that Reconstruction, on reflection, rejected and that the New Deal never considered. It is thus only by disregarding the concrete contexts in which the New Deal and Reconstruction generations rendered their judgments, and the qualifications which those contexts imply, that Ackerman's synthetic defense of *Brown* can work.

I do not deny that Ackerman convincingly demonstrates that application of this complex synthetic process can generate powerful and heretofore unanticipated arguments for important court precedents, like *Brown* and *Griswold*.[66] Nor do I doubt that those decisions are the causal result of the intellectual, economic, political, and social dynamics set in motion by the New Deal. What I do question is whether they can be explained, as he claims, as faithful interpretations of the considered judgments of the people rendered during the three transformative moments. More generally, even were Ackerman's claim more persuasive, it seems at least peculiar that he would be committed both to a bottom-up populist style of constitutional politics, which celebrates the role of the people in actively determining the principles that guide their common political life, and, at the same time, to a method of constitutional interpretation that so broadly licenses elite interpreters to determine the content of constitutional law.[67]

Bickel

The burden on Ackerman to establish that his account is consistent with his democratic premises is especially heavy, not only because he insists that the sources of constitutional meaning are limited to rare past moments, but also because the role assigned the people in constitutional interpretation is solely prospective—the people render their judgments and then have nothing further to say until the next constitutional moment. In contrast, at least in principle, a theory like Bickel's has a lesser burden, first, because the legitimate sources of interpretive meaning are more varied and include contemporaneous materials and, second, because the people are involved on both sides of the interpretive process, prospectively in making constitutional law and retrospectively in pronouncing their disagreement with the Court's judgments. Thus, the burden of preservation is not entirely on the Court, but is shared with the people themselves. They can correct misjudgments when they occur and, in doing so, speak directly to a specific issue rather than render a more abstract prospective judgment.

Bickel's theory, however, raises a host of problems. He failed, for example, to offer a fully persuasive interpretive strategy for uncovering and elaborating the evolving moral consensus that putatively underlies our complex social practices. No more than Ackerman would Bickel have the Court simply follow the opinion polls or "th' iliction returns."[68] The heart of Bickel's solution, however, seems to rely heavily upon a romanticized portrait of heroic Justices (followed, perhaps inevitably, by a despairing disillusionment) and a too sanguine belief in their ability to persuade the wider public through the force of their reasoning and moral vision.[69] Nor did Bickel give a fully adequate account of the mechanisms which make possible the people's role as the ultimate court of appeal with the ability to revise, and even override, the Court's principles when they stray too far from an existing moral consensus. The mechanisms Bickel identifies are messy—necessarily so, he would say—and it remains murky how they are supposed to operate in a society where judicial supremacy has increasingly become an article of faith.[70]

Without underestimating the difficulties that these challenges pose, I nevertheless want to focus on a different problem more directly related to Ackerman's project. If Ackerman's exclusive focus on past moments and mobilized deliberation are problematic for the reasons I have suggested, they nevertheless provide an important corrective to Bickel's account and to a more general failure in much contemporary constitutional theory. Citizens, Ackerman reminds us, are capable of taking center stage and of actively engaging in reasoned deliberation on fundamental political values. The principles they affirm at such times, moreover, may have wide-ranging significance, profoundly altering the status quo. When citizens do so act, as they have at critical junctures and may yet again, the fruits of their mobilized deliberation are entitled to the greatest weight, for such moments represent the closest approximation to the ideal of republican self-government of which we are capable. Bickel's emphasis on gradualism and actual ongoing consent, and his skepticism about the capacity of citizens to engage in deliberation on a mass scale, tends to obscure this crucial point.

At the most general level, Ackerman's project urges us to recapture the revolutionary enlightenment tradition in the cauldron of which the nation was formed.[71] His constitutional moments are especially important acts of self-government precisely because they involve heightened deliberation by large numbers of engaged citizens on fundamental questions of political value. When we obscure their significance, we deny crucial parts of our own history and of our future possibilities. Ackerman is right when he claims that these moments inaugurate new constitutional regimes. He is right, though, not because, as he seems to claim, the principles the people endorse are sufficient on their own to determine the shape of the new constitutional regime. Rather, although they do not control, they do dramatically shift the direction of future constitutional development. Thus, as I have explained, in my view, the principles that the people endorsed during the New Deal were not alone sufficient to produce *Brown* and *Griswold*. They did, however, set in motion a process of profound moral growth and development, a process that was propelled forward by the very beliefs, institutions, and practices that those principles had themselves legitimated. It was this process of growth that eventually yielded the moral consensus—or, perhaps, the possibility of such a consensus—justifying those decisions. The new constitutional regime that the New Deal inaugurated was not closed in 1936 but has been and continues to be an ongoing project.

What is missing in Bickel, then, is a recognition of the special importance that should be accorded to principles endorsed during periods of mobilized deliberation. Without necessarily being foundational, they are at the foundation of a developing constitutional regime, and, if the constitutional moment was genuine, they quickly become systematically and inextricably intertwined with the values, institutions, and practices that define the system. It is not that these principles are entirely beyond modification or even rejection until the next Ackermanian constitutional moment. Citizens can reach considered judgments in different modes at different times, and these too must be given effect. In light of the provenance of such principles and their continuing role in the constitutional order, however, they ought to be disturbed only on the basis of the most weighty evidence of a fundamental and widespread shift in political orientation.

It would be misleading, however, to suggest, as I have tried hard to avoid doing, that Bickel was entirely unwilling to credit the kind of plebiscitary style constitutional politics that Ackerman prizes. When we take into account the more flexible approach that Ackerman actually deploys in practice, moreover, the differences between the two dramatically narrow. Thus, for example, what appears to Ackerman as affirmative constitutional politics often appeared to Bickel to be justified political resistance to decisions of the Court not supported by the kind of consensus essential to their legitimacy. The most obvious case in point is the New Deal revolution itself. According to Bickel,

> [t]he course of opposition to the Court's law . . . , calling for inaction and for political action inconsistent with the law, and embodying what is loosely called disobedience of the law of the land on the part of both private and official persons—this course was widely pursued, for example, after the Court declared minimum-wage legislation unconstitutional in 1923, in *Adkins v. Children's Hospital*, until it succeeded fourteen years later with a judicial retreat in *West Coast Hotel Co. v. Parrish*.[72]

Likewise, just as Ackerman views the 1896 election as providing important support for *Lochner*, Bickel (and Ackerman) viewed the election of 1960, in which Kennedy and Nixon both pledged support for the principle of school desegregation, combined with the ensuing politics of the Kennedy years, as validating *Brown*.[73] Contrariwise, the election of 1968 and the politics leading up to it were an unfortunate vote of no-confidence in the Warren Court's criminal procedure decisions, including *Miranda*.[74] Thus, despite their many theoretical differences, Bickel and Ackerman, in practice, tend to converge on many important points. This convergence should perhaps not be so surprising, given their mutual adherence to democratic constitutionalism and its insistence that the principles of constitutional law derive their legitimacy from the ongoing consent of the people.

Synthesis

Having identified strengths and weaknesses in the views of both Bickel and Ackerman, and having narrowed the gap apparently dividing them, we are now in a position to glimpse the possibilities for a synthesis that offers a stronger, more defensible version of democratic constitutionalism. We need not follow Ackerman in insisting that the constitutional meaning can only be created in moments of mobilized deliberation and in limiting the Court strictly to a preservationist function. At the same time, we need not follow Bickel in obscuring the real possibilities, historic and potential, for the people to engage actively and self-consciously in the production of new constitutional meaning. Rather, we can instead embrace the role that transformative political movements have sometimes played in shifting the path of constitutional development along radically new lines, while at the same time refusing to exaggerate the breadth of the principles the people have endorsed even during the most transformative of constitutional moments. We can also acknowledge that any theory that aims to legitimate our constitutional law by rooting it in the exercise of popular sovereignty must recognize that constitutional meaning is in a constant state of flux. Such a synthesis of the views of Bickel and Ackerman offers a potentially powerful basis for a revised version of democratic constitutionalism—an account that is both cognizant of the weight and significance that ought to be accorded to judgments rendered by the majority of the people during moments of heightened deliberation and sensitive to the always ongoing process of moral growth and development that cannot await the next constitutional moment to find expression in constitutional law.

Notes

1. Alexander M. Bickel, *The Least Dangerous Branch* (Indianapolis, IN: Bobbs-Merrill, 1962), 16. Subsequent references to this work are cited in the text and notes with the following abbreviation: LDB.

2. For a recent effort to preserve the democratic character of the Constitution by recognizing that the people, not the Court, retain interpretive authority at least in some areas, see Larry D. Kramer, "Foreword: We the Court," *Harvard Law Review* 115 (2001): 4. As Kramer develops at length, moreover, democratic constitutionalism has deep roots in the Founding and in our continuing traditions. See Kramer.

3. I note that my account of Bickel's work is integrative, deemphasizing late-career shifts in his thinking that others have often highlighted. Of course, there were changes, but I believe they loomed so large to his contemporaries mostly because of their political and biographical significance. With historical

distance, the profound theoretical continuities and overall intellectual integrity that characterizes the whole body of his work is now easier to appreciate.

4. Bruce Ackerman, *We the People: Foundations* (Cambridge, MA: Belknap Press, 1991), 280. Subsequent references to *We the People: Foundations* are cited in the text and notes with the following abbreviation: WPF.

5. See, e.g., Ackerman, WPF, 10, 15; Bruce Ackerman, "Rooted Cosmopolitanism" *Ethics* 104 (1994): 517. Subsequent references to "Rooted Cosmopolitanism" are cited in the text and notes with the following abbreviation: RC.

6. Ackerman succinctly describes the higher lawmaking process in Ackerman, WPF, 266–94; Bruce Ackerman, *We the People: Transformations* (Cambridge, MA: Belknap Press, 1998), 15–27. Subsequent references to *We the People: Transformations* are cited in the text and notes with the following abbreviation: WPT.

7. See, e.g., Ackerman, WPT, passim.

8. Ackerman has not only defined four distinct phases through which higher lawmaking must pass—signaling, proposal, mobilized popular deliberation, and codification, see, e.g., Ackerman, WPF, 266–90, and adding a fifth, triggering, in more recent writings, see, e.g., Ackerman, WPT, 85–86—he has also identified a set of institutional patterns which are at least typical of the process if not, indeed, mandatory—constitutional impasse, electoral mandate, challenge to dissenting institutions, switch in time, and consolidating election. See Ackerman, WPF, 49; WPT, 20.

9. Some of these, of course, have been incorporated into formal Article V Amendments. Since the New Deal, Ackerman has identified two more moments—the internationalist movement spawned by the experience of World War II and the Civil Rights Movement. See Bruce Ackerman and David M. Golove, "Is NAFTA Constitutional?", *Harvard Law Review* 108 (1995): 799; Ackerman, WPF, 108–11, 137. For Ackerman's discussion of other constitutional movements, see ibid., 70–80, 108–13.

10. By claiming that self-government is a first principle for Bickel, I do not mean to imply that it is foundational. For further discussion of Bickel's underlying normative premises, see infra notes—and accompanying text. In *The Least Dangerous Branch*, he defended self-government on both skeptical grounds and on the basis of a commitment to political equality. See Bickel, LDB, 28.

11. Bickel, LDB, 24. See also Ibid., 29–30; Alexander M. Bickel, *The Supreme Court and the Idea of Progress* (New York: Harper and Row, 1970), 86–87; Bickel, MC, 11–12, 18–19, 23–25, 77. Subsequent references to *The Supreme Court and the Idea of Progress* are cited in the text and notes with the following abbreviation: SCIP.

12. See Bickel, LDB, 24–27; Alexander M. Bickel, *Politics and the Warren Court* (New York: Da Capo Press 1973), 134; Bickel, SCIP, 86–88; Bickel, MC, 26. For Bickel's increasing emphasis on the ability of the politi-

cal branches to uphold constitutional values, and corresponding decreasing faith in the Supreme Court, compare Bickel, LDB, 24–27; Bickel, MC, 8; Alexander M. Bickel, "Congress, the President and the Power to Wage War," *Chicago-Kent Law Review* 48 (1971): 131. Subsequent references to *Politics and the Warren Court* are cited in the text and notes with the following abbreviation: PWC.

13. Bickel, LDB, 25. Bickel also emphasized the obstacles faced by majoritarian political institutions in consistently upholding legitimate minority interests. See Bickel, SCIP, 86–88; Bickel, MC, 16–17.

14. Bickel, SCIP, 82. See also Bickel, LDB, 24.

15. Ibid. See also Bickel, PWC, 134; Bickel, SCIP, 86–88. On the role of the "passive virtues,"see Bickel, LDB, 111–98. Bickel's discussion of the death penalty nicely reveals his larger conception of the Court's special role. See ibid., 240–43.

16. Bickel, LDB, 199. Bickel, of course, formulated his view of judicial review prior to the systematic critiques of the Legal Process school developed in subsequent decades.

17. Bickel, LDB, 236. See Ibid., 93–94, 108–10; Bickel, SCIP, 87; Bickel, MC, 25–26.

18. Bickel, LDB, 30. See also Bickel, MC, 25–26.

19. See Bickel, LDB, 111–98, 240; Bickel, PWC, 147; Bickel, SCIP, 90–94; Bickel, MC, 26.

20. See Bickel, LDB, 240. For Bickel's increasing pessimism about the ability of the Court to live up to his ideal conception of its role, see Bickel, SCIP, 176–81.

21. Bickel, PWC, 13. See also Bickel, LDB, 27–29, 200, 237, 261; Bickel, PWC, 10–13; Bickel, SCIP, 87–88, 179–81; Bickel, MC, 105–06.

22. Bickel, MC, 180–81.

23. See Bickel, LDB, 244, 256–67; Bickel, PWC, 7, 10–14, 147–49, 155; Bickel, SCIP, 87–94, 179, 180–81. On civil disobedience, see, e.g., Bickel, PWC, 87–91; Bickel, MC, 100–04, 108–17.

24. See, e.g., Bickel, LDB, 258–64; Bickel, PWC, 13–14, 87–91; Bickel, MC, 101–02, 110–12.

25. See Bickel, LDB, 257–59, 265–67; Bickel, PWC, 87–91.

26. Bickel, LDB, 258. See also Bickel, LDB, 244–45, 252, 258, 262; Bickel, PWC, 7, 10–14, 147–49; Bickel, SCIP, 87–94. Of course, the nature and degree of public resistance to an unpopular Supreme Court opinion is not a fact wholly exogenous to the normative question.

27. Bickel, PWC, 155. See also Bickel, PWC, 13.

28. Ackerman, WPF, 10. On the Supreme Court as a preservationist institution, see, e.g., ibid., 60, 71–73, 86–103, 113–29, 137–40.

29. See Ackerman, WPF, 98–99.

30. See Ackerman, WPF, 99.

31. See, e.g., Ackerman, WPF, 230–65 (describing normal politics); Ibid. 266–94 (describing constitutional politics).

32. Ackerman, WPF, 231. See, e.g., Ibid., 230–32, 234–43, 259–61, 297–314.

33. See, e.g., Ackerman, WPF, 44–56, 272–90; Ackerman, WPT, 10–27.

34. See Ackerman, WPF, 232–43.

35. See, e.g., Ackerman, WPF, 305–14.

36. See, e.g., Ackerman, WPF, 24–32.

37. See, e.g., Ackerman, WPF, 265.

38. See, e.g., Ackerman, WPF, 260. Ackerman asserts that elected officials in Washington "are just stand-ins, that's all. The mass of *private* citizens are too busy right now to engage in the kind of sustained and mobilized debate and decision that would justify any of their stand-ins declaring that they have a decisive mandate for fundamental change."

39. See, e.g., Ackerman, WPF, 242–43, 263–64; Ackerman, RC, 527–29. Ackerman offers various reasons for his privileging of judgments reached after sustained popular deliberation. At times, his preference appears to derive from a claim, rooted in a conception of political equality, about the intrinsic value of reasoned dialogue in establishing "a sense of rational community between us" and expressing "a mutual recognition of one another" as members of a political community seeking "a common understanding of the appropriate terms for our coexistence" (RC, 530). As a result, even though we may collectively err in our search for truth, it is better on the whole "to sustain the conversation itself rather than any particular truth" (Ibid., at 531). At other times, he seems to appeal to an epistemic theory. The considered judgments of the people, formed during periods of public-regarding mobilized debate, are more likely than other less considered judgments to reflect true principles of justice. At other points, however, Ackerman seems tentative about the persuasiveness of these sorts of claims, particularly in his willingness to embrace the idea of entrenching against amendment certain fundamental rights. See WPF, 16, 320–21; RC, 532–33. Moreover, he seems willing to embrace his commitment to democratic constitutionalism only so long as things do not go too wrong (RC, 535). In any case, at still other points, he offers another more speculative explanation for his insistence on considered judgments—that private citizens themselves during periods of normal politics do not view their own opinions as informed and would be horrified to learn that those opinions were being used as a basis for overriding or making higher law. See supra note 34 and accompanying text. Thus, the majoritarian principle itself requires that only Ackermanian considered judgments be given the status of constitutional law.

40. Bickel, LDB, 94. See also Bickel, SCIP, 87.

41. Bickel, LDB, 30. See also Bickel, MC, 100.

42. At various points, Bickel offered different reasons for his foundational commitment to consent. At times, he rooted this claim in a relativistic

philosophical conception strikingly similar to the views of Michael Walzer or, perhaps, to the later Rawls. See John Rawls, *Political Liberalism* (New York: Columbia University Press, 1993); MC, 20. At other times, he offered a more skeptical version of this claim, combined with a prudentialist account. Thus, quoting Burke, he claimed

> that power must be based on consent to ensure stability, "stability being a prime value, both as an end and as a means"; as an end, because though truth may be preferable to peace, "as we have scarcely ever the same certainty in the one that we have in the other, I would, unless the truth were evident indeed, hold fast to peace"; and as a means, because stability is a source as well as a fruit of consent, making the beneficent exercise of power possible though by no means certain. (MC, 15)

43. See Bickel, PWC, 184; Bickel, MC, 15–18, 100.

44. Bickel, PWC, 11–14; Bickel, MC, 102, 110–11.

45. Bickel, MC, 17–18. There were exceptional cases. See PWC, 185–86.

46. Bickel, MC, 26. See also Bickel, PWC, 134; Bickel, SCIP, 87–88. Indeed, more than anything else, it was his growing doubts about the Court's capacity to meet this deliberative ideal that led him late in life to question the possibilities of judicial review. See Bickel, SCIP, 95–100.

47. See Ackerman, WPT, 406–20.

48. See, e.g., Ackerman, WPF, 268, 283–85.

49. See Ackerman, WPF, 104, 264–65, 268, 288; Ackerman, RC, 528–29. Ackerman even seriously considers, though ultimately rejects, the possibility that the Court's 1937 switch might have been too early not too late. See Ackerman, WPT, 335–50.

50. Ackerman, WPF, 263. See Ackerman, RC, 527–29.

51. See supra note 9 and accompanying text.

52. Ackerman, WPF, 263. See Ackerman, WPF, 241–42; Ackerman, RC, 527–29. Even when citizens do have considered judgments on questions of principle, there are pragmatic as well as theoretical (e.g., Arrow's Theorem) obstacles to aggregating their judgments into a social decision. Kenneth J. Arrow, *Social Choice and Individual Values* (New York: Wiley, 1951).

53. Ackerman might alternatively wish to reformulate his position not as a second-best argument but, rather, as an argument more directly rooted in democratic premises. Although during normal politics citizens have generally not formed considered judgments on questions of principle, they do hold one considered judgment—that government should stick strictly by the considered judgments made by earlier generations until superseded by a considered judgment of the current generation. If this claim were true, it would mean that the citizens do, in a (weak) sense, give their endorsement to the constitutional principles by

which they are governed. They exercise self-government by deferring, at least in the first instance, to the considered judgments made by prior generations. It seems at least as plausible, however, to think that citizens have a different mind-set—that they prefer to have their current legislators or the Supreme Court decide fundamental questions in the first instance, taking into account not only history and tradition, but contemporary values as well, and to become involved only when things go too wrong. It seems most plausible, however, to suppose that citizens are no more likely, and probably a good deal less likely, to have considered judgments on this question than on any others and that, in any case, they would not be of one mind were they to reflect upon the problem. To the extent that citizens would, if asked, articulate the first view, the reason, I suspect, would be, at least in part, their naive understanding of the nature of judicial review and of the extent to which constitutional interpretation has, in fact, altered original understandings over time.

54. Ackerman has sometimes, especially in more recent writings, suggested a greater openness to the possibility of evolutionary change as a secondary mode of constitutional development. See Ackerman, WPT, 392, 395, 403; Bruce Ackerman, "Revolution on a Human Scale," *Yale Law Journal* 108 (1999): 2080, 2288. However, these are only suggestions, and they appear to go against the grain of his principal arguments.

55. See supra note 9.

56. *Lochner v. New York*, 198 U.S. 45 (1905).

57. Ackerman, WPF, 101. See also Ibid., 83–84.

58. See Ackerman, WPF, 94–99, 114–29, 150–59. The source asserts that "the path of the law is from particularistic to comprehensive synthesis" and describes this process in connection with the Reconstruction and the New Deal.

59. See Ackerman, WPF, 86–103, 113–29, 140–62; Ackerman, RC, 520–22.

60. *Brown v. Board of Education*, 347 U.S. 483 (1954).

61. *Plessy v. Ferguson*, 163 U.S. 537 (1896). See Ackerman, WPF, 145–48. I accept Ackerman's account of *Plessy* for purposes of discussion.

62. See Ackerman, WPF, 146–48.

63. Ackerman, WPF, 150. See Ibid., 152.

64. Perhaps surprisingly, Ackerman himself makes precisely the same argument in reply to the claim that the New Deal undermined any effort to treat social institutions—not only the marketplace but, for example, the family too—as natural and hence outside the responsibility of the state. Ackerman argues that such a broad reading of the anti-laissez-faire premises of the New Deal, although appealing from a philosophical perspective, is ultimately unrealistic from a historical point of view (RC, 523–24).

65. I speak only hypothetically, accepting Ackerman's account. I mean to make no claims about the original intentions of the framers of the Fourteenth Amendment.

66. *Griswold v. Connecticut*, 381 U.S. 479 (1965).

67. See Frank I. Michelman, "Foreword: Traces of Self-Government," *Harvard Law Review* 100 (1986): 4, 63–65 (1986).

68. Peter Finley Dunne, Mr. Dooley's Opinions (1901), in http://www.boondocksnet.com/dooley/dooley6.html, taken from Jim Zwick, ed., Anti-Imperialism in the United States, 1898–1935, http://www.boondocksnet.com/ail98-35.html (Jan. 5, 2002). See supra notes 14–16 and accompanying text.

69. See Gerald N. Rosenberg, *The Hollow Hope: Can Courts Bring about Social Change?* (Chicago: University of Chicago Press, 1991).

70. See Kramer, supra note 2.

71. See Ackerman, WPF, 200–29.

72. Bickel, PWC, 13. See also Bickel, LDB, 262–63.

73. Compare Bickel, LDB, 256–67; Bickel, PWC, parts II and III; Bickel, SCIP, 91–94, with Ackerman, WPF, 108–10. For other examples of Bickel's positive reception of engaged citizen political action, see Bickel, LDB, 258–62 (discussing, *inter alia*, resistance to *Dred Scott v. Sanford*, 60 U.S. (19 How.) 393 (1857)); *McCulloch v. Maryland*, 17 U.S. (4 Wheat.) 316 (1819); and *Pollock v. Farmers' Loan and Trust Co.*, 157 U.S. 429 (1895)); Bickel, PWC, 13–14, 156 (discussing same and other cases).

74. *Miranda v. Arizona*, 384 U.S. 436 (1966). See Bickel, SCIP, 93.

Chapter 5

The Countermajoritarian Difficulty

Tradition versus Original Meaning

Stanley C. Brubaker

I. The Countermajoritarian Difficulty

How can we reconcile judicial review with the democratic character of the American regime? The problem has coexisted with the Constitution, but in *The Least Dangerous Branch*, Alexander Bickel developed it so effectively that his expression—"the countermajoritarian difficulty"—quickly became the standard in constitutional theory. Similarly, his own response, while gaining few ardent adherents, has also remained a touchstone of sorts; even while rejecting it, commentators have felt compelled to measure their theories against it.

Originalism was the most prominent of the alternatives that Bickel rejected and in turn originalists have become Bickel's most severe critics. They offer two reasons for rejecting Bickel's solution: It requires that judges play an unlawful political role, and it fails to recognize the authority of democratic will in enacting and amending the Constitution. I shall argue that neither Bickel nor the originalists provide an adequate solution to the countermajoritarian difficulty; together, however, they indicate the direction in which one may be found.

II. Bickel's Solution: Principle, Tradition, and the Passive Virtues.

Although the countermajoritarian difficulty cannot be denied, it can be alleviated and counterbalanced, Bickel argues, if judicial review can be shown to perform a unique and vital function for our constitutional order.

> The search must be for a function which might (indeed, must) involve the making of policy, yet which differs from the legislative and executive functions; which is peculiarly suited to the capabilities of the courts; which will not likely be performed elsewhere if the courts do not assume it; which can be so exercised as to be acceptable in a society that generally shares Judge Hand's satisfaction in a "sense of common venture"; which will be effective when needed; and whose discharge by the courts will not lower the quality of the other departments' performance by denuding them of the dignity and burden of their own responsibility.[1]

That function is to be the voice of enduring moral principle. The political branches of government are inevitably more concerned with the immediate and material interests of the people. "Judges have, or should have, the leisure, the training, and the insulation to follow the ways of the scholar in pursuing the ends of government" (LDB, 25–26). In the words of Henry M. Hart, Jr., which Bickel twice quotes, the Court appears "predestined in the long run, not only by the thrilling tradition of Anglo-American law, but also by the hard facts of its position in the structure of American institutions, to be a voice of reason, charged with the creative function of discerning afresh and of articulating and developing impersonal and durable principles. . . ." (LDB, 27, and 83).

But how to be this voice of reason and principle without either abrading the "sense of common venture" or "denuding" the political branches of "the dignity and burden of their own responsibility?" Bickel's answer to this question is complex, but consists essentially of two parts. One part lies in the provenance and character of these principles themselves. They were to be drawn from "tradition"—a concept central to Bickel's thought. "The function of the Justices . . . is to immerse themselves in the tradition of our society and of kindred societies that have gone before, in history and in the sediment of history which is law, and, as Judge Hand once suggested, in the thought and the vision of the philosophers and the poets. The Justices will then be fit to extract 'fundamental presuppositions' from their deepest selves, but in fact from the evolving morality of our tradition" (LDB, 236). In this sense, the principles are democratically grounded, if not democratically enacted; they bespeak self-government, though it is our "deepest self"—and not the self that emerges in the democratic process—that does the speaking (LDB, 239).

The other, complex, and not entirely separable part of Bickel's answer—which space will not allow me to detail[2]—lies in the *manner* in which these principles are to be articulated, permitting the Court a measure of "prudence."[3] Principle alone can justify judicial review, but practical exigencies as well as democratic politics cannot always abide principle. Bickel's solution lay in a set of doctrines and devices—"passive virtues—that allow the Court to avoid ruling on the merits of a case, but that engage the political branches in a sort of Socratic colloquy by which the Court may "elicit the correct answers," or least prepare them to accept the Court's pronouncement (LDB, 70).

Although the point is made rather quietly in *The Least Dangerous Branch* (LDB, 103–05), we should stress that for Bickel there are really two constitutions. There is the "structural" constitution, or "manifest" constitution, as he was later to call it, "the constitution of the mechanics of institutional arrangements and the political process, of power allocation and the division of powers."[4] And there is the constitution of "open texture"—of due process, equal protection, privileges and immunities, and first amendment freedoms—a constitution to be woven through time, in common law style, from the fabric of our evolving traditions. It is the second Constitution on which *The Least Dangerous Branch* focuses and on which the dispute with the originalists is joined.

III. The Originalist Response

For originalists, judicial review in accordance with the original understanding of the Constitution provides a far more straightforward, fully adequate, and singularly legitimate answer to the countermajoritarian difficulty. Echoing Alexander Hamilton and John Marshall, originalists hold that when the Court properly declares a law unconstitutional it is merely imposing the sovereign will of the people, declared and manifest in the Constitution, against the subordinate authority of the legislature. So long as—and only so long as—the Court follows the original meaning of the Constitution, the countermajoritarian difficulty is fully answered by the supermajoritarian authority of the Constitution. Conversely, when the Court deviates from the original meaning, it forfeits any claim to oppose the authority of the legislature.

This simple statement holds two divergent emphases within originalism, each of which has distinct reasons for objecting to Bickel's argument. The first is grounded in a premise of positivism and focuses on the objectivity of original meaning; apart from this standard, a judge has only his subjective preferences to oppose against the authority of enacted law—and for all his fancy language, in the end, Bickel can offer only such subjective preferences. Thus, the function he urges on the Court is simply not judicial in character. The second objection is grounded in a theory of democratic sovereignty; its concern is less with the objectivity of original meaning than its authority. Both arguments have force, but in the end the positivists provide a standard with no greater objectivity than Bickel's tradition and the democratic theories provide a standard with no greater authority.

The Positivist Originalists versus Bickel

For positivist originalists, to judge is to decide concrete cases on the basis of standards that are given. If a Justice reaches into his "deepest self" rather than the text and original meaning of the Constitution, he is making up these standards, not discovering them. He has forfeited the title to his office. Only originalism, they argue, can supply a genuine object for the courts to discover and thus rescue judicial review from the swamp of subjectivity and illegitimacy; "no other method of constitutional adjudication"[5] can do this. Originalism alone permits the Court to function as a court.

Notably, positivist-originalists do not precisely ignore the question of the authority of the Constitution in its original meaning—central to the second school of originalists—but they do submerge it into their stress on objectivity. From the perspective of the judge, they would argue, there is no need to press further the question of authority, for that much is given; such is the "ground-rule" of our constitutional system.[6] Law is enacted and courts must be bound by that meaning. "What does it mean to say that a judge is bound by the law?" asks Judge Bork. "It means that he is bound by the *only* thing that can be called law, the principles of the text, whether Constitution or statute, as generally understood at the enactment."[7] Here stands the firm reality of what the law is and what it means to be a judge, and from here the positivist-originalist would sling his opposition into the muck of subjectivity.

At first blush, the positivist-originalist's charge seems to have considerable force. Even if justices did have the time and inclination, as Bickel urged, to "immerse themselves" in the history, poetry, philosophy of our society and from this to extract "fundamental presuppositions" from "the evolving morality of our tradition" (LDB, 236),—even if they did all this, their judgments would remain inevitably subjective. As Bork argues, "A man or woman who read everything Bickel suggests could easily vote either way on such questions as whether the Court should create constitutional rights to abortion, to engage in homosexual conduct, to receive welfare payments, to take addictive drugs in the home . . ." (TA, 191).

But how objective is originalism? The essential difficulty is not one of access to evidence, but of determining what we should mean by originalism. Even if we had access to every speech uttered or document written at the time of enactment, we would have to decide such questions as whose intentions or meanings should count? What kinds of intentions should count? Should we look at concrete or abstract intentions or whichever is dominant? And we could not answer these questions without drawing upon exactly the sort of theoretical, or "subjective," considerations that the positivist-originalist seeks to avoid, that is, "some system of moral or ethical values that has no objective or intrinsic validity of its own and about which men can and do differ."[8]

One might be tempted to think such questions precious and thus not a serious challenge to positivist-originalism. But consider what momentous questions of constitutional law might turn on them.[9] Take for instance the distinction between abstract versus concrete intentions and ask whether the Equal Protection Clause of the Fourteenth Amendment bars segregation by race in the public schools. If we count concrete intentions, we might well conclude that the framers and ratifiers sought to extend to black Americans the same "civil" rights, preeminently property rights, as enjoyed by whites.[10] Focusing on such intentions, one could easily uphold segregation in the public schools. But if we count more abstract intentions, we might conclude that the framers and ratifiers wished to achieve racial equality before the law. Of such equality, property rights are certainly a major component, but so too is the right to be free from racial classifications whose purpose and effect is to stigmatize and subordinate. Raoul Berger, emphasizing concrete intentions, finds *Brown* lawless. Robert Bork, emphasizing abstract intentions, finds it lawful.[11]

Or consider the distinction between framers and ratifiers, and ask whether the Fourteenth Amendment "incorporates" the Bill of Rights. Though the evidence is disputed by the historians, on balance it seems that if we count the intentions of principal authors, or framers, then the answer is "yes," rights mentioned in the Bill of Rights are to be applied to the states. But, if we count the intentions of the ratifiers in the state legislatures, the answer would seem to be "no."[12]

Even if we could somehow resolve these controversies without recourse to moral or ethical values, it's not clear that originalism would provide a standard more objective than Bickel's. Let's simply take as given the choices favored by many originalists today: moderately abstract meanings over specific intentions, and the understandings of the ratifiers (or the public at large) over those of the framers. And let's take as given the further specification suggested by Justice Scalia: "We should look for a sort of 'objectified' intent—the intent that a reasonable person would gather from the text of the law, placed alongside the remainder of the *corpus juris*."[13] To paraphrase Judge Bork, a man or woman who read everything the originalist suggests, could easily vote either way on such questions as whether the Court should recognize federal authority to establish a national bank, ban seditious libel, prohibit slavery in the territories, or make fiat money legal tender. Further, there is little reason to suppose that the intent a reasonable person would gather from the text *at the time of enactment* should be any more objective than what a reasonable person would gather from the text *today*.

So if the case for originalism rests on its ability to supply the objective meaning that will allow the Constitution to be law and the Court a court, that honor must be shared with "contemporary" meaning. Actually, we might expand this point. Originalism must share that honor with any number of approaches to constitutional interpretation. For once its interpretive premise is accepted as authoritative, most theories confine judicial choice about as well as original meaning does: Richard Epstein's neo-Lockean theory, Ronald Dworkin's neo-Kantian theory, or John Hart Ely's representation reinforcing judicial review.

And the same is true of Bickel's tradition. Indeed, one might argue that at least as Bickel urges its use—that is, with restraint, with principles that "are to be traced and evaluated from the roots up, their validity in changing material and other conditions convincingly demonstrated, and their application to particular facts carried to the last decimal"—tradition suggests a stronger claim to objectivity.[14] The originalist might still reply that tradition is not "enacted."[15] But of course neither is the common law. And in the Anglo-American tradition, it is exceedingly difficult to claim that in their articulation of the common law, judges were not being judicial. So in the end, the "not judicial" argument must fail.

Popular Sovereignty Originalists versus Bickel

If originalists have a superior response to the countermajoritarian difficulty, it must lie in the realm of *authority*. On this dimension, both Bickel and originalists appeal to a concept of self-government. But Bickel appeals to a "deep self" found in tradition; originalists to the will of the people, or popular sovereignty, as expressed in constitutional enactment.

1. POPULAR SOVEREIGNTY ORIGINALISM. The originalists' theory of popular sovereignty has a distinguished lineage, tracing to Alexander Hamilton in Federalist 78 and John Marshall in *Marbury v. Madison*.[16] Yet in recent years, this aspect of the originalist argument is surprisingly underemphasized; also, it turns out to be more complex than initially meets the eye. If our criteria for an authentic expression of popular sovereignty are permissive, the people will have spoken too often. Thus, by Bruce Ackerman's criteria of popular sovereignty, we re-founded the Constitution with the New Deal without ever enacting any formal amendment.[17] If our criteria are restrictive, the people will not have spoken yet. Thus, by Cass Sunstein's criteria we must re-interpret the Constitution to allow for this more authentic expression to emerge.[18] But perhaps the criteria can be set so that the people have spoken just once extra legally, with the founding and then, legally defined, once for each of the amendments. And that is the theory presented by Keith E. Whittington in *Constitutional Interpretation: Textual Meaning, Original Intent, and Judicial Review*,[19] the most compelling account yet of popular sovereignty originalism.

For Whittington, as for Jean Jacques Rousseau, to whom he is explicitly indebted (CI, 122–59), the will of the people is not to be measured by any standard external to it—not God, or nature, or even reason.[20] Instead, authority derives from the concept of man as free and self-governing: the "right of the people to govern themselves does not arise from *what* they decide but from *who* they are."[21] If they are to retain that identity under government, if they are to maintain "human dignity," they must be makers of the law that binds them (CI, 137).

Whittington concedes we cannot reasonably expect citizens constantly to be engaged in the processes of self-government; nor is this essential to their identity as self-governing. What is essential is they have the opportunity to make the fundamental law. All other authority derives from this fundamental law and must be exercised tentatively, mindful of the limits expressed in the will of the people. Hence, Whittington tracks Rousseau's distinction between "law" (made by the people) and "executive" power (what we would call "government"), by separating the elements of politics into its "constitutional" realm (where popular sovereignty is, or has been, active) and "the merely administrative" (where the elected representatives, in a very broad sense, carry out the will of the people). Citizens are then free, both in the positive sense of making the laws that bind them and in the negative sense of being free from any laws that are not in this sense self-made.

As time passes from the moment of founding or amending the Constitution to the present, of course, the people are not governing themselves, but their posterity. Whittington's special insight is to note that if we wish *now* to hold this conception of ourselves as autonomous, self-governing individuals, with the capacity to make the laws that bind us, logically we must recognize that authority in our predecessors. "It is this spectral presence—the actual consent of the past and the possible consent of the future—that grounds the Constitution" (CI, 152). True, as a "placeholder" for future expressions of our sovereign authority, the Constitution's current authority is not as potent as when the people have freshly made or remade it, but it is more legitimate than any alternative (CI, 133).

With this appreciation of the authority of original meaning, grounded in democratic theory, Whittington believes he has resolved Bickel's countermajoritarian difficulty:

> By construing the Constitution in terms of the intent of its creators, originalism both enforces the authoritative decision of the people acting as sovereign and, equally important, preserves the possibility of similar higher-order decision making by the present and future generations of citizenry. In doing so, an originalist Court avoids the counter-majoritarian difficulty by adhering closely to its authorized role entailed by the binding written text. Moreover, it subsumes the difficulty

> within a larger democratic theory. The Court is not simply an antidemocratic feature of American politics but is an instrument of the people in preserving the highest promise of democracy. (CI, 111)

By defining what counts as an authentic expression of popular sovereignty in terms of the very acts of writing, ratifying, and amending a constitution, Whittington does neatly align it with original meaning. But there are three major difficulties in grounding the Constitution with this conception of popular sovereignty.

First, the ground itself becomes weak. Whittington's definition stretches popular sovereignty well beyond the conditions that for Rousseau gave the concept its strength. For Rousseau, popular sovereignty, or the "general will," must be expressed by the people themselves; representation is a form of enslavement. Further, the people must meet together, not just send in their results, for they must deliberate and listen to one another. Individual interest must be utterly subordinated to the general will. Only certain sorts of people have even the potential to achieve this sort of unity: the population must be small enough so that "each member can be known by all," yet large enough to achieve self-sufficiency; the people must be bound "by some union of origin, interest, or convention," yet not so tightly bound that they are no longer malleable. And these people would still need the good fortune to encounter a "Lawgiver," the crucial precursor to the expression of popular sovereignty, able "*to change human nature*, to transform each individual, who by himself is complete and solitary, into a part of a much greater whole, from which that same individual will then receive, in a sense, his life and his being."[22] Only thus may a people be formed, but further devices are necessary to maintain their capacity of expressing a general will. They must not form into "partial societies," or interest groups. They must believe they have no rights other than those the general will gives to them. They must impose a thoroughgoing system of censorship to guard against backsliding in the public mores. They must banish from the state anyone who fails to subscribe to the dogmas of the polity's civil theology. All of this is necessary if the people are to realize moral freedom—obedience to self-imposed laws—the ultimate moral ground for Whittington as for Rousseau. Although scholars debate Rousseau's guiding intent, the most persuasive explanation is that he wished to show the near impossibility of moral freedom, and hence political legitimacy, under modern conditions.

Whittington does not dispute this assessment of Rousseau's intent (CI, 135). His solution however is to argue that self-government in this profound sense remains the sole source of our constitutional authority and the basis for adherence to original intent because it is *metaphorically* true (CI, 142). Okay, the people of the United States didn't really gather together at the founding in one assembly. Okay, they didn't even get together in the states. Okay, they sent in representatives instead of presenting themselves. And okay, only a minority of the people were enfranchised and only a minority of them voted to send representatives to the ratifying conventions.[23] And okay, self-interest instead of the general will did often manifest itself in the deliberations. So, okay, "our constitution is [only] like self-government, but is not actually self-government." Its self-government is "true enough" (CI, 142). But "true enough" to resolve the countermajoritarian difficulty, with no further support from standards of right external to the general will? Doubtful.

Second, not only would we need to give Rousseau's theory a procrustean stretch if it is to ground our constitution, we would need similarly to refashion our current political self-understanding. And recall, under Whittington's theory of potential sovereignty, it is *our* willingness to accept this Rousseauian foundation *now* which grounds the logic of our embracing *their* expression of authority from back *then*. But are we willing to give up all prior claims of right in order to realize self-government and moral freedom as 1/250,000,000 part of a larger whole?[24] Are we willing to regard a new constitution as fully legitimate simply because it emerges from a national referendum with majority support—regardless of its circumvention of the Constitution's amendment procedure, regardless of the new government's form, and regardless of the rights that it would or would not protect?[25]

Third, the Whittington/Rousseau version of popular sovereignty—unassisted and unqualified by claims of natural rights, or indeed, any standard external to it—simply does not square with the content of our Constitution: its division and separation of powers; its limited powers; its rights of association, religious liberty, freedom of speech, property; the difficulty of its amendment process—all of this suggests an inherent suspicion of concentrated power and an affirmation of rights held antecedent to any social contract. Most fundamentally, the central clause of the *Social Contract*, "the *total alienation* of each associate, with all his rights, to the whole community," jars harshly with the premise implied in our constitutional statements of rights and expressly stated in our *Declaration of Independence*: we have rights that are "*un*alienable."

By this premise, we can not form Rousseau's social compact even if all of its other improbable demands were met. Our rights can*not* be alienated.

In sum, originalism grounded in pure popular sovereignty is inherently weak and mismatched with both our self-understanding and with the Constitution. But how well grounded is Bickel's tradition?

2. BICKEL'S TRADITION. While originalists stress the Constitution's firmness in the hard facts of its original meaning, Bickel stresses, in effect, its softness or even its absence of meaning. It is this "open texture" of the Constitution that permits the people "to pour into it and draw from it the sense of union and common purpose, past and future" (LDB, 105). And it is through this open texture that the Supreme Court is to serve the nation in weaving its tradition of principle. For Bickel, the Constitution, or at least that portion which lies beyond structure, in effect *is* this evolving tradition.

Though his characterization of the Constitution as one of "open texture" is maddeningly vague, the general direction of his thought is clear enough to see its accommodation with democracy. The Court would play a part, but only a part in the articulation of the fundamental values of the nation. The Court would largely employ the passive virtues, posing good questions in its colloquy with the political institutions, rather than imposing answers. And when he would have the Court impose an answer, or fundamental principle, Bickel demands proof of its place in the "evolving morality of our tradition." It is not sufficient that our "fundamental presuppositions" be merely "alluded to," they "are to be traced and evaluated from the roots up, their validity in changing material and other conditions convincingly demonstrated, and their application to particular facts carried to the last decimal" (LDB, 236–37). *Brown v. Board of Education*'s antidiscrimination principle[26] met that demanding standard. *Roe v. Wade*'s "privacy" fell woefully short (MC, 25–30). Even *Roe*'s more modest ancestor, "marital privacy," affirmed in *Griswold v. Connecticut*, was too forward for Bickel. He would have preferred that the Court engage its "passive virtues" and employ the more reserved doctrine "desuetude," leaving open the final question of the constitutionality of Connecticut's ban on the use of contraceptives and keeping on the state the "burden of self-government" (LDB, 143–156).

Yet the modesty of Bickel's jurisprudence does not compensate for its unconstitutionality. At its firm core, the Constitution must be the text. To this document, all must swear or affirm allegiance as a condition for holding public office.[27] Tradition may inform the text, and Bickel for the most part employs tradition in this regard. But he would also allow tradition to defeat the text, as when he urges the Court to begin a colloquy which would conclude with a judicial ban on the use of the death penalty—even though the death penalty is clearly authorized in three points in the text.[28] Bickel would effectively have the Justices wink as they take the oath required by Article VI to support "*this* Constitution." "Yes, we took an oath to the Constitution, but then what that constitution is is a matter of debate, and in the longer, wiser view of things, it must really mean the evolving traditions of the people." That's an argument that doesn't quite pass the straight face test.

If we cannot accept Bickel's replacement of the Constitution's text with evolving tradition, what about the use of tradition to provide the text with its essential moral support and thereby its illumination, the meaning that the Court would impose through judicial review against a current majority? Although Bickel relies on tradition extensively in the *Least Dangerous Branch*, only in his later work does he begin a defense of tradition, a task for which he turns to Edmund Burke. "Civil society is a creature of its past," he writes in *Morality of Consent*, "of a 'great mysterious incorporation,' and of an evolution which in improving never produces anything 'wholly new,' and in conserving never retains anything 'wholly obsolete'" (MC, 20). The passage from Burke's *Reflections on the Revolution in France*, from which Bickel draws, is worth quoting at length:

> Our political system is placed in a just correspondence and symmetry with the order of the world, and with the mode of existence decreed to a permanent body composed of transitory parts; wherein, *by the disposition of a stupendous wisdom*, moulding together the great mysterious incorporation of the human race, the whole, at one time, is never old, or middle-aged, or young, but, in a condition of unchangeable constancy, moves on through the varied tenor of perpetual decay, fall and renovation, and progression. Thus, by preserving the method of nature in the conduct of the state, in what we improve, we are never wholly new; in what we retain, we are never wholly obsolete. By adhering in this manner and on those principles of our forefathers, we are guided not by the superstition of antiquarians, but by the spirit of philosophic analogy.[29]

Tradition, in this Burkean sense, resists purely rational assessment, because it appeals to a standard that lies beyond individual human rationality; it proceeds instead upon a trust in the "disposition of a stupendous wisdom" evident in the whole of our political tradition. For Bickel, as for Burke, Anthony Kronman has observed, there is "an affectionate (though not uncritical) regard for the organic mysteries of established institutions."[30] In these institutions there is more "latent wisdom"[31] than could be held in the thought of mere individual rationality. And it is also this "mature skepticism"[32] (as well as his regard for the dignity of democratic choice) that guides Bickel's counsels of prudence in the exercise of judicial review. As Kronman emphasizes, the "affectionate regard," is "not uncritical;" it is not "an apology for the status quo," for "[a]ny institution of even moderate complexity will also have an aspirational component."[33] Still, the aspiration is *only* a component, and ultimately dependent, part of tradition.

Bickel offers many reasons to doubt the sufficiency of abstract moral reasoning: too often it simplifies an inevitably complex morality, ignores tradeoffs, is impatient with the concrete reality of politics and the claims of self-government, exaggerates its capacity to grasp all that is at stake, underestimates how much wisdom is accumulated in time-tested institutions and practices, and fails to realize how much that is good depends on adherence to institutions that may not withstand the full test of rational inquiry. Tradition corrects these tendencies.

Yet the Bickel/Burkean understanding of tradition goes one disturbing step further to trust more in the *process* of history than in rational understanding of moral philosophy, or in the possibility of "good government from reflection and choice."[34] And when tradition no longer looks at moral reality, filtered to be sure through the history and practices of a particular people, but looks instead simply at the history and practices of a people as sufficient in themselves, it is in danger of collapse. If we believe something—say, freedom of speech—is good because in our tradition it is thought good, but without appeal to whether it is really good, the temptation, in the name of democracy, is to move from history to the standard of "contemporary practice." But then if I believe that freedom of speech is good because you think that it is good, and you think it is good because I think it is good, but neither of us has any ultimate thought to whether it is really good, all we have left is our own will. Either we lapse into an enfeebling nihilism or we assert a strident righteousness as we come to believe that the test of moral reality is our own willfulness.[35]

And it was precisely these outcomes that Bickel was brought to face near the end of his life as he surveyed the social wreckage of the sixties. "What is happening to morality today?" he asked in *Morality of Consent*. "It threatens to engulf us" (MC, 119). The legal order was heaving under the demands of the "dictatorship of the self-righteous" (MC, 142). Later, in even greater despair, he looked at what had become of the Constitution: "All we ever had was a tradition, and now that is shattered."[36]

IV. What the Constitution Really Means

Ironically, originalism suffers a similar defect. For like tradition, originalism also takes as the final test of words the meaning or will of the persons using them. And this point holds whether we follow the arguments of the positivist or the popular sovereignty originalists. Positivists, doubting the existence or the relevance of moral reality, insist upon adhering to the meaning of those who wrote or ratified the Constitution—outside of this, there is only subjectivity. And advocates of popular sovereignty, viewing the will of the people as the final authority—with no further reference to nature or natural rights—likewise insist on that will as the final measure of meaning. Both seem to agree with the claim of John Locke: "Words in their primary or immediate signification, stand for nothing, but the Ideas in the Mind of him that uses them."[37]

By virtue of their oath, office holders must be bound to the text of the Constitution, but not necessarily to the original meaning of the text or to an evolving tradition of meaning. What we need is an explanation of what the Constitution "really" means, a meaning that can account for the various claims of authority the Constitution makes. In such an approach, we should understand the words of the Constitution to refer not to "Ideas in the Mind of him that uses them,"[38] but to phenomena and functions, ultimately a moral reality, independent of our ideas or usages. Traditions and original understandings, to be sure, afford us insight into real meanings, but we must examine more carefully the question that both originalists and Bickel implicitly pose, but answer imperfectly. What is the nature of the self that "constitutes," or gives authority to the Constitution, and is presupposed in that act of oath taking? For the originalist, as I have argued, it is most persuasively put as a Rousseauian self, one capable of moral freedom. For Bickel, it is our "deepest self," as found in the aspirations of our tradition. Neither answer is persuasive as an account of what is presupposed in the oath "to support this Constitution,"[39] but at least together they have posed the right question.

If the nature of constitutional authority and meaning lie in this direction, what should be the role of the Court? Given the republican character of the Constitution as well as the lack of firm proof as to what the Constitution really means, the "counter-majoritarian difficulty" persists. Bickel was right that this difficulty cannot be eliminated, only alleviated and counterbalanced. And he was right that the primary device for doing so are the "passive virtues" through which the Court engages the country in a Socratic colloquy as to the nature of constitutional meaning. But the object of this interpretation must be a reality that is only evoked, and not fully captured, either by an evolving tradition or by an original understanding.

Notes

1. Alexander Bickel, *The Least Dangerous Branch* (Indianapolis, IN: Bobbs-Merrill, 1962), 24. Subsequent references to this work are cited in the text and notes with the following abbreviation: LDB.

2. For a more extensive consideration of the passive virtues, see Christopher J. Peters and Neal Devins, "Alexander Bickel and the New Judicial Minimalism" in this volume.

3. For an elaboration of prudence as the central concept in Bickel's political philosophy and jurisprudence, see Anthony T. Kronman, "Alexander Bickel's Philosophy of Prudence," *Yale Law Journal* 94 (1985): 1567–1616.

4. Alexander Bickel, *The Morality of Consent* (New Haven, CT: Yale University Press, 1975), 29–30. Subsequent references to this work are cited in the text and notes with the following abbreviation: MC.

5. Robert H. Bork, *Tempting of America* (New York: Free Press, 1990), 155. Subsequent references to this work are cited in the text and notes with the following abbreviation: TA.

6. As Professor Henry P. Monaghan argues, "[O]ur legal *grundnorm* has been that the body politic can at a specific point in time definitely order relationships, and that such an ordering is binding on all organs of government until changed by amendment." "Our Perfect Constitution," *New York University Law Review* 56(1981): 353, 376. Bork makes a similar point in *The Tempting of America*, 174.

7. Bork, TA, 5, emphasis added. See also, Antonin Scalia, "Originalism: The Lesser Evil," *University of Cincinnati Law Review* 57 (1989): 849; Monaghan, "Our Perfect Constitution," 353, 375. Raoul Berger, *Government by Judiciary* (Cambridge, MA: Harvard University Press, 1977); Frank Easterbrook, "Approaches to Judicial Review," in *Politics and the Constitution* (Washington, DC: National Legal Center for the Public Interest, 1990).

8. Robert H. Bork, "Neutral Principles and Some First Amendment Problems," *Indiana Law Journal* 47 (1971): 1, 10.

9. The point of this argument does not hinge on the precise accuracy of the historical claims. It is sufficient that this account *could* be true to show the theoretical problems that the originalist must still confront.

10. Berger, *Government by Judiciary.*

11. Bork, TA, 74–84; Berger, *Government by Judiciary*, 1–19, and 166–83.

12. The literature is vast. For a sampling see Justice Hugo Black's appendix to his dissent in *Adamson v. California*, 332 U.S. 46 (1947); Horace Flack, *The Adoption of the Fourteenth Amendment* (Gloucester, MA: P. Smith, 1908); Charles Fairman, "Does the Fourteenth Amendment Incorporate the Bill of Rights? The Original Understanding," *Stanford Law Journal* 2 (1949): 5; Stanley Morrison, "Does the Fourteenth Amendment Incorporate the Bill of Rights?", *Stanford Law Journal* 2 (1949): 140; Joseph B. James, The Framing of the Fourteenth Amendment (Urbana, IL: University of Illinois Press, 1956); Berger, *Government by Judiciary*; Michael K. Curtis, *No State Shall Abridge: The Fourteenth Amendment and the Bill of Rights* (Durham, NC: Duke University Press, 1986); Akhil Reed Amar, *The Bill of Rights* (New Haven, CT: Yale University Press, 1998), 163–214.

13. Scalia, *A Matter of Interpretation* (Princeton, NJ: Princeton University Press, 1997), 17, 37–38. See also Bork, TA, 144; Michael McConnell, "On Reading the Constitution," *Cornell Law Review* 73 (1988): 359; and Gary McDowell, *The Constitution and Contemporary Constitutional Theory* (Cumberland, VA: Center for Judicial Studies, 1985), for similar expressions of how to approach original understanding.

14. Note Justice Scalia's concession that on the countermajoritarian problem, restraint with proof of evolving principle is as defensible as originalism. "Originalism: The Lesser Evil," *Cincinnati Law Review* 57 (1989): 849, 864.

15. See note 7.

16. *Marbury v. Madison*, 5 U.S. 137, 176.

17. Bruce Ackerman, *We the People: Foundations* (Cambridge, MA: Harvard University Press, 1991), and *We the People: Transformations* (Cambridge, MA: Harvard University Press, 1998).

18. Cass Sunstein, *The Partial Constitution* (Cambridge, MA: Harvard University Press, 1993).

19. Keith Whittington, *Constitutional Interpretation* (Lawrence, KS: University of Kansas Press, 1999). Subsequent references to this work are cited in the text and notes with the following abbreviation: CI.

20. Or public virtue. Whittington, CI, 138–39.

21. Whittington, CI, 138. (Emphasis added). Note the parallel rejections of God and Nature in Rousseau's *Social Contract* Bk. I, chs. 1–2. See also, Michael Walzer, "Philosophy and Democracy," *Political Theory* 9 (1981): 379, 383, very much in the tradition of Rousseau.

22. Jean Jacques Rousseau, *Social Contract* Bk. II, ch. vii (emphasis added). Although the Lawgiver presents his authority as an instrument of God, Rousseau regards this as simply a necessary artifice. The sort of truth known to the Legislator cannot be comprehended by ordinary people in other forms; thus Lawgivers must "attribute their own wisdom to the Gods."

23. Forrest McDonald, *E Pluribus Unum* (Indianapolis, IN: Liberty Press, 1965), 319.

24. For Rousseau, self-government required that "each member can be known to all." Even a polity of ten thousand members would begin to compromise the possibility of realizing moral freedom as obedience to self-made law; one's sense of "self" identified with this larger whole would start to lose its touch with reality *Social Contract* Bk. II ch. x.

25. Whittington, CI, 202, and n. 126, p. 292.

26. Bickel, LDB, 63: "[T]here shall be no distinctions of race ordained by the state."

27. U.S. Constitution, art. VI, par. 3.

28. Bickel, LDB, 240–43. The death penalty is twice contemplated in the Fifth Amendment. "No person shall be held to answer for a capital, or otherwise infamous crime, unless on a presentment or indictment of a Grand Jury" (i.e., one can be prosecuted with capital punishment if the person is indicted by a Grand Jury) and "nor shall any person . . . be deprived of life, liberty, and property, without due process of law," Fifth Amendment," (i.e., one can be deprived of life, as long as it is with due process of law). This latter clause is reiterated in section one of the Fourteenth Amendment.

29. Edmund Burke, *Reflections on the Revolution in France*, ed. J. G. A. Pocock (Indianapolis, ID: Hackett Publishing Company, 1987), 30. (Emphasis added).

30. Kronman, "Alexander Bickel's Philosophy of Prudence," 1572.

31. Burke, *Reflections*, 91.

32. Bickel, MC, 4.

33. Kronman, "Alexander Bickel's Philosophy of Prudence," 1608.

34. *The Federalist*, No. 1, ed. W. Carey and James McClellan (Indianapolis, IN: Liberty Fund, 2001). See Bickel's dismissal of this notion in Bickel, MC, 22–23.

35. Burke sought to preserve his reflections from this risk by positing God's wisdom—the "stupendous wisdom"—behind the history that man could only trust, but not comprehend. But Bickel finds no such ultimate refuge beyond history.

36. Quoted in Bork, TA, 193.

37. John Locke, *Essay Concerning Human Understanding*, ed. Vere Chappell (New York: Oxford University Press, 1998), III:ii.2.

38. Or to "usages" in a "language game," as Ludwig Wittgenstein argued. *Philosophical Investigations*, trans. By G. E. M. Anscombe, (New York: Macmillan, 1958).

39. U.S. Constitution, art. VI, par. 3.

Chapter 6

An Empirical Analysis of Alexander Bickel's *The Least Dangerous Branch*

Terri Peretti

In each of the last ten years, I have taught a seminar entitled Theories of Judicial Review. Many theorists have come and gone from the course reading list, but Alexander Bickel has been a mainstay. As I tell my students, Bickel is required reading in any course on judicial review. The last day of class, students vote on their favorite and least favorite constitutional theorist (with Robert Bork typically winning both categories). Before voting, one student was refreshing her memory regarding the various scholars we studied and found herself stuck on Alexander Bickel. Another student volunteered that he was "the guy who couldn't make up his mind whether he liked judicial review or not." That is an apt characterization of the central contradiction or tension in Bickel's work. He was quite uneasy about judicial review, particularly how it was used by the Warren Court, yet he desperately sought to identify its virtues and thereby defend it.

This chapter will argue that Bickel failed in his struggle to reconcile judicial review with democratic values and that the cause is empirical error in his key assumptions. I begin with a brief summary of Bickel's argument and then proceed to a refutation of its various components.

In *The Least Dangerous Branch*, Alexander Bickel confronted and attempted to solve what he regarded as the central problem of judicial review—the "counter-majoritarian difficulty." In a frequently cited passage, he argued that

> The root difficulty is that judicial review is a counter-majoritarian force in our system. . . . [W]hen the Supreme Court declares unconstitutional a legislative act or the action of an elected executive, it thwarts the will of representatives of the actual people of the here and now; it exercises control, not in behalf of the prevailing majority but against it. That, without mystic overtones, is what actually happens . . . and it is the reason the charge can be made that judicial review is undemocratic.[1]

Especially important is that judicial review, in contrast to statutory construction, "is the power to apply and construe the Constitution, in matters of the greatest moment, against the wishes of a legislative majority, which is, in turn, powerless to affect the judicial decision" (LDB, 20). Because the Court's rulings of unconstitutionality cannot be reversed by a popular or legislative majority through ordinary political processes, "judicial review. . . . [is] a deviant institution in the American democracy" (LDB, 18).

In searching for a special justification for this deviant institution, Bickel settled upon its unique capacity for reasoned elaboration of principle. While the legislature is a proper arena for the unrestrained advancement of various private interests, we should expect more of government generally. It "should serve not only what we conceive from time to time to be our immediate material needs but also certain enduring values" (LDB, 24). It is here that the Court has much to offer.

> [C]ourts have certain capacities for dealing with matters of principle that legislatures and executives do not possess. Judges have, or should have, the leisure, training, and the insulation to follow the ways of the scholar in pursuing the ends of government. . . . Their insulation and the marvelous mystery of time give courts the capacity to appeal to men's better natures, to call forth their aspirations, which may have been forgotten in the moment's hue and cry. This is what Justice Stone called the opportunity for "the sober second thought." (LDB, 25–6)

Thus, the Court performs a valuable and otherwise unfulfilled function, insisting that the government act consistently with our enduring values and principles. It is in this way that Bickel reconciled judicial review with democratic values.

I. Evaluating the Countermajoritarian Difficulty

Contained within Bickel's characterization of the countermajoritarian difficulty are several assertions which can be examined empirically. Bickel variously claims or assumes that: legislation reflects majority preferences; Supreme Court decisions are inconsistent with majority preferences; Supreme Court decisions are final and irreversible; and the Court is unique or "deviant" in its countermajoritarianism. As will be discussed below, each assumption is faulty and consequently dooms from the start Bickel's efforts to reconcile judicial review with democratic values.

I certainly do not claim to be the first to challenge the accuracy of the countermajoritarian paradigm.[2] I do hope, however, that I have offered a new twist or two, particularly in the final section regarding the pluralist character of American democracy and its implications for determining Court legitimacy.

Does Legislation Reflect Majority Preferences?

The first claim is that when the Court strikes down a law as unconstitutional, it is thwarting the majority will. An initial problem in evaluating this assertion is vagueness and variability in how Bickel defines the term "majority will." At times, Bickel refers merely to a "legislative majority" or "the will of representatives of the . . . people" (LDB, 17, 20). However, this conception is not particularly helpful as it merely states a truism. (When the Court strikes down a law as unconstitutional, it necessarily disallows the choices of a majority of elected representatives; it is, thus, by definition thwarting the majority will.) At other times, Bickel emphasizes that legislation is majoritarian in the sense that it can be traced to a popular majority. For example, in response to the claim that interest group politics and "minorities rule" are more helpful concepts than majority rule for understanding the legislative process, he asserts that

> [i]t remains true nevertheless that only those minorities rule which can command the votes of a majority of individuals in the legislature who can command the votes of a majority of individuals in the electorate. In one fashion or another, both in the legislative process and at elections, the minorities must coalesce into a majority. (LDB, 19)

Additionally, he argues that, even if Congress and the presidency do not independently represent a national majority, inequities in representation occurring in each tend to balance out and produce, in combination, a national majority (LDB, 18). Yet another Bickelian formulation of majority will is that a majority retains the critically important power of reversal of policies it opposes. For example, Bickel acknowledges that "[m]ost assuredly, no democracy operates by taking continuous nose counts on the broad range of daily governmental activities" and that "[t]he whole operates under public scrutiny and criticism—but not at all times or in all parts . . . Nevertheless, although democracy does not mean constant reconsideration of decisions once made, it does mean that a representative majority has the power to accomplish a reversal" (LDB, 17). However, Bickel then adds yet another twist; he qualifies this view of majority will further by noting that the power of reversal "is of the essence and no less so because it is often merely held in reserve" (LDB, 17). This suggests that majority will perhaps means little more than the majority passively acquiescing in policy in the process of granting general support to the government. Finally, Bickel sometimes advances a more traditional conception of majority will—that it violates the majority's specific policy preferences. For example, he asserts that "when the Court invalidates the action of a state legislature, it is acting against the majority will within the given jurisdiction" (LDB, 33).

I do not propose testing each of these various formulations. However, it is important to acknowledge the considerable carelessness with which the term "majority will" is used, a common problem in normative constitutional scholarship.[3] Testing the validity of the claim that laws are majoritarian is accordingly made more difficult. Two types of analysis will nonetheless be offered. The first examines whether and how often government policy reflects public opinion. The second assesses the degree to which the political system is designed to discern and vindicate the majority's policy preferences. This inquiry leads to the conclusion that the policymaking process is not majoritarian or populistic in design; additionally, its record of responsiveness is good but "hardly impressive,"[4] producing policy decisions consistent with majority opinion one-half to two-thirds of the time.

The first question is whether and how often public policy in the United States reflects majority opinion. Unfortunately, the relevant studies are not ideally constructed for my purposes, as they typically examine not whether legislative decisions or the policy products of the legislature and executive correspond to public opinion, but whether government policy, *including* that produced by the Court, corresponds to public opinion. In fact, this is a more realistic approach than Bickel's, recognizing that public policy in the United States is more than mere legislative choice; it is the product of interaction among many different policymaking institutions.

While some research does focus solely on the legislature, it does not examine whether legislation (produced by the institution as a whole) corresponds with public opinion. Instead, studies examine whether individual legislators vote consistently with their constituents' preferences.[5] They typically find variation in responsiveness, with the salience of the issue to constituents serving as the key determinant.[6]

With regard to public policy-public opinion congruence more generally, various studies agree that government policy is consistent with public opinion roughly 55 to 65 percent of the time. For example, Alan D. Monroe examined survey data from 1960 to 1974 and found a correspondence between public opinion and public policy 64 percent of the time.[7] Additionally, civil rights and civil liberties policies, which were more likely to be made by the judiciary, matched public opinion 67 percent of the time. In updating his analysis, Monroe found that government responsiveness has been lower in recent years, with policy decisions matching public opinion a bare majority of the time (55 percent from 1980 to 1991 and only 53 percent from 1992 to 1999).[8] Benjamin Page and Robert Shapiro tested whether public opinion change on several hundred survey items between 1935 and 1979 produced a corresponding policy change. They found congruence in two-thirds of the cases, with policy change more likely when the opinion shift was substantial and stable and with policy change no less likely for the judiciary compared to the other branches. Additionally, causation (with opinion change causing policy change) could be attributed in only half of the cases.[9] Richard Sutton examined over one hundred state policies and found a match with statewide majority opinion 60 percent of the time.[10] Finally and more directly to the point are Thomas R. Marshall's findings that, when relevant poll data was available, 72 percent of the federal laws and 58 percent of the state and local laws brought before the Court from 1935 to 1986 were consistent with the views of a national majority.[11]

These studies lead us to conclude that government policy reflects public opinion more often than not and that a majority of laws reviewed by the Court are indeed supported by public opinion. Nonetheless, a significant minority of laws, especially state and local laws, are not. Thus, we cannot automatically equate legislation with majority preferences, nor can we say with confidence that majority opinion was the certain and proximate cause of every piece of legislation enacted.[12] As one important study in this field concludes, "[p]ublic opinion is powerful but not all-powerful."[13]

These perhaps curious findings can be readily explained by several factors—the nature of American public opinion, the existence of other influences on public policy, and the countermajoritarian structure of elections and governing institutions in the United States. First, it is well-known that many Americans simply have no opinion on major political issues and that, at least at the individual level, their opinions are unstable, nonideological, and often weakly held.[14] The absence of firm and coherent majority-opinion groupings obviously inhibits the ability of government to enact policy that reflects "the majority will." Moreover, in recent years, only half of the age-eligible population has voted in presidential elections. As a result, victorious presidential candidates receive the support of barely a quarter of the electorate, hardly "majority" support. Turnout in midterm congressional elections is even worse, often below 35 percent, and turnout in state and local elections is lower still. Additionally, those who vote are unrepresentative; the electorate is older, better-educated, wealthier, and whiter.

A second factor that complicates the translation of majority will into public policy is the existence of other influences on policymaking, such as interest groups and political parties. It is well-known that interest groups influence government policymaking, especially when public opinion on an issue is divided or when those opinions are weakly held.[15] Furthermore, the number of interest groups exploded in the 1960s and 1970s, further splintering public opinion.[16] And special interests, relative to general interests, are more likely to overcome free rider problems. They have advantages that allow them more easily to form and maintain organizational structures. It is therefore not surprising that business groups far outnumber and "outmoney" other groups.[17]

Third, and more importantly, even when a policy-specific majority emerged, American elections and governing institutions are not structured so as to vindicate its preferences. After all, a "Constitution that provides for federalism, the separation of powers, a bicameral legislature, a Bill of Rights, six-year Senate terms, and an electoral college certainly was not designed to translate public opinion directly into public policy."[18]

For a variety of reasons, the American electoral system inhibits the transmission of majority preferences to government. First, many government officials—the president, judges and, originally, senators—are not even directly elected. The people are thus permitted a direct voice in only part of government—the House and, since 1913, the Senate. Additionally, members of Congress are elected by states and localities, not a national majority.

Another notable characteristic of American elections is that they are separate, independent, and staggered. A majority, should it exist, is not permitted to elect the entire national leadership in a single election. Instead, we elect different leaders at different times for different terms of office. Because house, senate, and presidential elections are independent of one another, divided party control of government is permitted, and majority rule is thereby impeded. In fact, with the growth in ticket-splitting, divided control is increasingly common and a typical feature of modern American government.

Another significant impediment to the electoral transmission of majority preferences is the heavy reliance in the United States on winner take all and plurality rules. These rules cause votes to be ignored or weighed unequally. To win a seat in Congress or a state's electoral votes in a presidential election, a candidate need only win the most votes, not necessarily majority voter support. The votes of those who supported losing candidates, potentially a majority, are therefore ignored; such voters in effect receive no representation. Proportional representation systems employed by most democracies are regarded as more effective and accurate representational devices.

Moreover, members of Congress have also developed highly effective, nonideological strategies for winning reelection. By devoting substantial energies to pork barrel and casework, members avoid angering constituents with controversial policy choices and can additionally "claim credit," a difficult task with lawmaking.[19] Low voter turnout, winner take all rules, and a profitable dependence on constituency service together mean that responding to a policy-specific majority (whether in the district, state, or nation) is not a necessary condition for winning congressional office.

The electoral college is also capable of distorting majority preferences, primarily due to the winner take all rule and the guarantee of three electoral votes to sparsely populated states. It may even award the presidency to a candidate who failed to receive a majority of the popular votes (occurring eighteen times), or who actually lost the popular vote count (occurring four times, including in the 2000 presidential election).

A final distortion worth mentioning occurs in the Senate, where small states receive equal representation with large states. As a result, interpreting voter preferences in senatorial elections as the expression of a "majority will" can be tricky. For example, Republicans gained control of the Senate in 1980 and confirmed in the minds of many that the Reagan Revolution had arrived. However, Democrats in fact received three million more senatorial votes nationally than the Republicans. When the Democrats then regained control of the Senate in 1986, marking the supposed end to the Reagan Revolution, the Republicans had actually increased their percentage of the national senatorial vote compared to 1980.[20] In these instances, control of the Senate went to the party that won narrow victories in a sufficient number of small states, not the party that won national voter support.

Not only do American elections fail to transmit majority preferences accurately, translating them into national policy is further inhibited by the existence of considerable structural fragmentation in government. Due to checks and balances and a bicameral legislature in which both houses depend heavily on committee organization, policy requires the simultaneous agreement of many different officials, which even a powerful and united majority may find difficult to attain. By implication, minorities are empowered by virtue of these many independent sites of power. They can defeat a policy proposal or win important concessions at many points throughout the policymaking process. Deserving special notice as an antimajoritarian tool is the filibuster, which is increasingly used today[21] and which allows a minority of senators to frustrate the majority's efforts to pass legislation, even when desired by many Americans.

Characterizing the laws that the Court strikes down as the expression of majority will is not necessarily erroneous, but at best misleading. Majority opinion often does not exist on an issue or is shallow and transient. Additionally, public policy is influenced by interest groups and political parties, not public opinion alone. Finally, American elections and government structure distort the transmission of majority preferences and impede their translation into government policy. Thus, while legislation often reflects majority opinion, there is no guarantee of this outcome, nor does it occur by design.

Are Supreme Court Decisions Countermajoritarian?

In automatically and thus erroneously equating legislative decisions with majority will, Bickel is led to another faulty assertion—that the Court's rulings of unconstitutionality are necessarily countermajoritarian. That simply cannot be concluded from the mere fact that the Court has struck down a law. There are in fact two separate empirical issues here. The first is whether we can infer that the Court's decisions are countermajoritarian since legislative decisions reflect majority preferences. As just discussed, we cannot since legislative decisions sometimes reflect majority preferences, but sometimes do not.

A second empirical approach is to test directly whether Supreme Court decisions are countermajoritarian by comparing them to public opinion. As will be discussed, such studies consistently show that the Court rules in favor of majority opinion more often than not. In other words, the Court is "an essentially *majoritarian* institution."[22]

Thomas R. Marshall has provided the most important and comprehensive study in this area.[23] He compared 146 Supreme Court decisions from 1935 to 1986 with national poll data on the issues on which the Court ruled. He found that 62 percent of its decisions were consistent with public opinion.[24] Additionally, the Court was more likely to uphold state or federal laws that were consistent with national opinion as compared to laws that were inconsistent with national opinion. Finally, its "consistent" decisions were not confined to instances in which it upheld laws as constitutional. About half of the Court's rulings of unconstitutionality reflected rather than contradicted nationwide public opinion.

David G. Barnum's study of the post-New Deal Court similarly found that it typically ruled consistently with public opinion (with school prayer being a notable exception), leading him to conclude that the Court's "countermajoritarian reputation . . . is greatly exaggerated."[25] For example, its birth control, school desegregation, and sex discrimination decisions were supported by a majority or a growing and sizable plurality of Americans. When the public was sharply divided on or opposed to a particular policy, such as affirmative action, busing, and homosexual rights, the Court was more equivocal or deferential. Additionally, the Court often sided with national opinion in striking down a state law. In so doing, Barnum concluded, the Court is "making a direct contribution to the operation of majoritarian democracy in the United States."[26]

Several other studies have also found a high degree of consistency between Court rulings and public opinion. For example, William Mishler and Reginald S. Sheehan found that, for most of the period from 1956 to 1989, the Court's decisions "conformed closely to the aggregate policy opinions of the American public."[27] Thomas R. Marshall and Joseph Ignagni also demonstrated that the Court's record in "rights claims" followed public opinion. For example, from 1953 to 1992, the

Court ruled in favor of a civil rights, civil liberties, or equality claim 73 percent of the time when it was supported by the public, compared to only 40 percent of the time when the public opposed the claim.[28] Finally, an empirical study by James A. Stimson, Michael B. Mackuen, and Robert S. Erikson demonstrated that "court decisions do, in fact, vary in accord with current public preferences" though less strongly and quickly as compared to the president, House, and Senate.[29]

Overall, the research refutes Bickel's characterization of the Court as a countermajoritarian institution. While the Court does indeed often rule against majority opinion (about one-third of the time, according to Marshall), it *more often* sides *with* majority opinion. Of course, this should not be surprising, given that Supreme Court Justices are chosen by recently elected officials, the president and senate, primarily because of their partisan affiliation and ideological views.[30] Furthermore, we know that a justice's ideology exerts a considerable influence on her decisions,[31] and that Justices live up to presidential expectations about 75 percent of the time, with that figure increasing in modern times and for presidents who carefully screen their nominees.[32]

Most scholars agree that the appointment process is the dominant path through which public opinion influences Supreme Court decisions and the best explanation for the majoritarian character of most Supreme Court decisions. However, some additionally observe an "anticipated reactions" phenomenon, with "strategic" or policy-oriented justices taking public opinion into account in order to increase the acceptance and thus the success of their rulings.[33] Some scholars more controversially claim that the Supreme Court directly and independently responds to public opinion.[34] Ascertaining the precise path by which public opinion influences the Court is not the primary task here. It is enough to note that the Court's decisions do reflect and vary with public opinion, contrary to the traditional claim that its rulings of unconstitutionality necessarily flout the majority will and are, thus, undemocratic.

Interestingly, Bickel at times acknowledges the fact of popular though nonelectoral influence on the Court. For example, he grants that "there are other means than the electoral process, though subordinate and subsidiary ones, of making institutions of government responsive to the needs and wishes of the governed. Hence, one may infer that judicial review, although not responsible, may have ways of being responsive" (LDB, 19). Unfortunately, Bickel is unwilling to follow through on this important concession. He instead provides a formalistic and ultimately unpersuasive response:

> But nothing can finally depreciate the central function that is assigned in democratic theory and practice to the electoral process; nor can it be denied that the policymaking power of representative institutions, born of the electoral process, is the distinguishing characteristic of the system. Judicial review works counter to this characteristic. (LDB, 19)

The lack of a formal electoral sanction is, in Bickel's view, fatal and defeats this potential claim that the Court is politically responsive and, hence, democratically defensible. However, with regard to the central assertion in contention here—that the Court is a countermajoritarian institution—the evidence is clear. The laws that the Court strikes down are not always majoritarian, and the Court itself decides consistently with public opinion a majority of the time.

Are Supreme Court Decisions Final?

According to Bickel, legislative policymaking is democratic because "a representative majority has the power to accomplish a reversal" (LDB, 17). In contrast, "[j]udicial review . . . is the power to apply and construe the Constitution, in matters of the greatest moment, against the wishes of a legislative majority, which is, in turn, powerless to affect the judicial decision" (LDB, 20). Thus, the Court is deviant and undemocratic in large part because its rulings are final or irreversible. The problem thereby created is, in Bickel's view, how to reconcile "authoritarian judicialism and the practice of democracy" (LDB, 244). As he even more strongly states it in *The Supreme Court and the Idea of Progress*, "the supreme autonomy that the Court asserts in many matters of substantive policy needs justification in a political democracy."[35]

As with Bickel's other assumptions, his claim of judicial finality or "supreme autonomy" lacks empirical support. Government officials charged with implementing Supreme Court decisions may refuse to offer their assistance to the Court. Lower court judges may fail to apply new doctrine faithfully. Congress may refuse to fund and the executive branch to enforce the Court's rulings. State and local officials opposed to the Court's policies will also have many opportunities to ignore or undermine them.

Gerald N. Rosenberg's study demonstrates these facts with regard to a variety of Court-led social reform efforts.[36] Whether in the area of school desegregation, abortion, or rights of the accused, the Court's efforts were largely unsuccessful. For example, *Brown*[37] had virtually no impact in the South until Congress passed the Civil Rights Act of 1964 and the executive branch began enforcing it in earnest. Similarly, despite *Roe* v. *Wade*,[38] women's access to abortion remains limited and widely uneven. Most hospitals have continued not to provide abortion services, and three-quarters of U.S. counties are without abortion providers. This is not surprising given that government officials have more often acted to restrict abortion access than ensure it. Rosenberg provides abundant evidence that the Court's policies are effective only to the degree that others in the private or public sector are willing to implement them.

Bickel's notion of judicial supremacy, thus, does not take adequate account of how legislators and citizens influence constitutional doctrine. Citizens and interest groups can (and do) protest Court decisions, and they can (and do) communicate their displeasure to their representatives. Leaders can, in addition to withholding implementation support, actively attack the Court.[39] Congress has a variety of formal powers it can use. It can impeach the Court's members, restrict its appellate jurisdiction, alter its size, propose constitutional amendments, fix the Court's terms, control its budget and staff, and set (though it cannot lower) judicial salaries. Although some of these powers are rarely used (impeachment and constitutional amendment, for example), they are not without their effects. For example, Court-curbing bills, even when not enacted, produced decisional reactions by the Court in six of the nine periods of "intense Congressional hostility" that Rosenberg studied.[40] The President has fewer formal Court-checking powers, but he can use the bully pulpit to attack the Court and can urge Congress to use its powers. (Of course, this is in addition to his power to nominate Supreme Court justices and to refuse to enforce the Court's decisions.) The key point here is that political opposition to the Court can be expressed in a variety of ways—presidential speeches, political campaigns, constitutional amendment proposals, or Court-curbing bills in Congress. And such opposition often leads the Court to overturn or alter its decisions. The Court responded to congresional attacks in the 1950s (such as the Jenner bill) with a "tactical withdrawal," choosing in *Barenblatt v. U.S.*[41] and *Uphaus v. Wyman*[42] to uphold both congressional and state authority to investigate subversive activities.[43] In 1937, political pressure forced it to abandon the legitimate constitutional task of protecting economic liberty. The Court's policy shift was then solidified through FDR's nine appointments, which represent another vehicle of politically enforced doctrinal alteration: membership change via deliberate Court-packing efforts. Bickel, thus, exaggerates the difficulty of altering the Court's policies via implementation, Court-curbing, and Court-packing.

Bickel does, at various times, acknowledge that there are limitations on the Court's power and thus on its decisional finality. For example, in discussing *Brown v. Board of Education*, he asserts that "[t]he Supreme Court's law . . . could not in our system prevail—not merely in the very long run, but within the decade—if it ran counter to deeply felt popular needs or convictions, or even if it was opposed by a determined and substantial minority and received with indifference by the rest of the country" (LDB, 258). He also notes that "the judiciary is wholly dependent upon the Executive. The Court commands no significant police power of its own. It is true that . . . the Executive is obliged to come to the judiciary's support in any . . . [enforcement] crisis . . . But there are degrees of enthusiasm in rendering executive support" (LDB, 252). Thus, "[t]he effectiveness of the [Court's] judgment . . . depends on consent and administration" (SCIP, 91). Bickel further admits that "judges are subject to controls similar to those that operate on other policy-making elites" and that "society is not without recourse" in the face of judicial policy it opposes (SCIP, 88,90).

Bickel's views on this issue are clearly contradictory: the Court's decisions are final, yet they are not final. He partially reconciles these competing ideas by, on occasion, distinguishing between judicial finality in theory and in practice. For example, he notes that "[t]he principle [that the Court enunciates] can be revised or reversed—*at least in theory*—only by the Court itself. The other institutions . . . are bound."[44] He also asserts that the Court's "authority, although asserted in absolute terms, is *in practice* limited and ambivalent, and with respect to any given enterprise or field of policy, temporary."[45] He even acknowledges that the need for popular and elite support for the Court's decisions "in the end, is how and why judicial review is consistent with the theory and practice of political democracy" (LDB, 258). Yet Bickel remains uneasy about this "ambivalent practical accommodation" (SCIP, 112).

Bickel recognizes that the Court's judgments are provisional, not final. Why not then conclude that the countermajoritarian difficulty is not, in the end, all that difficult? For a reason I still cannot fathom, Bickel is unwilling to follow the logical implications of his concessions. He instead clings to the idea that democratic values are threatened by judicial finality, even if that finality is only theoretical or rhetorical. His claim of judicial finality, in the end, seems fake. It serves as a necessary prop in his countermajoritarian difficulty construct, but one in which he only halfheartedly believes.

Is the Court Deviant?

The final claim to be evaluated is the Court's supposed deviance. It is the fact that the Court is *uniquely* countermajoritarian that, in Bickel's view, requires a special justification for judicial review. When the Court strikes down a law as unconstitutional, "it exercises control, not on behalf of the prevailing majority, but against it" (LDB, 17). This final section will refute this claim regarding the Court's deviance with three points—two empirical and one conceptual.

The first empirical point is that the Court reflects public opinion in its decisions about as often as other institutions. As discussed earlier, the Court's decisions are consistent with public opinion nearly two-thirds of the time, making "majoritarian" a more accurate label for the Court than "counter-majoritarian." Additionally, the fact that the Court rules against national opinion up to one-third of the time does not mark it as unusual or deviant. Page and Shapiro found that the Court was as likely to respond to public opinion change as Congress and the executive branch.[46] The Court also fares quite well comparatively in Marshall's study. He notes that:

> 64 percent to 68 percent of nationwide polls were matched by similar policies . . . [while] 62 percent to 66 percent of Supreme Court decisions were consistent with available polls. Against these comparisons, the modern Court appears neither markedly more nor less consistent with the polls than are other policy makers.[47]

Finally, the study by Stimson, Mackuen, and Erikson found some modest differences between the Court's responsiveness to public opinion and that of the House, Senate and President, with the Court responding less strongly and after a significant time lag.[48] Overall, though, the evidence suggests that the Court is not unusual in its degree of responsiveness (or unresponsiveness) to majority preferences.

The second empirical response is that, in not being designed to respond promptly and directly to majority wishes, the Court is a typical rather than a deviant American political institution. In other words, American democracy is not majoritarian. I must admit that advancing such an obvious point feels rather silly. However, the persistence of the countermajoritarian paradigm in constitutional scholarship—a strawman argument if there ever was one—makes such silliness necessary.

As previously discussed, there are many obstacles to majority rule in the United States—plurality election rules, interest group power, the electoral college, staggered elections, equal state representation in the Senate, the committee system in Congress, and the Senate filibuster. Bickel acknowledges many of these countermajoritarian features, but regards them as "impurities and imperfections" in an otherwise majoritarian system (LDB, 18). However, the countermajoritarian features of American democracy far exceed the majoritarian ones and cannot be regarded as minor or random "imperfections." They were deliberately adopted by the Framers precisely because of their antimajoritarian effects.

Federalist 10 clearly expresses the Framers' strong fears of majority tyranny.[49] A leading concern was that a selfish majority would come to dominate government and would ignore minority rights and the national good. As a result, they favored a representative over a direct democracy. In the former, wise leaders could refine and elevate the majority's selfish views while, in the latter, the majority would always win, enabling if not guaranteeing majority tyranny. Furthermore, they expected that a large republic would dissipate majority unity and inhibit its development; instead of a monolithic majority, a multiplicity of competing interests would more likely develop.

Bickel acknowledges this point at times. For example, in *The Supreme Court and the Idea of Progress*, he notes that the "Madisonian model of a multiplicity of factions vying against each other and checking each other . . . more nearly fits our system" and that "our government is not, and ought not be, strictly majoritarian" (SCIP, 83). However, despite the occasional concession (though rarely made in *The Least Dangerous Branch*), Bickel stubbornly and irrationally clings to the majoritarian view.[50]

There is one last point to make in response to Bickel's claim that the Court is a deviant institution in American democracy. This largely conceptual point follows from a concession of my own: Bickel is correct that the Court is different from the elective branches, and it is indeed less democratic. Its members are not elected, and they enjoy life tenure. The Justices, thus, possess relatively greater room in which to maneuver; they will not face voter anger and retribution in the next election if they decide in an unpopular fashion. The Court's ability to rule persistently against school prayer and, in the early twenthieth century, child labor laws, is proof of its relatively greater freedom to act. However, concluding that the Court is different or less democratic does not require that we also conclude that it is less legitimate. Instead, institutional differentiation is a central feature of American democracy. Ironically, the fact that the Court is "deviant" or different from other governing institutions makes it a normal and integral part of American democracy.

The Framers sought to frustrate the majority's efforts to win selfish policy benefits at the expense of others and the nation as a whole. In doing so, they also secured the positive good of increasing the opportunities of all groups to stop government action perceived as harmful to their interests. That end is accomplished through three institutional design principles: redundancy, diversity, and nonhierarchy.[51] *Redundancy* means that there are many institutions that contribute to policy-making rather than one that dominates policy-making. As a result, there are more arenas in which citizens and groups can express their desires and more channels for influencing and contesting policy. *Diversity* means that those institutions are designed differently. If every institutional site was identical, then a group's likelihood of success would be the same for each. However, varying the selection method and term length for each institution improves the chances of winning in at least one arena; group claims and resources may be ignored in one branch, but valued in another. Finally, *nonhierarchy* means that these various governing institutions are ordered, through checks and balances, in a nonhierarchical manner. No single institution is regarded as superior or dominant. It cannot alone enact policy; instead, widespread and simultaneous agreement among many institutions must be secured. This guarantees that a group's victory in one arena is meaningful. Whether it occurs in the Senate, the White House, or the courts, a single victory is sufficient to forestall an unfavorable policy course. A group's interests have thus been effectively protected.

While judicial review would indeed be considered odd or illegitimate in a majoritarian democracy, in the Madisonian or pluralist system described above, it is neither. In American democracy, an institution's rightful authority to act is not determined by the closeness of its connection to the people, or by its ability to reflect the majority will. If that were the case, why tolerate the Senate or the electoral college? Or why not let the most democratic unit, the House, alone decide policy? Legitimacy is instead determined by an institution's contribution to the policy-making process. Does it offer a meaningful opportunity for groups to have their say in the policy process, thereby promoting interest representation and system legitimacy? Does it represent interests overlooked in other institutions, thereby expanding the bases of consent? Does it bring a different set of strengths and a different perspective to policy-making? Viewed in this light, the fact that the Court is different is a blessing, not a curse. The Court's deviance (and "difference" is a more appropriate term) need not require an apology or extraordinary justification.

In suggesting that the Court is to be judged by its contribution to effective policy-making and the meaningful representation of America's diverse interests, certain types of research become critically important. Historians can document the Court's periodic protection of groups that could not win elsewhere—for example, business at the turn of the twentieth century and criminal defendants and racial and religious minorities in the mid-twentieth century. Policy analysts can inform us about when (or whether) the Court improves upon the policy product of the other branches.[52] Research on who litigates in the courts and with what degree of success also helps us to learn about the Court's distinctive contribution to interest group representation and consensual policy-making.[53] Less important in determining the Court's legitimacy is the traditional legal-academic enterprise of ascertaining the veracity of the Court's judgements regarding the Constitution's meaning.

II. Conclusion

If time and space allowed, I would have included an evaluation not only of how Bickel constructs the countermajoritarian difficulty, but also how he then solves it. He argues that the legitimacy of judicial review is saved by the Court's unique capacity to serve as the guardian of society's enduring principles. This follows from Bickel's assessment, though largely an erroneous one, of the relative virtues of the legislature and the judiciary. I must save for another day analysis of his belief that legislatures are almost completely devoid of principle while courts possess it in abundance. Suffice it to say that Bickel was often disappointed with the Court in this regard, and I doubt that his assessment would improve with its performance since (with *Bush* v. *Gore* immediately coming to mind).[54]

In the end, Bickel's solution to the countermajoritarian difficulty is bound to fail since his characterization of the problem is so weakly grounded empirically. First, the laws that the Court strikes down are not necessarily, specifically, or peculiarly majoritarian. Second, the Court's decisions match majority opinion more often than not and about as often as the other branches. Third, the Court's rulings are not final, but are instead subject to popular and elite revision and even reversal. Finally, the Court is not a unique, countermajoritarian institution in a predominantly majoritarian democracy. American democracy is not in *any* way directed to the goal of majority rule. It instead requires policy agreement among many different interests and many different officials, in order to secure broad-based consent, prevent tyranny, and promote political stability. The Court, like other redundant, diverse institutions, is an integral component of this system and needs no special defense.

Barry Friedman correctly observes that "the counter-majoritarian problem simply will not go away . . . [d]espite a growing literature indicating that this particular lens on judicial review is profoundly flawed."[55] He attributes its puzzling persistence, first, to constitutional scholars' "grave discomfort with normativity" and, second, to the "high esteem accorded to the iconic figures of the profession" who first advanced it—Thayer, Holmes, Hand, and Frankfurter.[56] Our hero worship has continued with Alexander Bickel. Although Bickel has, in Kronman's apt phrase, "many admirers but few followers,"[57] his impact on constitutional scholarship has been profound. The legal academy's long-standing (and Friedman argues, "pathological")[58] obsession with the countermajoritarian difficulty is proof of that.

This obsession has come at a price, however. Because the countermajoritarian paradigm is defective, it has produced much scholarship but little progress. We continue to spin our wheels, trying to solve an unresolvable dilemma—reconciling the countermajoritarian practice of judicial review with majoritarian democracy. Compounding the futility of the enterprise is the fact that there is, in any case, no dilemma to resolve: judicial review is not countermajoritarian, and American democracy is not majoritarian. Thus, our search is pointless. To borrow Ely's phrase, "[n]o answer is what the wrong question begets."[59]

The result of asking the wrong question is the now familiar (and endless) cycle in constitutional scholarship. A new, promising theory of judicial review is introduced, followed by its thorough "trashing" by scholars of various ideologies and approaches, followed by yet another exciting interpretive theory, followed by more critiques and our consensual dismissal of it. The end result is a surfeit of theories discarded on the trash heap, endorsed by a community of one (the author). Little wonder that two leading scholars have given up and urge us simply to eliminate judical review altogether.[60]

Although we have been ill-served by Bickel's faulty formulation of the problem, I will probably always include his work in my seminar on judicial review. I will know we have progressed, however, when I present it, not as the dominant paradigm in constitutional scholarship, but as an historical artifact.

Notes

1. Alexander M. Bickel, *The Least Dangerous Branch*, 2d ed. (Yale University Press , 1986), 16–17. Subsequent references to this work are cited in the text and notes with the following abbreviation: LDB.

2. For example, Martin M. Shapiro, *Freedom of Speech: The Supreme Court and Judicial Review* (Englewood Cliffs, NJ: Prentice-Hall, 1966); Mark A. Graber, "The Nonmajoritarian Difficulty: Legislative Deference to the Judiciary," *Studies in American Political Development* 7 (1993): 35.

3. See my discussion in *In Defense of a Political Court* (Princeton, NJ: Princeton University Press, 1999), 190–191 and chapter seven more generally.

4. Alan D. Monroe, "Public Opinion and Public Policy, 1960–1999" (paper presented at the annual meeting of the American Political Science Association, San Francisco, California, 2001), 15.

5. Warren E. Miller and Donald E. Stokes "Constituency Influence in Congress," *American Political Science Review* 57 (1963): 45; John Kingdon, *Congressmen's Voting Decisions* (New York: Harper and Row, 1973); Robert S. Erikson, "Constituency Opinion and Congressional Behavior," *American Journal of Political Science* 22 (1978): 511.

6. Barbara Hinckley, *Stability and Change in Congress* (New York: Harper and Row, 1983).

7. Alan D. Monroe, "Consistency between Public Preferences and National Policy Decisions," *American Politics Quarterly* 7 (1979): 3.

8. Monroe, "Public Opinion and Public Policy, 1960–1999."

9. Benjamin Page and Robert Shapiro, "Effects of Public Opinion on Policy," *American Political Science Review* 77 (1983): 175.

10. Richard Sutton, "The States and the People: Measuring and Accounting for 'State Representativeness," *Polity* 5 (1973): 451.

11. Thomas R. Marshall, *Public Opinion and the Supreme Court* (Boston, MA: Unwin Hyman, 1989), 83, 85.

12. In addition to the Page and Shapiro study ("Effects of Public Opinion on Policy"), see Lawrence R. Jacobs and Robert Y. Shapiro, *Politicians Don't Pander: Political Manipulation and the Loss of Democratic Responsiveness* (Chicago: University of Chicago Press, 1999).

13. James A. Stimson, Michael B. Mackuen, and Robert S. Erikson, "Dynamic Representation," *American Political Science Review* 89 (1995): 543, 558.

14. Norman H. Nie, Sidney Verba, and John R. Petrocik, *The Changing American Voter* (Cambridge, MA: Harvard University Press, 1976); W. Russell Neuman, *The Paradox of Mass Politics* (Cambridge, MA: Harvard Unviersity Press, 1986); Michael X. Delli Carpini and Scott Keeter, "U.S. Public Knowledge of Politics," *Public Opinion Quarterly* 583 (1991); Benjamin Page and Robert Shapiro, *The Rational Public* (Chicago: University of Chicago Press, 1992); Richard Morin, "What Informed Public Opinion?" *Washington Post National Weekly Edition*, April 10–16, 1995, p. 36.

15. How powerful interest groups are is, of course, subject to dispute. For example, see Jonathan Rauch, *Demosclerosis* (New York: Random House, 1994); Dan Clawson, Alan Neustadtl, and Denise Scott, *Money Talks* (New York: Basic Books, 1992). But see Michael Pertschuk, *Giant Killers* (New York: W. W. Norton, 1986); John P. Heinz, Edward O. Laumann, Robert L. Nelson, and Robert H. Salisbury, *The Hollow Core: Private Interests in National Policy Making* (Cambridge, MA: Harvard University Press, 1993).

16. Kay Schlozman and John Tierney, *Organized Interests and American Democracy* (New York: Harper and Row, 1981); Mark Petracca, ed., *The Politics of Interests* (Boulder, CO: Westview Press, 1992).

17. Jack Walker, *Mobilizing Interest Groups in America* (Ann Arbor, MI: University of Michigan Press, 1991); Mancur Olson, *The Logic of Collective Action* (Cambridge, MA: Harvard University Press, 1965); Schlozman and Tierney, *Organized Interests and American Democracy.* The classic argument can be found in E. E. Schattschneider, *The Semi-Sovereign People* (New York: Holt, 1975).

18. Morris P. Fiorina and Paul E. Peterson, *The New American Democracy*, 2nd ed., (New York: Longman, 2001), 157.

19. Morris P. Fiorina, *Congress: Keystone of the Washington Establishment, 2nd ed.* (New Haven, CT: Yale University Press, 1989). Pork barrel refers to a representative's efforts to channel federal projects and monies to the local district, while casework involves performing favors for individual constituents, typically helping with bureaucratic red tape.

20. Morris P. Fiorina and Paul E. Peterson, *The New American Democracy* (Boston, MA: Allyn and Bacon, 1999), 362–363.

21. Michael Malbin, "Leading a Filibustered Senate," in *Extensions* (Norman, OK: University of Oklahoma, Carl A. Albert Center, 1985); Richard

E. Cohen, "Crackup of the Committees," *National Journal* (July 31, 1999): 2210–2217 (citing Barbara Sinclair's research).

22. Thomas Marshall, *Public Opinion and the Supreme Court* (Boston, MA: Unwin Hyman, 1989), 192 (emphasis added).

23. Thomas R. Marshall, *Public Opinion and the Supreme Court*, 192.

24. Ibid., 78.

25. David G. Barnum, "The Supreme Court and Public Opinion: Judicial Decision-Making in the Post-New Deal Period," *Journal of Politics* 47 (1985): 652.

26. David G. Barnum, *The Supreme Court in American Democracy* (New York: St. Martin's Press, 1993), 280.

27. William Mishler and Reginald S. Sheehan, "The Supreme Court as a Countermajoritarian Institution? The Impact of Public Opinion on Supreme Court Decisions," *American Political Science Review* 87 (1993): 87, 97.

28. Thomas R. Marshall and Joseph Ignagni, "Supreme Court and Public Support for Rights Claims," *Judicature* 78 (1994): 146.

29. James A. Stimson, Michael B. Mackuen and Robert S. Erikson, "Dynamic Representation," *American Political Science Review* 89 (1995): 543, 555.

30. Henry J. Abraham, *Justices, Presidents, and Senators* (Lanham, MD: Rowman and Littlefield Publishers, 1999); Terri Peretti, *In Defense of a Political Court*, 85–100.

31. Jeffrey A. Segal and Harold J. Spaeth, *The Supreme Court and the Attitudinal Model* (New York: Cambridge University Press, 1993); Jeffrey A. Segal and Albert D. Cover, "Ideological Values and the Votes of U.S. Supreme Court Justices," *American Political Science Review* 83 (1989): 557. For my review of this voluminous research, see Peretti, *In Defense of a Political Court*, 101–111.

32. Peretti, *In Defense of a Political Court*, 111–131; Laurence Tribe, *God Save This Honorable Court* (New York: Random House, 1985).

33. See generally Lee Epstein and Jack Knight, *The Choices Justices Make* (Washington, DC: Congressional Quarterly Press, 1998).

34. Mishler and Sheehan, "The Supreme Court as a Countermajoritarian Institution?"; William Mishler and Reginald S. Sheehan, "Popular Influence on Supreme Court Decisions: A Response to Helmut Norpoth and Jeffrey A. Segal," *American Political Science Review* 88 (1994): 716; Roy B. Flemming and B. Dan Wood, "The Public and the Supreme Court: Individual Justice Responsiveness to American Policy Moods," *American Journal of Political Science* 41 (1997): 468.

35. Alexander M. Bickel, *The Supreme Court and the Idea of Progress* (New Haven, CT: Yale University Press, 1978), 86. He also refers to "supreme judicial autonomy" on pages 82 and 84. Subsequent references to this work are cited in the text with the following abbreviation: SCIP.

36. Gerald N. Rosenberg, *The Hollow Hope* (Chicago: University of Chicago Press, 1991).

37. *Brown* v. *Board of Education*, 347 U.S. 483 (1954).

38. *Roe v. Wade*, 410 U.S. 113 (1973).

39. See a fuller discussion in Peretti, *In Defense of a Political Court*, ch. 5. See also Walter F. Murphy, *Congress and the Court* (Chicago: University of Chicago Press, 1962); Stuart S. Nagel, "Court-Curbing Periods in American History," *Vanderbilt Law Review* 18 (1965): 925; Roger Handberg and Harold F. Hill Jr., "Court Curbing, Court Reversals, and Judicial Review: The Supreme Court versus Congress," *Law and Society Review* 14 (1980): 309; Jeffrey A. Segal, "Courts, Executives, and Legislature," in *The American Courts*, eds. John B. Gates and Charles A. Johnson (Washington, DC: Congressional Quarterly Press, 1991), 373.

40. Gerald N. Rosenberg, "Judicial Independence and the Reality of Political Power," *Review of Politics* 54 (1992): 369.

41. *Barenblatt* v. *U.S.*, 360 U.S. 109 (1959).

42. *Uphaus* v. *Wyman*, 360 U.S. 72 (1959).

43. Walter F. Murphy, *Congress and the Court* (Chicago: University of Chicago Press, 1962), 246.

44. Bickel, *The Least Dangerous Branch*, 203. Emphasis added.

45. Bickel, *The Supreme Court and the Idea of Progress*, 181. Emphasis added.

46. Page and Shapiro, "Effects of Public Opinion on Policy."

47. Marshall, *Public Opinion and the Supreme Court*, 80.

48. Stimson, Mackuen and Erikson "Dynamic Representation."

49. *The Federalist, No. 10* (James Madison) (New York: New American Library, 1961), 77.

50. I had initially planned to write on "The Contradictions of Alexander Bickel." I have already pointed out several of these and remain confused about why he advances these contradictory claims. My guess is that Bickel is desperate to conclude that judicial review is deviant and in dire need of justification; this in turn requires the various assumptions disputed here, even if they lack empirical validity and even if Bickel occasionally acknowledges that fact.

51. For a fuller explanation, see Peretti, *In Defense of a Political Court*, 209–216.

52. One excellent example is Robert H. Mnookin, ed., *In the Interest of Children* (New York: W. H. Freeman and Company, 1985).

53. Gregory A. Caldeira and John R. Wright, "Amici Curiae before the Supreme Court: Who Participates, When, and How Much?", *Journal of Politics* 52 (1990): 782; Lee Epstein, "Courts and Interest Groups," in *The American Courts: A Critical Assessment*, eds. John B. Gates and Charles A. Johnson (Washington, DC: Congressional Quarterly Press, 1991), 343–45; Reginald S. Sheehan, William Mishler, and Donald R. Songer, "Ideology, Status, and the Differential Success of Direct Parties before the Supreme Court," *American Political Science Review* 86 (1992): 464; S. Sidney Ulmer, "Governmental Litigants,

Underdogs, and Civil Liberties in the Supreme Court: 1903–1968 Terms," *Journal of Politics* 47 (1985): 899.

54. *Bush v. Gore*, 531U.S. 98 (2000). Ironically, Justice Breyer, in his dissent in the case, cited several passages from *The Least Dangerous Branch*, repeating for the majority's benefit its argument for judicial restraint in political disputes that are unusual, momentous, or ill-suited to principled resolution.

55. Barry Friedman, "The Counter-Majoritarian Problem and the Pathology of Constitutional Scholarship," *Northwestern University Law Review* 95 (2001): 933.

56. Ibid., 933, 939.

57. Anthony T. Kronman, "Alexander Bickel's Philosophy of Prudence," *Yale Law Journal* 94 (1985): 1567, 1568.

58. Friedman, "The Counter-Majoritarian Problem."

59. John Hart Ely, *Democracy and Distrust* (Cambridge, MA: Harvard University Pres 1980), 72.

60. Mark Tushnet, *Taking the Constitution Away from the Courts* (Princeton, NJ: Princeton University Press, 1999); Robert H. Bork, *Slouching Toward Gomorrah: Modern Liberalism and American Decline* (New York: Regan Books, 1996).

Chapter 7

Bickel and the New Proceduralists

Kenneth D. Ward

The countermajoritarian difficulty remains a puzzle more than forty years after Alexander Bickel published *The Least Dangerous Branch.* He introduced the term to describe the problem of justifying judicial review, a nondemocratic institution in a government that derives its legitimacy from citizens' participation. Constitutional theorists first sought to solve the countermajoritarian difficulty and then tried to move past it. They have disagreed about what the puzzle is and have even sought to explain its allure. The countermajoritarian difficulty has indeed gained a life of its own. Bickel, by contrast, has lost his allure. Though he is often cited for coining a memorable phrase, his significance to constitutional theory is measured by his response to the countermajoritarian difficulty, a response that has been judged deficient. Constitutional theorists have concluded that Bickel fails to justify judicial review. But it is hard to assess this conclusion, because the conventional view of the countermajoritarian difficulty does not reflect the problem that Bickel addressed.

The conventional view assumes that political institutions derive authority by representing a popular will, and that the legislature and the executive have a plausible claim to be representing such a will because they are elected institutions. It is a problem, according to this view, when an unelected judiciary invalidates acts of these institutions. The problem is solved by grounding judicial authority in principles that can satisfy a test of democratic legitimacy; judicial review is justified when judges enforce principles that reflect a popular will.

Bickel did not believe governments derive legitimacy by advancing such a will. He, instead, explained political legitimacy in terms of citizens' attitude about the political community. He contended that elected institutions promote political legitimacy by helping citizens develop a "sense of common venture."[1] The countermajoritarian difficulty arises because judicial review interferes with their developing such an attitude. More importantly, because theorists focus on whether Bickel identified principles that reflect a popular will, they ignore how he framed the problem of justifying judicial review. Bickel's conception of judicial review has significance for contemporary constitutional theory.

This essay illustrates its significance. Section one provides a brief summary of Bickel's view of the countermajoritarian difficulty and contrasts it with the conventional view as epitomized by John Hart Ely's *Democracy and Distrust*. This contrast emphasizes two features of Bickel's argument. First, Bickel connected the question of judicial review to the problem of how to legitimate the authority of a *system* of political institutions; he asked whether judicial authority complements elected authority in a manner that strengthens the broader government's claim of legitimacy. Ely, on the other hand, measured the legitimacy of judicial review by a standard of democracy that he applied separately to individual institutions. Second, because Bickel tethered judicial authority to a broader system of government, he was less concerned than Ely was with the substance of judicial decisions. Though Ely gained prominence from his process-based defense of judicial review, Bickel had previously emphasized the processes we should use to make various political decisions, including the types of questions that judges should answer and how they should approach these questions.

Section two illustrates how Bickel's conception of judicial review resonates in the work of contemporary constitutional theorists. We will see that theorists who have sought to move beyond the countermajoritarian difficulty have conceived of judicial review in terms that are similar to Bickel's. We will also see that many contemporary theorists repeat a mistake that Bickel made when they consider judicial review from a perspective that emphasizes how judges should decide cases. It is Bickel's focus on judicial decisions that helps explain why so many people misinterpreted his argument. Today, theorists who adopt this perspective cannot grasp an important division that characterizes debates among those who reject the conventional view of the countermajoritarian difficulty. Some theorists continue to believe that we must justify judicial review based on the substantive decisions that we expect judges to make. Others ground this authority in considerations that are independent of such decisions.

In particular, the section uses recent work by Ronald Dworkin and Jeremy Waldron to illustrate that Bickel's conception remains relevant to contemporary debates. Both Dworkin and Waldron assess judicial review based on its contribution to a system of governmental institutions. Moreover, Waldron contends that we must defend judicial review in terms that are independent of the decisions that we expect judges to make. And this leads him to emphasize the advantages of the legislative process over the judicial process and thus to reject Dworkin's defense of judicial review. Theorists who view judicial review solely in terms of the decisions they expect judges to make cannot grasp Waldron's argument.

I. Two Views of the Countermajoritarian Difficulty

Bickel believes that political legitimacy flows from citizens' consent to government, and that citizens' consent depends on elected institutions. But we must be careful. This idea of consent suggests that people accept the authority of government, because their vote ensures that elected institutions express their will. And many constitutional theorists believe that Bickel sought to solve the countermajoritarian difficulty by demonstrating that the legal principles judges enforce could substitute for the popular will expressed by legislation.

But Bickel does not press this line of argument. He, instead, links consent to citizens' attitude toward the political community. He contends that elected institutions promote consent by fostering a sense of common venture, and that this sense of common venture is the source of political legitimacy (LDB, 20). Therefore, judicial review threatens political legitimacy to the extent that it undermines elected institutions that promote this attitude. This, according to Bickel, is the countermajoritarian difficulty. What does it mean for elected institutions to promote citizens' sense of common venture? We can trace Bickel's idea to a tradition of constitutional theory associated with James Bradley Thayer. This tradition emphasizes that elected institutions encourage citizens to develop a quality of character they must have if constitutional government is to succeed. We know that Bickel was greatly influenced by Felix Frankfurter who was a follower of Thayer.[2] We also know that Bickel adopts the notion of a common venture from Learned Hand, and

Thayer was Hand's favorite teacher.[3] More significantly, Bickel delves deeply into this tradition when he examines the countermajoritarian difficulty. He discusses two problems that arise when judicial review impedes elected institutions, and draws on both Thayer and Hand to suggest that judicial review might prevent citizens from developing the virtues that would advance the ends of constitutional government. First, Bickel notes that judicial review weakens democratic processes, by encouraging legislators and their constituents to shift the responsibility of governance to courts. Reduced responsibility invites legislative negligence because legislators then have an incentive to acquiesce in unconstitutional demands of their constituents and trust the Court to correct their mistakes (LDB, 21–22). This dependency also diminishes the capacities of citizens. Bickel cites Thayer's contention that ". . . the people thus lose the political experience, and the moral education and stimulus that comes from fighting the question out . . . and correcting their own errors. The tendency of a common and easy resort to this great function . . . is to dwarf the political capacity of the people, and to deaden its sense of moral responsibility."[4]

Second, Bickel discusses a related difficulty, the weakness of judicial review in a democratic society. Because judges ultimately lack the power to counteract sustained abuses by majorities, a democratic society must look to an alternative means to control individual passions and to promote stable government. The Court can not save society from itself. Bickel cites Hand to link these two discussions. Hand states that:

> . . . a society so riven that the spirit of moderation is gone, no court *can* save; that a society where that spirit flourishes, no court need *save*; that in a society which evades its responsibility by thrusting upon the courts the nurture of that spirit, that spirit in the end will perish.[5]

Bickel, thus, suggests that the political experience that nurtures a morally responsible citizenry would teach citizens to moderate their passions.

The countermajoritarian difficulty, according to Bickel, describes the problem of judicial review undercutting elected institutions that foster the sense of common venture that animates a legitimate government. Although Bickel believes judicial review "must achieve some measure of consonance" with democracy, he does not believe that it can be made democratic (LDB, 27); he does not attempt to solve the countermajoritarian difficulty by showing that judges enforce principles that reflect a popular will.

Bickel, instead, frames the problem of justifying judicial review as follows:

> The search must be for a function which might . . . involve the making of policy, yet which differs from the legislative and executive functions; which is peculiarly suited to the capabilities of the courts; which will not likely be performed elsewhere if the courts do not assume it; which can be so exercised as to be acceptable in a society that generally shares Judge Hand's satisfaction in a "sense of common venture"; which will be effective when needed; and whose discharge by the courts will not lower the quality of the other departments' performance by denuding them of the dignity and burden of their own responsibility. It will not be possible fully to meet all that is said against judicial review . . . we can only fill the other side of the scales with counter arguments on the real needs and the actual workings of our society and . . . with our portions of faith and hope. (LDB, 24)

Bickel, then, hopes to justify judicial review by identifying a role for judges that complements the authority exercised by elected institutions without impeding their ability to foster citizens' sense of common venture and the quality of character it represents.

The conventional view of the countermajoritarian difficulty departs from Bickel's view in at least two ways. First, Bickel assumes that judicial authority must be justified by its contribution to a legitimate system of government institutions. The conventional view, by contrast, looks at judicial authority in isolation from other institutions. It treats law and politics as autonomous realms, and assumes the judiciary, a legal institution, should not intrude in the political realm unless it satisfies the standard of democratic legitimacy that characterizes that realm.

John Hart Ely's *Democracy and Distrust* epitomizes the conventional view. He identifies conditions in which it is legitimate for judges to override the political decisions of elected institutions. He contends that judicial review undercuts two bases of democratic legitimacy. Elected institutions: (1) define norms that better reflect a popular will, and (2) allow citizens to control their government. Ely suggests that constitutional theorists must ground judicial review in principles that can overcome these concerns. Judges, according to this view, derive authority when they enforce principles that the community endorses or should endorse *and* that at the same time limit judicial discretion. Such principles subject judges to something like democratic control.

Ely considers judicial authority in isolation. While Bickel believes that judges derive authority by contributing to a system of government that is itself legitimate, Ely distinguishes the question of judicial legitimacy from the question of how elected institutions derive their legitimacy or the question of what makes a government legitimate.

Ely's argument also illustrates the second way that the conventional view of the countermajoritarian difficulty departs from Bickel's conception. Ely, in contrast to Bickel, suggests that judicial authority follows from the principles that judges enforce, and consequently that judges must decide cases correctly in order to sustain their authority.

Consider his critique of Bickel's justification of judicial review. He associates Bickel with various non-originalist—what he calls "non-interpretivist"[6]—theories of judicial review. These theories assign judges a lawmaking function, the power to enforce principles not found in the text of the Constitution.[7] Ely contends that these theories fail to solve the countermajoritarian difficulty, because they do not identify an acceptable source of principles, and the principles they identify would not limit judicial discretion (DD, 43–72). Moreover, Ely joins the quest to solve the countermajoritarian difficulty. He contends that judges should enforce certain core procedural principles that define American democracy, and that these principles will limit the discretion of judges. His argument, then, depends on judges deciding cases in a manner that advances such principles.[8]

Ely's critique of Bickel seems devastating. But it rests on a faulty premise: it misunderstands the conception of political legitimacy that underlies Bickel's argument. Bickel does not claim that legal principles must constrain judicial discretion or that judges derive authority by deciding cases in a manner that advances principles that reflect a popular will. Although he believes that judges complement elected institutions by enforcing principles that elected institutions tend to ignore, he does not concentrate on—or even identify—the principles that should inform particular judicial decisions. Nor does he claim that judges derive authority by deciding cases in accordance with applicable principles. Instead, Bickel illustrates how judges can help the political community identify principles without unduly impeding elected institutions that promote citizens' sense of common venture.[9]

II. Bickel and Contemporary Constitutional Theory

Contemporary constitutional theorists have rejected the conventional view of the countermajoritarian difficulty rather than the view Bickel defined. And in moving beyond the countermajoritarian difficulty, oddly enough, they move back toward Bickel's original view. Consequently, Bickel remains relevant to contemporary debates. Like Bickel, many constitutional theorists now recognize that judges will have discretionary authority and do not try to ground judicial review in principles that reflect a popular will. Instead, they assess judicial authority based on its contribution to a system of political institutions. Consider, for example, the recent deluge of arguments claiming that judicial authority makes the political process more deliberative, representative, just, or free, or advances some other important goal.[10] This section will examine two such arguments when it considers Waldron's recent criticism of Dworkin's defense of judicial review.

We must be careful, however, in identifying Bickel's significance for contemporary debates. Many theorists associate Bickel with the conventional view they reject and do not claim to be his followers. Therefore, it would be a mistake to say that they apply or extend his insights. Nonetheless, these theorists follow a path Bickel trod when they approach the problem of justifying judicial review, and they can learn from his missteps.

Bickel believes that judicial decisions could advance the ends of a legitimate government, even though judges would have discretion in enforcing principles. But Bickel's emphasis on how judges should decide cases distracts attention from his claim about the source of judicial authority. Indeed, this focus suggests that judges derive authority by correctly interpreting principles that are applicable to the cases they decide. Consequently, it invites the conventional view of the countermajoritarian difficulty.

The confusion begins with Bickel's claim that judges contribute to a legitimate government by enforcing principles that elected institutions would otherwise fail to consider adequately (LDB, 24, 27–28, 67–68, 200, 204). Bickel argues that a legitimate government must be principled and democratic, and consequently he gives the impression that judges operate in a realm outside of politics and that the principles they enforce originate in this realm. But this is a false impression. Bickel claims that these principles are the product of our history of democratic government, and they reflect a moral consensus that he considers the foundation for democratic constitutionalism (LDB, 30).

Bickel recognizes, however, that this consensus breaks down when the principles have to be interpreted and applied to resolve political conflicts. Similarly, he recognizes that the principles are too abstract to control judicial discretion (LDB, 47, 199). Consequently, Bickel does not link judicial review to the particular principles that judges enforce. Rather than claim that judges derive authority when they decide cases correctly, he emphasizes how judges should approach cases. Judges, according to Bickel, promote principled government when their decisions engage elected institutions in colloquies that encourage citizens to clarify and extend the moral consensus that makes self-government possible (LDB, 200–206). And *The Least Dangerous Branch* should be read as a treatise on the strategies judges can use to manage political conflict with elected institutions.

Nonetheless, Bickel focuses on particular cases and this exacerbates the confusion. *The Least Dangerous Branch* can also be read as a defense of the Court's decision in *Brown v. Board of Education,* and Bickel offers commentary on numerous other decisions as well.[11] More significantly, his rhetoric sometimes suggests that judges must decide cases correctly. For example, he describes how judges identify principles by "immers[ing] themselves in the tradition of our society . . . in history and the sediment of history which is law. . . . The Justices will then be fit to extract 'fundamental presuppositions' from their deepest selves, but in fact from the evolving morality of our tradition" (LDB, 236). This rhetoric implies that judges derive authority from the principles they enforce and thereby distracts attention away from Bickel's claim that judges gain authority by contributing to a legitimate system of government. It invites a misreading that would explain why so many theorists have associated Bickel with the conventional view of the countermajoritarian difficulty.

Today, many constitutional theorists continue to ground their theories in claims about how judges should decide cases. Because they are clearer than Bickel was in distinguishing the general claim that judges contribute to a system of political institutions from particular examples of how judges should decide cases, these theorists avoid the suggestion that principles control judicial decisions. But these theorists continue to focus on judicial decisions. They seek to justify or limit judicial review based on the decisions—or the consequences of the decisions—that they expect judges to make.[12] This narrow perspective makes it difficult to grasp arguments that assess judicial review based on considerations that look beyond the question of how judges should decide particular cases.

And constitutional theory has seen a recent trend towards arguments that defend judicial review in light of values that are independent of the substance of judicial decisions.[13] Steven Macedo, for example, links judicial review to the goal of public justification. He contends that judges respect citizens as reasonable beings by justifying the exercise of government authority in terms that litigants can grasp.[14] His conception of judicial review demands that judges justify their decisions in certain terms, but it does not depend on legal principles constraining judges or even the particular principles that judges enforce. Judges, according to this view, can decide cases for either party so long as their decisions are properly justified.[15]

Moreover, though Macedo's argument appears to be focused on adjudication, the value that drives his argument lies outside the adjudicative arena. It is also possible that an institutional structure without judicial review could better satisfy Macedo's conception of reasonability. Similarly, Waldron's criticism of Dworkin follows from his conclusion that an institutional structure without judicial review would better satisfy the values that should characterize the process by which we make decisions about justice. The critical response to this claim illustrates how people fail to grasp Waldron's argument because they are looking at judicial review from a perspective that emphasizes how judges should decide cases.

Both Waldron and Dworkin view judicial review in terms of the broader question of how a system of political institutions should make collective decisions. But they disagree about whether we should assess judicial review based on the decisions that we expect judges to make. While Dworkin contends that judicial review is justified if judges' decisions make it more likely that the political community will manifest integrity, Waldron concludes that judicial review offends the value of equality that should animate the political process that resolves disagreements about justice. According to Waldron, it would offend this value no matter how judges decide cases.

In *Freedom's Law*, Dworkin defends judicial authority based on how it contributes to a system of political institutions. He contends that judicial review can be justified as consistent with democracy, if it increases the likelihood that a political community would treat citizens with equal concern and respect.[16] It would do so by securing for citizens genuine membership in the political community.[17] This notion of genuine membership connects Dworkin's justification of judicial review to the conception of law he defends in *Law's Empire*.[18] In that work, he contends that law derives authority when it exhibits the virtue of integrity.[19] Integrity in law suggests that citizens enjoy the equal concern that characterizes membership in a "true" or genuine community. Dworkin considers equal concern, in turn, the hallmark of a political community in which citizens have an obligation to obey law (LE, 198–202, 211, 213–14).

Dworkin's view depends on the decisions that judges would make. Judicial review, according to this view, is justified if judges reach decisions that promote integrity. Judicial holdings should reflect the best interpretation of the political community's principles of justice, and judges should extend the norms these principles express to all applicable contexts (FL, 10–11, 83). It is not surprising, therefore, that Dworkin spends considerable time describing how judges should decide cases. In much of *Law's Empire*, he demonstrates how integrity should guide adjudication (LE, 167, 276–399). And he presents *Freedom's Law* as an exercise in interpreting principles of American constitutional law in light of this virtue (FL, 2, 10–11, 34–35, 37–38).

Waldron also assesses judicial authority in terms of how it might contribute to the broader political process. He contends that people must develop political institutions to respond to the "circumstances of integrity." In a pluralistic society, people not only hold competing conceptions of the good life, they also disagree about justice. Therefore, they must develop procedures that can address the conflicts that arise from these conditions and can do so in a manner that respects the fact of disagreement (LD, 191).

Waldron, of course, rejects Dworkin's defense of judicial review and argues against judges having such authority. Many constitutional theorists have had trouble grasping his criticism of Dworkin, however, because they tend to assume that the case for judicial review depends on the decisions we expect judges to make. But Waldron's criticism of Dworkin depends on his assumption that we justify institutional authority based on considerations that are independent of the substantive decisions those institutions might make.

Waldron's argument turns on a distinction between the process that we—a collective—should use to settle our disagreements about justice and the substantive norms that I—an individual—believe should guide the Court or other institution that resolves these disagreements. Constitutional theorists, according to Waldron, should concentrate on the political question of how to respond, procedurally, to disagreements about justice as opposed to the philosophical question of what is the best conception of justice. He favors political institutions that can resolve these conflicts without reference to the substantive norms that are the subject of their disagreements about justice (LD, 3–4, 7, 159–61).

Waldron challenges Dworkin's suggestion that judicial review might promote democracy—and the norm of equality that underlies it. He seeks to maintain the association between democracy and majority rule. He claims that there is a loss to democracy when citizens do not get to participate in a collective decision, even if the decision concerns the meaning of democracy. Dworkin, Waldron contends, elides the notions of a decision about democracy and a decision made by democratic means. Waldron believes that this elision prevents Dworkin from accounting for the cost to democratic values when a decision about democracy is made through nondemocratic means. While Dworkin wants to define democracy before determining the institutional process that best secures it, Waldron believes that people cannot resolve their disagreements about the meaning of democracy. He, thus, concludes that there is a loss to democracy when a nonelected and unaccountable institution makes decisions about what democracy requires (LD, 292–94).

It appears that Waldron rejects Dworkin's suggestion that judicial review is consistent with democracy. But that is not the point of his criticism. Waldron's point is that majority rule is the only procedure that resolves disagreements about justice in a manner that respects citizens' interest in participating in the decision, and this would include disagreements about the meaning of democracy itself.

It also appears that Waldron and Dworkin disagree about the best way to advance equality. While Dworkin believes that judicial review could promote equal concern and respect, Waldron believes it offends that very value by excluding people from the process through which the political community resolves its citizens' disagreements about justice. Dworkin's defense of judicial review, according to Waldron, does not account for this loss to equality.

But Waldron does not challenge Dworkin's conception of equality on substantive grounds. He cannot do so consistent with his assumption that the political community should not rely on a controversial substantive claims to resolve disagreements about justice. It is easy for constitutional theorists to miss this point. Many tend to follow Dworkin's approach. They argue about how to apply legal principles to specific controversies or identify the norms judges should seek to advance when interpreting these principles.[20] Waldron, by contrast, emphasizes the values that the political community advances through the process of collective decision making.

Theorists who share Dworkin's focus on adjudication have trouble distinguishing the norms that judges advance through their decisions from the values that Waldron seeks to advance through the process by which we make collective decisions. They contend that Waldron should balance the loss from judicial review—whether measured in terms of democracy or equality—against the gains from judicial decisions that promote these norms.[21] In so doing, they miss the critical point of Waldron's argument, that we must justify institutional authority based on considerations that are independent of the substantive decisions that we expect those institutions to make.

It is also likely that these theorists will associate Waldron's emphasis on the process of collective decision making with Ely's famous process-based defense of judicial review. We have already seen that Ely's argument epitomizes the conventional view of the countermajoritarian difficulty and its focus on adjudication. He contends that judges derive authority by enforcing the core procedural principles of American democracy. Some of Ely's critics made powerful arguments that the distinction between substance and process is a meaningless one. However, we must be clear about the significance of Waldron's distinction between process and substance. By clarifying the assumptions that underlie each argument, we discover why the criticisms that devastated Ely lose their force when applied to Waldron.

Ely's critics contended that the procedural principles Ely thought judges should enforce presupposed a substantive ideal of democracy.[22] According to this view, procedural principles are too ambiguous to control judicial authority; judges can anticipate the substantive outcomes that follow from competing interpretations of these principles. Therefore, (1) judges would have discretion to pursue favored outcomes, and (2) their holdings would be too controversial to support the claim that people accept them as constitutional law.

We can see that these critics share Ely's view of the countermajoritarian difficulty and argue that the procedural principles he identifies do not solve the problem. Waldon is not vulnerable to this type of criticism, because he does not invoke procedural principles to solve this problem. He views judicial authority from a different perspective than that of Ely and Ely's critics. Indeed, Ely's argument presupposes the type of substantive claim that Waldron believes we must avoid.[23] Waldron assumes that because people have fundamental disagreements about justice, neither judges nor legislators can define principles that will resolve social conflicts without creating controversy. He uses the value of equality to answer the procedural question of which institution is best suited to exercise such authority.

Waldron's claim should be easy to grasp, especially given that many constitutional theorists now share the assumption that drives his argument: our disagreements prevent us from resolving conflicts about justice without appealing to controversial principles. Nonetheless, constitutional theorists continue to focus on how judges decide cases, and this perspective makes it difficult to comprehend arguments that assess judicial authority based on considerations that are independent of judicial decisions.

We can see a cycle repeating itself. Bickel anticipates much work in constitutional theory when he accepts the fact that judges could not resolve political conflicts without creating controversy. Therefore, he does not ground judicial review in the principles that judges enforce. Instead, he contends that judges could contribute to the political process that defines such principles. But Bickel's perspective remained fixed on adjudication as he describes how judges should engage elected institutions and help sustain citizens' sense of common venture. This perspective prevented him from adequately clarifying his argument's central claim. Today many constitutional theorists continue to have trouble seeing beyond the context of adjudication. And the narrowness of this perspective prevents them from grasping interesting debates that have real significance for constitutional theory.

Notes

1. Alexander Bickel, *The Least Dangerous Branch*, 2nd ed. (New Haven, CT: Yale University Press, 1986), 20. Subsequent references to this work are cited in the text and notes with the following abbreviation: LBD.

2. See Frederic R. Kellog, "Legal Scholarship in the Temple of Doom: Pragmatism's Response to Critical Legal Studies," *Tulane Law Review* 65 (1990): 46; Felix Frankfurter, "John Marshall and the Judicial Function," collected in *James Bradley Thayer, Oliver Wendell Holmes, and Felix Frankfurter on John Marshall*, ed. Philip B. Kurland (Chicago: University of Chicago Press, 1967), 149.

3. Ronald Dworkin, *Freedom's Law* (Cambridge, MA: Harvard University Press, 1996), 338.

4. LDB, 21–22 (*James Bradley Thayer, Oliver Wendell Holmes, and Felix Frankfurter on John Marshall*, 85–86).

5. See Ibid., 23. Quoting Learned Hand, "The Contribution of an Independent Judiciary to Civilization," ed. I. Dillard, *The Spirit of Liberty* (New York: Knopf, 1952), 155–65.

6. I follow Paul Brest in using the term non-originalist in order to avoid the mistaken impression that non-interpretivists do not interpret the text of the Constitution and to achieve clarity given that the primary critics of non-originalist judicial review call themselves originalists. See Paul Brest, "The Misconceived Quest for the Original Understanding," *Boston University Law Review* 60 (1979): 204.

7. See John Hart Ely, *Democracy and Distrust* (Cambridge, MA: Harvard University Press, 1980), 1. Subsequent references to this work are cited in the text and notes with the following abbreviation: DD.

8. Indeed, a central criticism of Ely is that his approach does not in fact limit judicial discretion, because judges' concern for the outcome of cases will inevitably determine which procedural principles they enforce. See generally, Laurence Tribe, "The Puzzling Persistence of Process-Based Constitutional Theories," *Yale Law Journal* 89 (1980): 1063.

9. See generally, Kenneth Ward, "The Counter-Majoritarian Difficulty and Legal Realist Perspectives of Law: The Place of Law In Contemporary Constitutional Theory," *The Journal of Law & Politics* 18 (2002): 867–71.

10. Dworkin, *Freedom's Law*; Steven Macedo, *Liberal Virtues* (New York: Oxford University Press, 1990); Terri Peretti, *In Defense of a Political Court* (Princeton, NJ: Princeton University Press, 1999); Michael Perry, *We The People: The Fourteenth Amendment And The Supreme Court* (New York: Oxford University Press, 1999); Sotirios Barber, *On What the Constitution Means* (Baltimore, MD: John Hopkins University Press, 1984); Gerald F. Gaus, "Public Reason and the Rule of Law," in *The Rule of Law*, ed. Ian Shapiro (New York: New York University Press, 1994); Christopher L. Eisgruber, *Constitutional Self-Government* (Cambridge, MA: Harvard University Press, 2001); Richard Fallon, *Implementing The Constitution* (Cambridge, MA: Harvard University Press, 2001); Louis Michael Seidman, *Our Unsettled Constitution: A New Defense of Constitutionalism and Judicial Review* (New Haven, CT: Yale University Press, 2001); See also, Jeb Rubenfeld, *Freedom in Time: A Theory of Constitutional Self-Government* (New Haven, CT: Yale University Press, 2001). See, Bruce Ackerman, *We The People—Foundations* (Cambridge, MA: Harvard University Press, 1991; Cass Sunstein, *One Case At A Time* (Cambridge, MA: Harvard University Press 1999). See, Keith E. Whittington, *Constitutional Interpretation* (Lawrence, KS: University Press of Kansas, 1999). See Richard S. Kay, "American Constitutionalism," (defending originalism as advancing the value of constancy and thus promoting order); Michael J. Perry, "'What is the Constitution'? and Other Fundamental Questions," (defending originalism as necessary to advance the Constitution's aim of coordinating social interaction); Jed Rubenfeld, "Legitimacy and Interpretation," (linking originalist interpreta-

tion to the value of freedom.) all collected in *Constitutionalism*, ed. Larry Alexander (New York: Cambridge University Press, 1998).

11. Note well, however, that his defense of *Brown* emphasizes how the Court's decisions engaged the other institutions of government as opposed to how the Justices interpreted the Constitution.

12. Dworkin, *Freedom's Law*; Peretti, *In Defense of a Political Court*; Barber, *On What the Constitution Means*; Fallon, *Implementing The Constitution*; Seidman, *Our Unsettled Constitution*; Ackerman, *We The People—Foundations.*

13. Macedo, *Liberal Virtues*; Gaus, "Public Reason and the Rule of Law"; Kay, "American Constitutionalism"; Perry, "'What is the Constitution'? (and Other Fundamental Questions"; Jeremy Waldron, *Law and Disagreement* (New York: Oxford University Press, 1999). Subsequent references to *Law and Disagreement* are cited in the text and notes with the following abbreviation: LD.

14. See Macedo, *Liberal Virtues*, 159–62.

15. This claim assumes circumstances in which judges can offer a properly justified decision in favor of either litigant. Such circumstances, however, would seem to be present in most of the cases where the Supreme Court issues controversial decisions.

16. Dworkin takes the "defining aim of democracy to be . . . that collective decisions be made by political institutions whose, structure, composition, and practices treat all members of the community, as individuals, with equal concern and respect" (*Freedom's Law*, 17). Subsequent references to *Freedom's Law* are cited in the text and notes with the following abbreviation: FL.

17. Dworkin, FL, 31. Dworkin believes that the political community must satisfy three conditions to secure genuine membership: (1) each citizen must have an opportunity to influence collective decisions; (2) the interests of each citizen must be considered equally in assessing the consequences of any collective decision; and (3) the political community respects the moral independence of citizens—its authority to resolve moral disputes among citizens does not entail the authority to force citizens to embrace particular moral views" (FL, 25–26).

18. Indeed, he states that the discussion summarizes the conclusions from the earlier work.

19. Ronald Dworkin, *Law's Empire* (Cambridge, MA: Belknap Press, 1986), 191–92. Integrity ". . . requires government to speak with one voice, to act in a principled and coherent manner toward all its citizens, to extend to everyone the substantive standards of justice or fairness it uses for some. Dworkin considers integrity a virtue that is distinct from justice and fairness. Subsequent references to *Law's Empire* are cited in the text and notes with the following abbreviation: LE.

20. Ackerman, *We The People—Foundations*; Bruce Ackerman, *We The People—Transformations* (Cambridge, MA: Harvard University Press, 1998; Peretti, *In Defense of a Political Court* ; Sunstein, *One Case At A Time.*

21. Donald Downs, review of *Law and Disagreement*, by Jeremy Waldron, *American Political Science Review* 94 (2000): 183; William N. Eskeridge, Jr., "The Circumstances of Politics and the Application of Statutes, *Law and Disagreement*," *Columbia Law Review* 100 (2000): 578–79; and Richard Posner, review of *Law and Disagreement*, by Jeremy Waldron, *Columbia Law Review* 100 (2000): 590. Eskeridge recognizes Waldron's point that people disagree about democracy. But he seems to attribute the disagreement to the disenfranchisement of certain groups. His argument suggests that we can criticize this disenfranchisement by appealing to a procedural value as opposed to a substantive norm. Eskeridge views the problem from the doctrinal perspective that I claim characterizes American constitutional theory. His claim seems to be that judicial decisions will address the problem of disenfranchisement.

22. Tribe, "The Puzzling Persistence of Process-Based Constitutional Theories"; Rogers M. Smith, *Liberalism and American Constitutional Law* (Cambridge, MA: Harvard University Press, 1985), 173–74; Mark Tushnet, *Red, White, and Blue: A Critical Analysis of Constitutional Law* (Cambridge, MA: Harvard University Press, 1988); 94–107; Robert Bork, *The Tempting of America: The Political Seduction of the Law* (New York: Free Press, 1990), 197–98; Paul W. Kahn, *Legitimacy and History: Self-Government in American Constitutional Theory* (New Haven, CT: Yale University Press, 1992), 149–50; Stephen M. Griffin, *American Constiutionalism: From Theory to Politics* (Princeton, NJ: Princeton University Press, 1996), 160; and Peretti, *In Defense of a Political Court*.

23. Before proceeding, it is helpful to make an additional point concerning the distinction between procedural values and substantive norms. We have seen that Ely's appeal to procedural principles depends on the presupposition that people accept these values—they are not controversial—and that they control judicial discretion. This gives the impression that these principles, in contrast to substantive norms, are nonnormative and apolitical. Both Ely and Waldron believe that this is a false impression. They recognize that procedural values are normative and political, and distinguish procedural values based on the type of political problem they address. Waldron dissents, however, when Ely appeals to procedural values to ground judicial review. He attacks Ely's assumption that these values are not controversial.

Lastly, it should be noted that Ely anticipates his critics when he concedes that procedural values are normative in the sense that they reflect a political judgment and presumably in the sense that our choice of procedural values will influence the substantive decisions of the institutions that embody them. In other words, our choice of institutional structure will make certain substantive outcomes more likely and other outcomes less likely (Ely DD, 75n.).

Chapter 8

Constitutional Theory and the Faces of Power

Keith E. Whittington

Modern constitutional theory was born at the intersection of *Lochner* and *Brown*, and Alexander Bickel was present at the creation. Bickel was one of a number of scholars who struggled to make sense of the Warren Court's increasing activism on behalf of progressive causes in light of the earlier progressive critique of judicial activism in the first decades of the twentieth century. Bickel captured this inherited understanding of the Court and the power of judicial review in his vision of the "counter-majoritarian difficulty."[1] For veterans of President Franklin D. Roosevelt's struggle with the Court over the constitutionality of the New Deal, such as Justice Felix Frankfurter for whom Bickel clerked, the *Lochner* Court was clearly and fundamentally a countermajoritarian institution. In this view, the Court stood against democratic majorities, asserting the rights and interests of individuals and the politically defeated against the public welfare. For the New Dealers and a generation of progressives, elections and the will of popular majorities were the touchstones of political legitimacy. The renewal of judicial activism in cases such as *Brown* may have operated to the immediate benefit of progressive causes, but it was a troubling challenge to democratic values and the commitment to popular rule. The *Lochner* Court had reshaped common understandings of how a constitutional government works and introduced the belief in a basic tension between constitutionalism and democracy that framed the scholarly reception of *Brown*.

The image of a powerful court capable of vetoing the political actions of popularly elected legislative majorities stands near the center of our modern conception of constitutional government, though subsequent commentators have evaluated the substantive merits of particular exercises of judicial review differently. The countermajoritarian Court is the starting point for much of modern constitutional theory. Though countermajoritarianism is an important feature of constitutionalism and well worth studying, it should not monopolize the agenda of constitutional theory. The countermajoritarian framework is not always adequate for understanding even its paradigm case, the explicit use of the judicial veto to strike down legislation. Equally importantly, constitutions affect political behavior and outcomes through a variety of mechanisms that do not adhere to the countermajoritarian framework. Constitutional theory has tended to focus on the legal to the exclusion of the political, and as a consequence has ignored important aspects of how constitutionalism works in practice. The countermajoritarian framework is adequate neither for understanding how constitutional government works, nor for evaluating the exercise of judicial review. Rather than being the central organizing theme of constitutional theory, countermajoritarianism should be one of many. The countermajoritarian Court should be understood as only one dimension of constitutional power to direct political outcomes. There are significant empirical and normative issues to be explored along each of these dimensions.

This chapter considers the limitations in traditional constitutional theory and the possibilities of future research into the ways in which the Constitution structures political results other than through an explicit judicial veto. In the first section, I develop the characteristic "higher law" perspective on the Constitution and identify some limitations of that perspective. This higher law perspective is analogized to how postwar political science attempted to understand political power. The two perspectives share some similar tendencies and also some related problems. In the second section, I consider several aspects of the Constitution as a structure of constraint on politics, emphasizing the ways in which political structures affect how political preferences are aggregated and expressed and the resources and incentives that guide political action. In the third section, I note several ways in which the Constitution helps to nurture and maintain a particular form of politics consistent with constitutionalist ends. Bickel began his seminal work with an examination of John Marshall's defense of judicial review and explanation of the relationship between law and the Constitution.[2] For most of the twentieth century, we have focused on John Marshall's Constitution. This paper seeks to reemphasize what might be regarded as James Madison's Constitution, a constitution embedded in politics.

I. Judicial Review and the Countermajoritarian Constitution

Judicial review became a newly prominent feature of constitutional government during the *Lochner* era in the late nineteenth and early twentieth centuries. The power of the courts to strike down laws that were contrary to the requirements of the Constitution was well established by the middle decades of the nineteenth century. Moreover, this extraordinary and textually implicit power had largely been justified and accepted as a routine aspect of the judicial function under a written, legal constitution. Nonetheless, it was not until the later decades of the nineteenth century that the power of judicial review was regularly employed and used against the federal as well as the state governments. The Supreme Court moved from invalidating fewer than one state law per year prior to the Civil War to invalidating nearly four per year by the turn of the century and more than a dozen per year in the 1920s. Similarly, the Court began to regularly invalidate federal laws, at a pace of about four per decade in the latter half of the nineteenth century but increasing drastically during the battles of the 1920s and 1930s. In addition to aggressively constraining the powers of various government bodies, the Court also gave greater emphasis and legal content to constitutional guarantees of individual rights.

Unsurprisingly, constitutional theory responded to the rise of judicial review by placing it at the center of the scholarly enterprise. It was not until the early twentieth century that a specific term, judicial review, was popularized to refer to the practice of the courts invalidating laws on constitutional grounds.[3] Of course, the substantive issue of how judicial review should be exercised was much disputed. Even so, judicial review became an increasingly prominent feature of the American constitutional order. Not coincidentally, Edward Corwin recovered the "higher law" background of the Constitution during the same period.[4] In his 1938–1939 Messenger lectures, Charles McIlwain influentially defined constitutionalism as "a legal limitation on government" and noted that the "one institution above all others" that is essential to it is "an honest, able, learned, independent judiciary."[5] Others asserted that a constitution lacking this "fundamental law" quality is not a "true constitution," but merely a "nominal" or even a "façade" constitution.[6] Constitutionalism may be made to complement democracy, but they are always in tension.[7]

Especially within judicial discourse, the Constitution is centrally regarded as an external constraint on political action. The Constitution is a second-order constraint on first-order preferences, coming into play only after those preferences are formed and registered and significant only to the degree that its requirements contradict those preferences. As John Marshall noted in *Marbury*, if the legislature could control or "alter" constitutional meaning then the effort to bind legislative power with a written constitution would be "absurd" and the constitutional project would be "reduce[d] to nothing."[8] "[C]onstitutionality became an external, continuously operating legal restraint on legislative and majority will analogous to the restraint of ordinary law on individuals."[9] As a later Court deduced from that assumption, it is an "indispensable feature of our constitutional system" that the constitutional interpretations "enunciated by this Court" must be "the supreme law of the land."[10] The Court stands not only outside of politics, but also outside of government. The New Dealers acutely felt that separation, and in his brief introduction to his public papers, Franklin D. Roosevelt repeatedly and explicitly juxtaposed "the Court" and "the Government."[11]

Embedded in this understanding of the Constitution is a separation and antagonism between democracy and constitutionalism. Constitutionalism is understood to be a check on democratic power, represented institutionally as the legislature. Indeed, "majority tyranny" is usually regarded as the animating problematic of American constitutionalism.[12] Especially in the twentieth century, the substantive constraints on political majorities have often been rendered in terms of individual rights. Ronald Dworkin has prominently articulated this view, stating that "individual rights are political trumps held by individuals."[13] American constitutional theory "is not a simple majoritarian theory. The Constitution, and particularly the Bill of Rights, is designed to protect individual citizens and groups against certain decisions that a majority of citizens might want to make, even when that majority acts in what it takes to be the general or common interest."[14] Constitutionalism allows individuals to effectively veto, or trump, the actions of democratic majorities.

As much as anyone, Alexander Bickel launched constitutional theory into a debate over the countermajoritarian court and higher law constitutionalism. Still in the shadow of the New Deal, Bickel thought such countermajoritarianism posed a profound "difficulty."[15] Others who set their sights by the light of the Warren Court instead saw a countermajoritarian promise, a "promise that the deepest, most fundamental conflicts between individual and society will once, someplace, finally, become questions of justice."[16] In either case, it is Bickel's understanding of the nature of American constitutionalism that has set the terms of the scholarly debate. To Bickel, it seemed an obvious "reality" that the Court "exercises control, not in behalf of the prevailing majority, but against it. That, without mystic overtones, is what actually happens." Constitutionalism and judicial review are simply "undemocratic."[17] Although Bickel coined the phrase "counter-majoritarian difficulty," he did not have to work hard to convince twentieth-century constitutional scholars that countermajoritarianism was the correct depiction of constitutionalism and the Court.

Bickel was undoubtedly most influenced by the memory of the *Lochner* experience, but his focus on the judicial veto was consistent with the ascendant mode of political analysis. Political scientists of the same period, led by Bickel's Yale colleague Robert Dahl, were centrally concerned with the exercise of "power." Dahl himself tended to be skeptical of the significance of the Constitution in American politics and, with unfortunate timing at the dawn of the Warren Court, questioned the likelihood of genuinely countermajoritarian behavior by the Supreme Court.[18] More important for present purposes, however, is how Dahl understood power to be exercised. Speaking for a generation of behavioralist political scientists, Dahl provided a classic formulation of power: "*A* has power over *B* to the extent that he can get *B* to do something that *B* would not otherwise do."[19] Given that a central tenet of behavioralism was that social science should be concerned with observable external behavior, power could only be known in the context of "concrete decisions," direct interventions in which the powerful turned aside the expressed preferences of the powerless.[20] Judicial review is a perfect fit for such an analytical perspective. We know the Constitution through its manifestation in the judicial veto, when the powerful Court strikes down the expressed will of a legislative majority. The Constitution is "powerful" to the extent that the Court can and does turn aside such majority decisions and establishes a legal outcome distinct from what the legislature would have created.

Constitutional theory has been primarily absorbed with debating the pros and cons of this "first face" of constitutional power, the concrete decisions of the Court altering and restraining political outcomes. This is an important and valuable debate, for the Court is an important institution in American politics and judicial review raises interesting questions for democratic theory. The Constitution does sometimes serve as a higher law, and the Court does sometimes behave in a countermajoritarian fashion. These are notable dimensions of American constitutionalism and worthy of study.[21]

The nearly exclusive scholarly attention to this first face of constitutional power is problematic, however. For instance, the embrace of the countermajoritarian framework of constitutionalism discourages investigation into its descriptive assumptions. That the Constitution serves as a higher law and the Court as a countermajoritarian institution are treated as axioms rather than propositions. Both propositions are open to doubt. Dahl's own pioneering work raised questions about whether the Court is likely to oppose, or oppose successfully, clear political majorities. Although Dahl's own study is open to methodological and theoretical criticism,[22] other empirical research similarly casts doubt on the reality of a strongly countermajoritarian Court.[23] In practice, the Court may be more likely to go with the prevailing political winds than lean against them. The imagery of the New Deal confrontation with the *Lochner* Court may be misleading rather than enlightening in guiding us toward an understanding of the role of the judiciary in a constitutional system.

Similarly, the higher law model of constitutionalism is theoretically problematic. The legalistic constitutionalism framework assumes the existence of effective and unproblematic external sanctions on transgressors. As Sylvia Snowiss has noted, "unlike statutes, a constitution contemplates compliance, not violation" and judicial enforcement of society's law against private individuals is conceptually quite different than judicial enforcement of a constitutional rule against a sovereign power that no longer regards the posited rule as authoritative.[24] Equally problematic, reasonable people often disagree about the meaning of the relevant constitutional rule. Whether conceptualized as an interpretative problem of understanding contested constitutional requirements,[25] or a philosophical problem of determining which rights should trump,[26] the substantive content of higher law constitutionalism is unavoidably controversial. The central political problem of higher law constitutionalism is one of interpretation as much as it is one of enforcement.[27] The disagreements within a political community often do not disappear when the debate is shifted from the realm of policy to the realm of constitutionalism. Such difficulties raise the disturbing possibility that constitutionalism does not work, or at least does not work in the manner envisioned by most constitutional scholars. They suggest that much of the normative constitutional theory debate is built on flawed foundations.

This foundation is not only flawed, it is distracting. In their attempt to identify the higher law that binds judges, legislators, and executives, constitutional theorists ignore broader questions of how the Constitution affects the political environment in which those actors operate. The most fruitful questions may be when and how the Constitution can shape political outcomes, not whether it can operate as a constraining fundamental law. The legalistic understanding of constitutionalism has blinkered our perspective and narrowed our research agenda. Constitutional scholars have tended not to look past the first face of constitutional power to observe or take seriously the other ways in which constitutions might be politically effective. Just as the examination of political power in the Dahlian mode was soon supplemented by studies of other dimensions, or faces, of power,[28] so constitutional scholars should supplement discussion of the exercise of judicial review with an appreciation of other dimensions of constitutionalism. Notably, constitutions create political structures that encourage certain outcomes over others and political visions that can call individuals toward favored destinations.

II. A Structure of Agency and Constraint

The Constitution can be conceptualized in ways other than as a higher law. Most notably, it can be viewed as a political structure. In one sense, this is trivially true, and as a consequence it has often been dismissed by those most interested in constitutionalism. Every government, by necessity, has a structure that can be described and categorized. Every government has a constitution, even if not all governments adhere to constitutionalism. The higher law concept seems to more directly distinguish constitutional governments from the constitutions of governments.

The structural perspective should not be dismissed so quickly, however. For one thing, an accurate understanding of the operation of the structural constitution is often essential to debates over the higher law constitution and judicial review. Even the basic empirical questions of whether and how a written constitution can in fact serve as an effective fundamental law point us toward the need for political and structural analysis. The mechanics of an operating constitutional system, and not just the correct principles of the fundamental law, should be of great concern to constitutional scholars.

More basically, the structural perspective need not be at odds with the legalistic perspective. Constitutional structures are not just part of a general political background against which the distinctive qualities of a fundamental law operate. Constitutional structures place systematic substantive limits on political outcomes, and thus can complement the direct restraints embodied in the higher law. The idea of the structural constitution is often traced back to Aristotle and regarded as merely "descriptive."[29] As such, it is thought to neglect the particular substantive "function of a constitution," "establishing and maintaining effective restraints on political and governmental action."[30] But a concern with constitutional structure need not be so sharply separated from a concern for constitutional purpose, and as students of political institutions recognize structures are often purposive and substantive.

Political institutions generally operate to privilege some outcomes at the expense of others. As E. E. Schattschneider observed, "all forms of political organization have a bias in favor of the exploitation of some kinds of conflict and the suppression of others because organization is the mobilization of bias. . . . The function of institutions is to channelize conflict, but they do not treat all forms of conflict equally."[31] "Some issues are organized into politics while others are organized out."[32] By organizing some issues and results out of politics, the structural constitution *ex ante* limits the actions government takes rather than *ex post* vetoing the actions that the government has already taken. In structuring the political process, the constitution can oblige the government to restrain itself.

A constitution creates a discourse of political authority and a hierarchy of favored political goods. A primary feature of a constitution is the distribution of political resources by prescribing "the legitimate distribution, types, and methods of control among government officials."[33] A constitution helps specify who has political power, what that power consists of, and how it might be employed. Although the distribution of constitutional powers may be defined relatively formally and abstractly, it nonetheless has specific and recognizable consequences. As Dahl (too strongly) notes, "Constitutional rules are mainly significant because they help to determine what particular groups are to be given advantages or handicaps in the political struggle."[34]

The power of constitutional review of legislation by judges can be seen as a special case of this more general phenomenon. A certain class of government officials (judges) may be empowered to lay aside legislation as inconsistent with prior, more fundamental legal commitments. Such officials may be selected by a variety of mechanisms from various pools of qualified candidates, and the particular selection mechanism and requirements are likely to affect the substantive decisions of such an institution.[35] Judges do not possess a general discretionary veto power, but rather possess a veto that has a limited set of triggers and thus encourages a specific kind of institutional discourse concerned with identifying when the veto should be exercised and justifying those decisions to various external constituencies.[36] Some constitutional systems restrict access to the constitutional courts to various government officials and often limit the power of constitutional review to a single specialized body, with potential consequences for political results.[37] By contrast, American-style judicial review empowers private individuals to initiate that decision-making process through normal litigation before any judge. Such constitutional choices are likely to have concrete implications for what social groups and political interests may be benefited by the courts. Even given relatively open access to the courts, however, individuals and groups have different capacities to effectively exploit that political resource—whether because they lack the organization and skill to mobilize the law, or because they lack the adequate footholds in the existing texture of the law.[38] Even higher law constitutionalism must ultimately be embedded within a particular institutional context in order to be politically effectuated, and the structural constitution is not irrelevant to the actual operation of the legalized constitution.

The provision for and form of constitutional review is just one example of how constitutional structures affect political outcomes. The U.S. Constitution creates a variety of institutions, empowering them with different resources and concerns, and making them responsive to different influences and constituencies. Although the particular distribution of political resources that go into the institution of judicial review—the judicial veto, individual rights to constitutional litigation, the fundamental law authority of constitutional claims—are important, they are not the only political resources that may be effectively used to shape and constrain political outcomes. Indeed, simply viewed in terms of the capacity to shape government activities, the resources available to the courts may be less formidable than those available to other political institutions.[39] The courts may only appear particularly important because of the location of their actions near the end of the sequence of political decisions and because of their peculiarly explicit constitutional discourse. The ultimate sustainability of a constitutional polity may depend more heavily on how nonjudicial political resources are more routinely employed and how their employment influences political outcomes.

The political institutions that perform constitutional functions importantly structure political outcomes. Politics involves collective action. As the economic new institutionalism has emphasized, the outcome of collective action is crucially shaped by the manner in which individual preferences are aggregated and the strategies that individuals are induced to follow in order to advance their goals.[40] Political structures generally, therefore, provide the strategic context within which individuals operate by "laying down the rules according to which (1) players are identified, (2) prospective outcomes are determined, (3) alternative modes of deliberations are permitted, and (4) the specific manner in which revealed preferences, over *allowable* alternatives, by *eligible* participants, occurs."[41] According to *Marbury* at least, the Constitution made the Court a player eligible to restrict the range of allowable policy alternatives under specific conditions. But this is obviously only a small part of the overall policy-making game that the Constitution has helped structure.

Over the course of American history, for example, the design of the U.S. Senate has had important consequences for policy outcomes.[42] A notable feature of this "strategic context" perspective is that the significance of constitutional institutions may vary over time. The structure of politics constrains the actions of government in understandable and predictable ways, but not necessarily in ways that were originally intended. For those who drafted the Constitution, the design of the Senate was to provide an added measure of wisdom and deliberation to the Congress and an added measure of security and influence for the small states in the new, "more perfect union." The particular electoral rules governing the composition of the Senate had expected consequences for the legislative outputs that would emerge from the new Congress, and they were designed with an eye toward directing that output toward the substantively desirable (and reducing the probability of substantively undesirable legislation).[43] Those resources were soon exploited, however, to restrain government in other unexpected ways. For example, the Senate became the crucial bulwark for the South's defense of slavery.[44] For a time, the constitutional structure of the Senate made the territorially expansive but relatively underpopulated South politically powerful and constrained the set of possible federal policies.[45] When the South was temporarily excluded from Congress during the

Civil War and Reconstruction, northern Republicans acted to exploit the structure of the Senate to consolidate their new policy-making power and tilt the protections of the political constitution the other way. Between 1861 and 1876, five new, safely Republican but sparsely populated states were carved out of the western territories and admitted to the union.[46] The stacked postbellum Senate gave the Republicans an important veto on federal policy even after the Democratic South rejoined the Congress and the Republicans lost control over the House of Representatives and the popular presidential vote.[47] This political arrangement insured that "as long as the Republicans sought to protect them, the policies begun in the 1860s would remain throughout the remainder of the century."[48]

By shaping the policy-making process, constitutional structures can encourage public policy to take forms more consistent with constitutional goals. For example, the American political system provides a multitude of access and veto points. One consequence of distributing political power widely in a constitutional system is that it becomes relatively difficult to pursue broadly tyrannical or narrowly majoritarian policies. The U.S. Constitution adopts rules that favor compromise and consensus. "Gridlock occurs, and occurs often," because the constitutional procedures for creating national policy make it difficult to alter a reasonably moderate status quo.[49] "[W]hen gridlock is broken, it is broken by large, bipartisan coalitions—not by minimal-majority or homogeneous majority-party coalitions."[50] The eventually successful coalitions behind important pieces of legislation are broad, averaging 82 percent of the Congress on all important postwar legislation and even averaging 78 percent of the Congress on such legislation passed during unified governments in which one party holds both Congress and the presidency.[51]

Although the constitutional structure of the legislative process works to prevent the adoption of narrowly majoritarian policies that negatively affect sizable minorities, it does so in a routine and largely unnoticed fashion. Whereas traditional constitutional theory (as did political science analysis oriented around the first face of power) has focused on explicit events in which the expressed majority will is displaced by a judicial veto, it has largely failed to grasp the broader political consequences of constitutional structure. Recognizing a second face of power calls our attention to "non-events" in which power is quietly exercised so as to keep the majority will from even being expressed in the form of legislation. Power is also exercised, and majority will is systematically restrained, by "confining the scope of decision making to relatively 'safe' issues."[52] Analytically, such "mobilization of bias" can be hard to observe. One virtue of institutional analysis is that it can call attention to such built-in biases. Effective political power, and constitutional restraint, resides in structure and not just in action. Distributing political resources to various actors necessitates that their interests be taken into account in policy-making. As a consequence, "power can work through anticipation, so a power relationship may exist even absent visible compulsion."[53] As one study of the presidential veto power notes, "the concept of the second face of power clearly suggests that *the veto* (a capability) can shape the content of legislation even if *vetoes* (uses of the capability) are rare."[54] The potential of a presidential veto or Senate filibuster requires legislatures to act to prevent them from becoming actualities, by, for example, only pursuing policies that can secure widespread support.

The constitutional structure of politics both enables government to take certain actions and channels political activity toward preferred outcomes, restraining government through the mobilization of the biases built into the system.[55] The "statistical democracy" that constitutional theorists often fear does not exist as an effective political force absent a particular institutional context that constitutes it.[56] Constitutions may either build up democratic politics on a narrowly majoritarian basis or force the development of broad-based, compromising coalitions. It may privilege certain actors and interests, or many actors and interests, through the distribution of various political resources, and not just through the formalization of fundamental law. In focusing on the drama of the occasional conflicts between the judiciary and the legislature, constitutional theory has neglected the routine operation of the constitutional system and the arguably more significant and effective restraints that it imposes on government.

III. Constituting Politics and Identity

The substantive commitments of the Constitution influence politics directly and not simply through the mediation of judicial review. There are many things that the government does not do. There are many things that it is almost unimaginable that the government would do. Some of those possibilities are off the political table because of the presence of the higher law Constitution and the promise of judicial review. But if the unimaginable were to become imaginable, the judiciary would be a thin reed upon which to rely. As James Bradley Thayer concluded, "under no system can the power of courts save a people from ruin; our chief protection lies elsewhere."[57] The most important restraints on government are not realized when the Court occasionally strikes down actions that already have political support and that the government has initiated, but when possible actions are kept off the political agenda altogether and prevented from gaining significant political support.

The immediate political effects of a constitution are important not only for determining which specific norms, rules, or rights might be recognized and enforced and thereby the particular ways in which the range of political action is constrained. They are also important for bolstering the political commitment to constitutionalism itself. The power of judicial review is at least as parasitic on a general acceptance of constitutionalism as it is a mechanism for constitutional maintenance.[58] When the Court speaks in the name of the Constitution, we generally take that seriously as a source of political authority. Even if we disagree about the specifics of our constitutional commitments, we at least share a commitment to our "thin Constitution" that elevates the ideal of a limited, consensual government.[59] Rights are trumps only to the extent that most of the political community is willing to play that game, and in many communities they are not.

The textual Constitution may be important in this context to the extent that it educates.[60] The Constitution may matter to political outcomes not only in how it structures the expression of political preferences and offers incentives to induce certain preferred behavior, but also in how it helps shape political preferences themselves. In this educative function, the Constitution would motivate political actors to do right as well as restrain them from doing wrong. We in fact expect the Constitution to perform in this fashion in the courts. The Constitution offers relatively few means by which judges may be restrained from doing wrong, but we at least hope that it motivates judges to take positive action. In conducting their offices, we expect judges to learn from the Constitution and to take action based on their learning. This has at least been plausibly the case in the context of the judiciary, and it might well be the case in other contexts. Rather than thinking of the judiciary as a world apart in terms of being affected by constitutional commitments, we might examine the ways in which other political officials and the public respond in analogous ways to the Constitution.

Put another way, the Constitution might show a "third face of power," in which it shapes "conceptions of the necessities, possibilities, or strategies of conflict."[61] The Constitution may encourage us to think about politics in some ways rather than others, to imagine some political outcomes as achievable and laudable and others as unrealistic or undesirable. In order to be effective, the Constitution must set the terms of political debate. An effective constitution cannot be readily abandoned, even when it becomes inconvenient. Political actors must find it easier to adhere to the terms of the Constitution than to violate them; the Constitution may not only restrain democratic majorities by blocking or redirecting their demands, but it also may do so "by changing their demands and expectations."[62] There is no guarantee that a constitution will have such an effect, but the "Constitution is binding to the extent that it continues to make a political people by providing the grammar by which they speak authoritatively about their public values."[63]

Constitutional theory needs to explore why and how a constitution might help "make a political people." One way in which the Constitution might do this is by altering the expectations of political actors so as to bias them toward accepting and reinforcing the constitutional status quo. Once a constitution has been established, it may become what game theorists call a "focal point," which provides "some coordination of the participants' expectations" in a bargaining situation. In a situation in which some collective agreement must be reached such as policy-making, but in which there are a range of possible outcomes available, focal points bring the expectations of the relevant parties "into convergence and bring the negotiation to a close." It "is the intrinsic magnetism of particular outcomes, especially those that enjoy prominence, uniqueness, simplicity, precedent, or some rationale that makes them qualitatively differentiable from the continuum of possible alternatives."[64] In a sense, the substantive content of the focal point is arbitrary. It is not the intrinsic worth of the focal point that makes it magnetic, but its cultural prominence. Once identified, individual expectations gravitate to the focal point, biasing collective action in that direction. The "ultimate focus of agreement did not just reflect the balance of bargaining power but *provided* bargaining power to one side or the other."[65] The influence of a "dramatic and conspicuous precedent," a mediator's proposal, or the results of "some previous but logically irrelevant negotiation" can drive collective action toward some predetermined outcome, even to the significant disadvantage of some seemingly powerful parties.[66]

The Constitution as coordinating device can make existing constitutional arrangements self-enforcing, even in the face of significant disagreement on the substantively appropriate constitutional commitment. It is not simply that an arbitrary "something" is better than "nothing"—as when, for example, it is better to have some rule governing on which side of the road to drive than to have no rule.[67] It is also the case that once we have "something" it is hard to convert to "something else," even if the something else is, at least for some, ab initio substantively preferable. The expectation that others will continue to adhere to constitutional terms discourages anyone from abandoning or subverting them, increasing constitutional stability. The coordinating effect is distinct from the usual difficulties of organizing support for a positive alternative to some default solution, such as the status quo. Indeed, the coordinating effect can help independently define the status quo as the default. It can be difficult to amend the Constitution not only because the existing constitutional text is protected by a supermajoritarian amendment procedure, but also because the existing constitutional text may come to seem "natural" and "obvious" in a way that no alternative does.[68] Interests and expectations become defined in terms of the culturally conventional baseline, which then becomes relatively difficult to alter. New constitutional rules must overcome the costs of social reorganization, as well as be substantively justifiable on their own terms.

An additional way in which a constitution might help constitute a particular political people is by contributing to the ideological formation of those who live under it. In doing so, a constitution would not only restructure preferences by altering social expectations, but also would reshape preferences directly by redefining what is regarded as substantively good. The constitution could be only one source of ideological formation among many, but at best a constitution may operate to promote others to adopt its own values. If fully successful, democratic outcomes would be consistent with constitutionalism, obviating the necessity of external legal checks on democratic power.

At a micro level, individuals who occupy particular constitutional institutions may be socialized to behave in particular ways and to adopt the distinctive routines and perspectives of the institution. As well as constraining choices, institutions constitute preferences, such that "the goals actors pursue are shaped by the institutional context."[69] Institutions "influence the self-conception of those who occupy roles defined by them in ways that give those persons distinctively 'institutional' perspectives." In influencing the "senses of purpose and principle" that individual political actors hold, institutions reorient political behavior and can even impose a sense of "duty" and identify "inherently meaningful action."[70]

A constitution creates and is composed of sets of such institutions that orient individual officeholders toward pursuing distinctively constitutional ends. The institutional environment created by the Constitution is diverse, however. The particular institutional missions nurtured by the legislature and the judiciary, for example, are quite divergent. Although all of these institutional goals may be constitutionally important, they may not all be equally directed at preserving constitutionalism. The normative goals, operational routines, and discursive environment of the judiciary, defined in large part by the ideal of the higher-law constitution, may make the courts particularly attentive to recognizing and enforcing the restraints on government and the rights of individuals.[71] On the other hand, the other branches of government may have constitutional virtues of their own. Even though some of those virtues (such as presidential concern with administrative efficiency or executive strength) may not be closely associated with or even in partial conflict with the ideal of constitutional restraints on political power, others (such as legislative concern with representation and deliberation) may well be more consistent with constitutionalism and yet may be underappreciated by a focus on the particular legalistic virtues of the courts.[72] The implicit operation of these institutions may also work to advance constitutional ends and restrict the range of political outcomes, for example, by fostering a national perspective that detaches federal officials from more parochial interests and desires, or by encouraging a greater appreciation for the virtue of tolerance.[73]

In framing the discursive field of political battle, the Constitution tilts the surface in ways that benefit some interests and actors and hampers others. Presidential scholar Stephen Skowronek illustrates the dual nature of the normative institutional order in arguing, "different institutions may give more or less play to individual interests, but the distinctive criteria of institutional action are official duty and legitimate authority. Called upon to account for their actions or to explain their decisions, incumbents have no recourse but to repair to their job descriptions."[74] The normative order can both explain and legitimate political actions. Individuals take action because it is their duty, the proper way of behaving for someone in their situation. Regardless of the motives for their actions, however, they can also appeal to others to recognize that they are behaving in the conventionally proper way. Established normative commitments can justify behavior to others who would otherwise have no interest in supporting it.[75]

At the macro level, the people at large must also be constituted as constitutional citizens. To some degree, this may also be accomplished through political institutions that incorporate or involve the broad citizenry. Relatively open immigration, religious disestablishment, and common schools all help establish the social framework within which political attitudes are formed and "liberal virtues" are cultivated.[76] The political universe is composed of broad normative and symbolic orders, however, as well as formal institutions. The Constitution clearly contributes to, even if it does not dominate, the normative environment of American politics.[77] By tapping into, mobilizing, and transforming the ideological commitments dominant in a nation's politics, a constitutional system can help stabilize itself and advance its own goals.

Constitutionalism is probably viable only to the extent that it can reinforce and expand preexisting ideological commitments. "We the people" is simultaneously interpretive and constitutive.[78] But necessarily the "Constitution, each constitution and reconstitution, makes citizens in its own image. . . . The citizens' conceptions of their identities, individual as well as collective, are irretrievably altered by the process of constituting themselves as a nation."[79] James Madison, who was skeptical of the value of the "parchment barriers" of a bill of rights, thought that ideological formation was one significant use of such statements in a popular government. He wrote to Thomas Jefferson: "The political truths declared in that solemn manner acquire by degrees the character of fundamental maxims of free Government, and as they become incorporated with the national sentiment, counteract the impulses of interest and passion."[80] In rejecting the usefulness of judicial review, Pennsylvania's Judge Gibson appealed to the "inestimable value" of a written constitution "in rendering its principles familiar to the mass of the people" and thereby building up the "inconceivably great" power of "public opinion" to restrain the government.[81] The greater the extent to which the Constitution's ideological commitments become the culturally accepted "maps of problematic social reality and matrices for the creation of collective conscience," the more effectively the Constitution can structure and restrain daily politics.[82] The Federalists were consciously active in creating just such an American political culture, one that would live "in the temper, the habits, and the practices of the people."[83]

Constitutions may be able to alter political outcomes by providing additional publicly recognizable means of legitimation than might not otherwise be available to particular actors and interests. Madison and Jefferson explicitly hoped to do this, looking to the written constitution to provide valuable symbols that could be exploited in political conflicts. Madison hoped that "a bill of rights will be a good ground for an appeal to the sense of the community," if the government were to usurp the boundaries of its powers. This was the same value that such written commitments might have in a monarchical government, "as a standard for trying the validity of public acts, and a signal for rousing & uniting the superior force of the community."[84] Jefferson similarly thought that for the jealous state governments a "declaration of rights will be the text whereby they will try all the acts of the federal government" in the court of public opinion, and that the federal government might do the same if the states exceeded their proper bounds. Jefferson warned that those who resist government actions "must have principles furnished them whereon to found their opposition."[85] In contemporary politics, various social and political interests have appealed to the text and "wrapped themselves in the Constitution" to gain advantage in the public sphere.[86]

IV. Beyond Bickel

The countermajoritarian difficulty has provided the organizing rubric for constitutional theory for much of the past half century. That framework has not always been a comfortable one. Some have questioned whether and why the judiciary's countermajoritarianism should be regarded as a difficulty at all. Others have raised doubts about the meaning of countermajoritarianism and whether the Court should even be described in that way. Despite recent efforts to shift the focus elsewhere, the Court remains at the center of academic constitutional theory and the Constitution is still largely conceptualized as our higher-law.[87]

Judge Richard Posner has defined academic constitutional theory as "the effort to develop a generally accepted theory to guide the interpretation of the Constitution of the United States."[88] This effort assumes the importance of higher-law constitutionalism and is often forced by its ambitions to overcome or mitigate the countermajoritarian difficulty. As would-be advice to the Court, academic theory has adopted the Court's perspective of the constitutional world and focused on the judiciary's particular problems. Such problems are real and worthy of consideration, but constitutional theory needs to move beyond them. It needs to supplement the Court's Constitution with the political constitution of institutions and ideals. Like the behavioral political science that emerged in the postwar period, constitutional theory has been largely concerned with only the most explicit displays of constitutional power to counter government action. It has neglected the more routine mechanisms by which government power might be effectively restrained and constitutional ends secured.

The Court is not the only constitutional actor. To the extent that constitutional theory is to be a largely prescriptive enterprise designed to provide generally accepted theory to guide government officials as they make constitutional decisions, then an exclusive concern with the judiciary is problematic. The wave of constitution making in the aftermath of the collapse of the Communist regimes in Eastern Europe has brought new attention to the problem of constitutional design. In the United States, constitutional design has understandably been of secondary concern. Far greater attention has been paid to the domestically more salient problem of interpreting an enduring constitution than the seemingly distant problem of creating a new one. The fall of the Berlin Wall, however, served as a reminder that constitutional design is very much a contemporary problem for much of the world. More recently, domestic events such as the impeachment of President Bill Clinton and the adoption of antiterrorism measures have also emphasized that nonjudicial political actors may have distinctive constitutional concerns even within the context of an established constitutional system. American constitutional theory has provided little systematic foundation for offering advice to those active in creating new constitutional systems or confronting problems outside the judicial context.

To the extent that constitutional theory is concerned with understanding and not just prescribing, an excessive concern with the legalized Constitution is hampering. Efforts to understand the Constitution as it exists and operates outside the courts will not progress very far unless they shed the analytical perspectives adopted for understanding the Constitution inside the courts. The true significance of the Constitution outside the courts may not lie in those moments and activities when nonjudicial actors behave most like judges or are most closely engaged with constitutional law. Understanding the Constitution outside the courts may be best advanced by focusing less on "the Constitution" of traditional constitutional theory than on constitutionalism. The most interesting questions in this area may relate to how the scope of government action is effectively delimited rather than on how well elected officials understand constitutional law. Such explorations will raise their own normative and prescriptive questions, focusing on such matters as the need for constitutional reform and on the appropriateness of various alternative mechanisms for limiting government.

Finally, looking beyond the first face of constitutionalism may be necessary to adequately contextualize judicial review itself. Some have begun to question the ultimate value of judicial review and have posited that judicial review is of little consequence.[89] More commonly, a variety of constitutional theories offer essentially functional defenses of judicial review that depend on assumptions about the operation of the constitutional system as a whole and of other political branches. These theories not only provide answers to the countermajoritarian difficulty and justify the power of judicial review, but they also advance particular understandings of how active the Court should be in exercising that power, what sorts of constitutional claims the Court should be most aggressive in advancing, and in what directions constitutional law ought to be developed. In other words, even a constitutional theory primarily concerned about judicial review and the higher-law constitution depends on a broader sense of constitutionalism and how it operates. Yet that critical background has been little explored.

The Supreme Court has been a prominent part of twentieth-century American constitutional history. Contemporary constitutional theory was born through the effort to come to grips with that development and continues to reflect those origins. Judicial review and constitutional law represent only one facet of the constitutional experience, however. Supplementing our understanding of the judiciary's Constitution will require a willingness not only to look beyond the courts but also to explore other, distinctive faces of constitutionalism.

Notes

1. Alexander M. Bickel, *The Least Dangerous Branch* (Indianapolis, IN: Bobbs-Merrill, 1962), 16.

2. Ibid., 1.

3. Matthew Franck has identified a few scattered earlier uses of the term in the constitutional context, but Princeton's constitutional historian Edward Corwin seems to have popularized it. Edward S. Corwin, "The Establishment of Judicial Review Supreme Court and the Fourteenth Amendment," *Michigan Law Review* 9 (1910): 102.7, (1909): 643. Competing terms to describe the phenomenon were being suggested at the same time, including "judicial supremacy," "judicial veto," and "judicial nullification." See Charles Grove Haines, *The American Doctrine of Judicial Supremacy* (New York: Macmillan,

1914), 16 n2. Corwin himself had previously tried out "judicial paramountcy." Edward S. Corwin, "The Supreme Court and Unconstitutional Acts of Congress," *Michigan Law Review* 4 (1906): 616.

4. Edward S. Corwin, "The 'Higher Law' Background of American Constitutional Law," *Harvard Law Review* 42 (1928–1929): 149, 365.

5. Charles Howard McIlwain, *Constitutionalism: Ancient and Modern* (Ithaca: Cornell University Press, 1947), 21, 140. McIlwain fudged the central issue of the fight over the *Lochner* Court, preferring to sustain the "balancing of jurisdictio and gubernaculum" and concluding that the "two fundamental correlative elements of constitutionalism for which all lovers of liberty must yet fight are the legal limits to arbitrary power and a complete political responsibility of government to the governed." Ibid., 146.

6. Giovanni Sartori, "Constitutionalism: A Preliminary Discussion," *American Political Science Review* 56 (1962): 855, 861.

7. Walter F. Murphy, "Constitutions, Constitutionalism, and Democracy," in *Constitutionalism and Democracy*, eds. Douglas Greenberg, et al. (New York: Oxford University Press, 1993), 3–7.

8. *Marbury v. Madison*, 5 U.S. 137, 177, 178 (1803).

9. Sylvia Snowiss, *Judicial Review and the Law of the Constitution* (New Haven, CT: Yale University Press, 1990), 119.

10. *Cooper v. Aaron*, 358 U.S. 1, 18 (1958). See also, *Baker v. Carr*, 369, U.S. 186, 211 (1962); *Powell v. McCormack*, 395 U.S. 486, 521 (1969); *U.S. v. Nixon*, 418 U.S. 683, 704 (1974); *City of Boerne v. Flores*, 521 U.S. 507, 529 (1997); *United States v. Morrison*, 529 U.S. 598, 617n7 (2000).

11. Gary D. Glenn, "The Venerable Argument against Judicial Usurpation," in *The End of Democracy II*, ed. Mitchell S. Muncy (Dallas, TX: Spence Publishing, 1999), 121.

12. See also, Jennifer Nedelsky, *Private Property and the Limits of American Constitutionalism* (Chicago: University of Chicago Press, 1990), 183–189.

13. Ronald Dworkin, *Taking Rights Seriously* (Cambridge, MA: Harvard University Press, 1978), xi. Robert Nozick offered a less telling but similar metaphor of rights as "side constraints." See Robert Nozick, *Anarchy, State, and Utopia* (New York: Basic Books, 1974), 29.

14. Dworkin, *Taking Rights Seriously*, 132–133. See also, Ibid., 194. ("A right against the Government must be a right to do something even when the majority thinks it would be wrong to do it, and even when the majority would be worse off for having it done.")

15. Bickel, *The Least Dangerous Branch*, 16.

16. Ronald Dworkin, *A Matter of Principle* (Cambridge, MA: Harvard University Press, 1985), 71.

17. Bickel, *The Least Dangerous Branch*, 17. See also, Ibid., 27. ("Democratic government under law—the slogan pulls in two opposed directions.")

18. Robert A. Dahl, *A Preface to Democratic Theory* (Chicago: University of Chicago Press, 1956), 135. ("If constitutional factors are not entirely irrelevant, their significance is trivial as compared with the non-constitutional."); Robert A. Dahl, "Decision-Making in a Democracy: The Supreme Court as a National Policy-Maker," *Journal of Public Law* 6 (1957): 284.

19. Robert A. Dahl, "The Concept of Power," *Behavioral Science* 2 (1957): 201–202.

20. Robert A. Dahl, "A Critique of the Ruling Elite Model," *American Political Science Review* 58 (1958): 464.

21. I have contributed to this literature myself. See Keith E. Whittington, *Constitutional Interpretation* (Lawrence, KS: University Press of Kansas, 1999).

22. See, e.g., Richard Funston, "The Supreme Court and Critical Elections," *American Political Science Review* 69 (1975): 795; Jonathan D. Casper, "The Supreme Court and National Policy Making," *American Political Science Review* 70 (1976): 50; Bradley C. Canon and S. Sidney Ulmer, "The Supreme Court and Critical Elections: A Dissent," *American Political Science Review* 70 (1976): 1215; David Adamany, "Legitimacy, Realigning Elections and the Supreme Court," *Wisconsin Law Review* 1973 (1973): 790; John B. Gates, *The Supreme Court and Partisan Realignment* (Boulder, CO: Westview Press, 1992).

23. Gerald N. Rosenberg, "Judicial Independence and the Reality of Political Power," *Review of Politics* 54 (1992): 369; Barry Friedman, "Dialogue and Judicial Review," *Michigan Law Review* 57 (1993): 91; William Mishler and Reginald Sheehan, "The Supreme Court as Countermajoritarian Institution? The Impact of Public Opinion on the Court," *American Political Science Review* 87 (1993): 87; Mark A. Graber, "The Passive-Aggressive Virtues: *Cohens v. Virginia* and the Problematic Establishment of Judicial Power," *Constitutional Commentary* 12 (1995): 67; Michael Klarman, "Rethinking the Civil Rights and Civil Liberties Revolution," *Virginia Law Review* 82 (1996): 1; Lucas A. Powe, Jr., *The Warren Court and American Politics* (Cambridge, MA: Harvard University Press, 2000).

24. Snowiss, *Judicial Review and the Law of the Constitution*, 199. See also, Stephen M. Griffin, *American Constitutionalism* (Princeton, NJ: Princeton University Press, 1996), 13–15.

25. See, e.g., James B. Thayer, "The Origin and Scope of the American Doctrine of Constitutional Law," *Harvard Law Review* 7 (1893): 139–149.

26. See esp., Jeremy Waldron, *Law and Disagreement* (New York: Oxford University Press, 1999).

27. Bickel was referring to this problem in noting that John Marshall in *Marbury* not only begs the question but also "begs the wrong question." As Marshall surely knew, "a statute's repugnancy to the Constitution is in most instances not self-evident." Bickel, *The Least Dangerous Branch*, 2, 3.

28. See, e.g., Peter Bachrach and Morton S. Baratz, "Two Faces of Power," *American Political Science Review* 56 (1962): 942; Bachrach and Baratz, "Decisions

and Nondecisions: An Analytical Framework," *American Political Science Review* 57 (1963): 632; Steven Lukes, *Power: A Radical View* (London: Macmillan, 1974); Jack Nagel, *The Descriptive Analysis of Power* (New Haven, CT: Yale University Press, 1975); John Gaventa, *Power and Powerlessness: Quiescence and Rebellion in an Appalachian Valley* (Urbana, IL: University of Illinois Press, 1980); Jeffrey C. Isaac, "Beyond the Three Faces of Power: A Realist Critique," *Polity* 20 (1987): 4; Douglas W. Rae, "Knowing Power: A Working Paper," in *Power, Inequality, and Democratic Politics,* eds. Ian Shapiro and Grant Reeher (Boulder, CO: Westview Press, 1988); Clarissa Rile Hayward, "De-Facing Power," *Polity* 31 (1998): 1.

29. E.g., Carl J. Friedrich, *Constitutional Government and Democracy* (Boston, MA: Little, Brown, 1941), 120.

30. Ibid., 112, 119.

31. E. E. Schattschneider, "Intensity, Visibility, Direction and Scope," *American Political Science Review* 51 (1957): 933, 935–936.

32. E. E. Schattschneider, *The Semi-Sovereign People* (Hinsdale, IL: Dryden Press, 1960), 71.

33. Dahl, *Preface*, 135.

34. Ibid., 137.

35. The persistent conservatism of Chilean judges, for example, is largely a function of an institutional structure that isolates judicial selection from the larger political environment and allows the Chilean judiciary to perpetuate its ideological origins in pre-democratic Chile. Elisabeth C. Hilbink, "Legalism Against Democracy: The Political Role of the Judiciary in Chile, 1964–1994," (Ph.D. diss., University of California at San Diego, 1999). In the United States, state judges selected by elections appear to be generally similar in terms of professional credentials as those selected by executive appointment. Henry R. Glick and Craig Emmert, "Selection Systems and Judicial Characteristics: The Recruitment of State Supreme Court Justices," *Judicature* 70 (1987): 228. Nonetheless, there is some evidence that selection mechanisms matter for judicial outcomes in state judiciaries. Paul Brace and Melinda Gann Hall, "The Interplay of Preferences, Case Facts, Context, and Rules in the Politics of Judicial Choice," *Journal of Politics* 59 (1997): 1206.

36. The judiciary has a particular "institutional mission" that is reflected and reinforced by its internal norms and routines. Howard Gillman, "The Court as an Idea, Not a Building (or a Game): Interpretive Institutionalism and the Analysis of Supreme Court Decision-Making," in *Supreme Court Decision-Making*, eds. Cornell W. Clayton and Howard Gillman (Chicago: University of Chicago Press, 1999), 78–86.

37. See, e.g., Georg Vanberg, "Abstract Judicial Review, Legislative Bargaining, and Policy Compromise," *Journal of Theoretical Politics* 3 (1998): 299.

38. See Herbert M. Kritzer and Susan Silbey, eds., *In Litigation Do the "Haves" Still Come Out Ahead?* (Stanford, CA: Stanford University Press, 2003).

39. On the relative limits of courts, see Bradley C. Canon and Charles A. Johnson, *Judicial Politics*, 2d. ed. (Washington, DC: CQ Press, 1999); Gerald N. Rosenberg, *The Hollow Hope* (Chicago: University of Chicago Press, 1991).

40. See generally, Keith Krehbiel, "Spatial Models of Legislative Choice," *Legislative Studies Quarterly* 13 (1988): 259; Terry M. Moe, "Political Institutions: The Neglected Side of the Story," *Journal of Law, Economics, and Organization* 6 (1990): 213.

41. Kenneth A. Shepsle, "Studying Institutions: Some Lessons from the Rational Choice Approach," *Journal of Theoretical Politics* 1 (1989): 131, 135. See also, Sue E. Crawford and Elinor Ostrom, "A Grammar of Institutions," *American Political Science Review* 89 (1995): 582; Roger B. Myerson, "Analysis of Democratic Institutions: Structure, Conduct and Performance," *Journal of Economic Perspectives* 9 (1995): 77.

42. Similar analyses could be made for the restraining effects of American federalism. See, e.g., David Brian Robertson, "The Bias of American Federalism: The Limits of Welfare-State Development in the Progressive Era," *Journal of Policy History* 1 (1989): 261; Barry R. Weingast, "Constitutions as Governance Structures: The Political Foundations of Secure Markets," *Journal of International and Theoretical Economics* 149 (1993): 286; Keith E. Whittington, "Dismantling the Modern States? The Changing Structural Foundations of Federalism," *Hastings Constitutional Law Quarterly* 25 (1998): 483.

43. On the creation of the Senate, see generally Elaine K. Swift, *The Making of an American Senate* (Ann Arbor, MI: University of Michigan Press, 1996), 9–82.

44. See generally, Mark A. Graber, *Dred Scott and the Problem of Constitutional Evil* (Princeton, NJ: Princeton University Press, forthcoming).

45. See also, David M. Potter, *The South and the Concurrent Majority* (Baton Rogue, LA: Louisiana State University Press, 1972).

46. Charles Stewart III and Barry R. Weingast, "Stacking the Senate, Changing the Nation: Republican Rotten Boroughs, Statehood Politics, and American Political Development," *Studies in American Political Development* 6 (1992): 223, 256. A population that would otherwise entitle a state to one House seat had been the historical standard for population readiness for statehood. Most severely, Nevada, which was admitted in 1864, did not meet that standard until 1970.

47. Ibid., 247. ("In the ten congressional elections from 1874 to 1892, the Democrats always out polled the Republicans in House elections, and in the five presidential elections during this period, the worst the Democrats did was a popular vote tie in 1880.") The Republicans lost control of the Senate for a total of only four years between secession and the turn of the century.

48. Ibid., 248.

49. Keith Krehbiel, *Pivotal Politics* (Chicago: University of Chicago Press, 1998), 39.

50. Ibid., 47.

51. Krehbiel, *Pivotal Politics*, 84–85; David R. Mayhew, *Divided We Govern* (New Haven, CT: Yale University Press, 1991), 119–135. The latter figure is particularly interesting because presidential vetoes are rarely exercised in such circumstances (important legislation during unified government) but are fairly common for such legislation during divided government. Vetoes occur in about 2 percent of the former cases, but in about 20 percent of the latter. Charles M. Cameron, *Veto Bargaining* (New York: Cambridge University Press, 2000), 49. Cameron argues that such vetoes should be understood as part of a bargaining context, rather than as single shot "bullets" designed to kill legislation.

52. Bachrach and Baratz, "Two Faces of Power," 948.

53. Cameron, *Veto Bargaining*, 84.

54. Ibid., 19.

55. Stephen Holmes has usefully highlighted how constitutions may channel political debate in constructive directions, such that constitutional restraints may facilitate positive government action. Stephen Holmes, *Passions and Constraint* (Chicago: University of Chicago Press, 1995).

56. Ronald Dworkin, *Freedom's Law* (Cambridge, MA: Harvard University Press, 1996), 20.

57. James Bradley Thayer, "The Origin and Scope of the American Doctrine of Constitutional Law," *Harvard Law Review* 7 (1893): 129, 156. See also, Learned Hand, *The Spirit of Liberty* (Chicago: University of Chicago Press, 1960), 190.

58. See also, Louis Hartz, *The Liberal Tradition in America* (New York: Harcourt, Brace and World, 1955), 9. ("Judicial review as it has worked in America would be inconceivable without the national acceptance of the Lockian creed, ultimately enshrined in the Constitution, since the removal of high policy to the realm of adjudication implies a prior recognition of the principles to be legally interpreted.") Bickel, *The Least Dangerous Branch*, 30. ("It is putting the cart before the horse to attribute the American sense of legitimacy to the institution of judicial review. The latter is more nearly the fruit of the former.")

59. Mark V. Tushnet, *Taking the Constitution Away from the Courts* (Princeton, NJ: Princeton University Press, 1999).

60. It should be emphasized that the textual Constitution is likely to be a limited factor in this regard. In addition to being concerned with whatever impact the textual Constitution might have, constitutional theory should also be concerned with the broader, informal constitution of a polity. The political constitution is more than the text.

61. Gaventa, *Power and Powerlessness* 19–20.

62. Murray Edelman, *Politics as Symbolic Action* (Chicago: Markham Publishing, 1971), 8.

63. William F. Harris II, *The Interpretable Constitution* (Baltimore, MD: Johns Hopkins University Press, 1993), 118.

64. Thomas Schelling, *The Strategy of Conflict* (Cambridge, MA: Harvard University Press, 1960), 70.

65. Ibid., 68. Emphasis added.

66. Ibid., 68, 67. In the Philadelphia constitutional convention, the compromise on the three-fifths clause for taxation and representation was facilitated by the fact that the Confederation Congress had used the same "Federal ratio" in an earlier revenue proposal. Max Farrand, *The Framing of the Constitution of the United States* (New Haven, CT: Yale University Press, 1913), 108. ("In the Massachusetts state convention, Rufus King very aptly said that 'this rule . . . was adopted, because it was the language of all America'.")

67. Larry Alexander and Frederick Schauer, "On Extrajudicial Constitutional Interpretation," *Harvard Law Review* 110 (1997): 1359, 1371; Russell Hardin, *Liberalism, Constitutionalism, and Democracy* (New York: Oxford University Press, 1999), 14, 16, 18.

68. Likewise, the supermajoritarian procedures are themselves difficult to displace, for example, by Akhil Amar's extraconstitutional majoritarian referendum. Akhil Reed Amar, "The Consent of the Governed," *Columbia Law Review* 94 (1994): 457.

69. Kathleen Thelen and Sven Steinmo, "Historical Institutionalism in Comparative Politics," in *Structuring Politics*, eds. Sven Steinmo, Kathleen Thelen and Frank Longstreth (New York: Cambridge University Press, 1992), 8. Emphasis omitted.

70. Rogers M. Smith, "Political Jurisprudence, the 'New Institutionalism,' and the Future of Public Law," *American Political Science Review* 82 (1988): 89, 95.

71. See also, Abram Chayes, "How Does the Constitution Establish Justice?", *Harvard Law Review* 101 (1988): 1026. ("The judiciary is the institutional custodian of justice."); Martin M. Shapiro, *Freedom of Speech* (Englewood Cliffs, NJ: Prentice-Hall, 1966); Terri Peretti, *In Defense of a Political Court* (Princeton, NJ: Princeton University Press, 1999); Christopher L. Eisgruber, *Constitutional Self-Government* (Cambridge, MA: Harvard University Press, 2001), 46–108.

72. See also, Jeffrey K. Tulis, *The Rhetorical Presidency* (Princeton, NJ: Princeton University Press, 1987); Waldron, *Law and Disagreement*, 19–208.

73. Evidence exists that legislators, among other political elites, tend to be more tolerant than the general public. The particular mechanisms by which tolerance is fostered have not been fully identified. See, e.g., David G. Barnum

and John L. Sullivan, "The Elusive Foundations of Political Freedom in Britain and the United States," *Journal of Politics* 52 (1990): 719.

74. Stephen Skowronek, "Order and Change," *Polity* 28 (1995): 91, 94.

75. See also, John W. Meyer and Brian Rowan, "Institutionalized Organizations: Formal Structure as Myth and Ceremony," in *The New Institutionalism in Organizational Analysis*, eds. Walter W. Powell and Paul J. DiMaggio (Chicago: University of Chicago Press, 1991), 47–60; Paul J. DiMaggio and Walter W. Powell, "The Iron Cage Revisited: Institutional Isomorphism and Collective Rationality in Organizational Fields," in *The New Institutionalism*, 70–76.

76. See also, Stephen Macedo, *Liberal Virtues* (New York: Oxford University Press, *The Liberal Tradition in America* 1990).

77. On that normative environment and its political consequences, see Hartz, *The Liberal Tradition in America*; Gordon S. Wood, *The Creation of the American Republic, 1776–1787* (New York: W. W. Norton, 1969); Rogers M. Smith, *Civic Ideals* (New Haven, CT: Yale University Press, 1997); Seymour Martin Lipset, *American Exceptionalism* (New York: W. W. Norton, 1997); Aaron L. Friedberg, *In the Shadow of the Garrison State* (Princeton, NJ: Princeton University Press, 2000).

78. See also, Stefan Voigt, *Explaining Constitutional Change* (Cheltenham, UK: Edward Elgar, 1999), 91–104; Mark E. Brandon, *Free in the World* (Princeton, NJ: Princeton University Press, 1998); Harris, *The Interpretable Constitution*, 1–45, 114–163.

79. Anne Norton, *Republic of Signs* (Chicago: University of Chicago Press, 1993), 128. As Norton emphasizes, this is more dialogue than dictate, as the constituted people actively interpret their constitutional inheritance.

80. James Madison, *The Writings of James Madison*, ed. Gaillard Hunt, vol. 5 (New York: G. P. Putnam's Sons, 1905), 273.

81. *Eakin v. Raub*, 12 Serg. and Rawle 330, 354–355 (Pa 1825).

82. Clifford Geertz, *The Interpretation of Cultures* (New York: Basic Books, 1973), 220.

83. Michael Lienesch, *New Order of the Ages* (Princeton, NJ: Princeton University Press, 1988), 164 (quoting Samuel Miller).

84. Madison, *Writings*, 5:273.

85. Thomas Jefferson, *The Papers of Thomas Jefferson*, ed. Julian Boyd, vol. 14 (Princeton, NJ: Princeton University Press, 1958), 660.

86. The political effect of judicial constitutional discourse can still be understood in this way—as a means of legitimating judicial actions to a political audience. Snowiss, *Judicial Review and the Law of the Constitution*, 13–89; Martin Shapiro, *Courts* (Chicago: University of Chicago Press, 1981), 1–64.

87. For recent efforts to shift the focus of constitutional theory away from the courts, see, e.g., Louis Fisher, *Constitutional Dialogues* (Princeton, NJ:

Princeton University Press, 1988); Bruce Ackerman, *We the People* (Cambridge, MA: Harvard University Press, 1991); Griffin, *American Constitutionalism*; Tushnet, *Taking the Constitution Away from the Courts*; Keith E. Whittington, *Constitutional Construction* (Cambridge, MA: Harvard University Press, 1999). In doing so, however, not all these works break from the higher law framework.

88. Richard A. Posner, "Against Constitutional Theory," *New York University Law Review* 73 (1998): 1.

89. See, e.g., Tushnet, *Taking the Constitution Away from the Courts*, 129–176; Waldron, *Law and Disagreement*, 285–289.

Contributors

Stanley Brubaker, Professor of Political Science at Colgate University, is the author of articles in the *American Political Science Review*, *Constitutional Commentary*, the *Review of Politics*, and the *Journal of Politics.*

Neal Devins, Goodrich Professor of Law, Director, Institute of Bill of Rights Law and Professor in Government at the College of William and Mary, is the author of *Shaping Constitutional Values: The Supreme Court, Elected Government and the Abortion Dispute* (John Hopkins University Press, 1996), and *The Democratic Constitution* (with Louis Fisher) (Oxford University Press, 2004).

David Golove, Professor of Law, New York University School of Law, is the author of articles in the Harvard, Stanford, Michigan, and New York University Law Reviews. He is also the co-author of *Is Nafta Constitutional?* (with Bruce Ackerman)(Harvard University Press 1995).

Robert F. Nagel, Rothgerber Professor of Constitutional Law, University of Colorado School of Law, is the author of *The Implosion of American Federalism* (Oxford University Press, 2001); *Judicial Power and American Character* (Oxford University Press, 1994) and *Constitutional Cultures* (University of California Press, 1989).

Terri Peretti, Associate Professor of Political Science at Santa Clara University, is the author of *In Defense of a Political Court* (Princeton University Press, 1999).

CHRISTOPHER J. PETERS, Associate Professor of Law at Wayne State University Law School, is the author of articles on judicial decision making and related subjects in the *Harvard Law Review*, the *Yale Law Journal*, the *Columbia Law Review*, and *Legal Theory*, among other journals.

MARK TUSHNET, Carmack Waterhouse Professor of Constitutional Law at Georgetown University Law Center, is the author of *A Court Divided: The Rehnquist Court and the Future of Constitutional Law* (W. W. Norton, 2005); *Taking the Constitution Away from the Courts*, (Princeton University Press, 1999) and is the co-author of leading course books on U.S. and comparative constitutional law.

KENNETH WARD, Associate Professor of Political Science at Texas State University, is the author of articles in the *University of Miami Law Review*, the *Journal of Law and Politics*, *Hasting Constitutional Law Quarterly* and *American Politics Research*.

KEITH E. WHITTINGTON, Associate Professor of Politics, Princeton University, is the author of *Constitutional Construction: Divided Powers and Constitutional Meaning* (Harvard University Press, 1999) and *Constitutional Interpretation: Textual Meaning, Original Intent, and Judicial Review* (University Press of Kansas, 1999).

Index